Model-Driven Software Development Using a Metamodel-Based Extension Mechanism for UML

INFORMATIONSTECHNOLOGIE UND ÖKONOMIE
Herausgegeben von Wolfgang Gaul, Armin Heinzl
und Martin Schader

Band 28

PETER LANG
Frankfurt am Main · Berlin · Bern · Bruxelles · New York · Oxford · Wien

Ralf Gitzel

Model-Driven Software Development Using a Metamodel-Based Extension Mechanism for UML

PETER LANG
Europäischer Verlag der Wissenschaften

Bibliographic Information published by Die Deutsche Bibliothek
Die Deutsche Bibliothek lists this publication in the Deutsche Nationalbibliografie; detailed bibliographic data is available in the internet at <http://dnb.ddb.de>.

Zugl.: Mannheim, Univ., Diss., 2005

D 180
ISSN 1616-086X
ISBN 3-631-54844-3
US-ISBN 0-8204-9845-9

© Peter Lang GmbH
Europäischer Verlag der Wissenschaften
Frankfurt am Main 2006
All rights reserved.

All parts of this publication are protected by copyright. Any utilisation outside the strict limits of the copyright law, without the permission of the publisher, is forbidden and liable to prosecution. This applies in particular to reproductions, translations, microfilming, and storage and processing in electronic retrieval systems.

www.peterlang.de

Preface

The book you are holding in your hands is the published version of my PhD thesis on the subject of metamodeling and model-driven development. It describes a new extension mechanism suitable for UML that allows a hierarchical definition of concepts and is intended to replace the light-weight Stereotype approach currently used. In my opinion, the Stereotype concept does not offer enough substance to use it effectively in the context of model-driven approaches. More importantly, only a hierarchical approach effectively supports the reuse of code generation templates for different domains, reducing the overhead involved in the creation of code generation environments. I hope that the reader will find the ideas in this book thought-provoking and inspiring.

While it is my name that graces its cover, it would not have been possible to finish this book without the help of many other people. First of all, I would like to thank my *Doktorvater*, Prof. Martin Schader, who supported me with important advice and kept distractions (such as routine work) away from me during the hottest phase of this book's creation. I deliberately use the German term here, for the English expression 'thesis supervisor' in my opinion does not do the difficult birth process taking place during a dissertation and the role of the (literally translated) 'doctorial father' any justice. Second, I would like to thank Prof. Armin Heinzl, the co-supervisor of my dissertation, as well as Prof. Niedereichholz and Prof. Kirchgässner for their participation in my oral exam.

Special thanks go out to Michael Schwind, who helped me with the programming of the prototype, Wendy Odell, who helped me with her native speaker's feel for language, and my parents, Werner and Rosa, who supported me during one of the more 'interesting' phases of my work. Markus Aleksy and Tilo Dickopp gave me valuable and sometimes very critical feedback for which I am grateful. Also, I would like to thank my other colleagues and my students for the good working climate and atmosphere at our institute. Last but not least, I would also like to thank my girlfriend Amma Mamphey, who gave me moral support during the final phases.

Mannheim, September 2005   Ralf Gitzel

Table of Contents

1 Introduction 1
   1.1 Motivation 1
   1.2 Objectives 3
   1.3 Chapter Overview 3
   1.4 Scientific Contributions 4

2 Metamodeling Hierarchies 5
   2.1 Conventional Applications of Metamodeling 5
   2.2 Metamodeling Related Standards 7
      2.2.1 Unified Modeling Language 7
      2.2.2 Meta Object Facility 7
      2.2.3 Java Metadata Interface 8
      2.2.4 XML Metadata Interchange 9
   2.3 Core Concepts of Object-Oriented Metamodeling 9
      2.3.1 Definitions 10
         2.3.1.1 Basic Definitions 10
         2.3.1.2 Metamodeling Definitions 11
         2.3.1.3 Comparison With Alternative Definitions 12
      2.3.2 Model Semantics 13
         2.3.2.1 Syntax versus Semantics 14
         2.3.2.2 A Pragmatic Approach to Semantics 15
      2.3.3 Principles and Examples 16
         2.3.3.1 Core Elements of MOF 16
         2.3.3.2 The Model/Metamodel Dualism 17
         2.3.3.3 Class Instantiation Semantics 19
         2.3.3.4 Association Instantiation Semantics 19
   2.4 A Design Space for Metamodel Hierarchies 21
      2.4.1 Linear Versus Nonlinear Metamodel Hierarchies 23
      2.4.2 Number of Layers 30
      2.4.3 General Instantiation Semantics 31
      2.4.4 Strictness Definition 32
      2.4.5 Shallow Versus Deep Instantiation 36

		2.4.6	Explicit or Implicit Real World Level 39
		2.4.7	Linguistic Model Element Definitions.................................. 40
		2.4.8	Axiomatic Versus Recursive Top Level 43
		2.4.9	Evaluation of a Metamodel Hierarchy.................................. 46
	2.5	Conclusion 48
3	Model-Driven Development 49
	3.1	Goals and Aspired Benefits of MDD... 49
		3.1.1	Resistance to Change 50
		3.1.2	Increased Level of Abstraction 51
	3.2	MDD Origins and State of the Art.. 53
		3.2.1	Origins of MDD 54
		3.2.2	MDD State of the Art... 55
		3.2.2.1	The Model-Driven Architecture 55
		3.2.2.2	ArcStyler.. 57
		3.2.2.3	Executable UML... 57
	3.3	A Critical Evaluation of MDD Approaches 58
		3.3.1	Open Questions 59
		3.3.2	Problems in the Context of MDD and Potential Solutions............. 60
		3.3.2.1	Platform Independence 60
		3.3.2.2	Code Generation 62
		3.3.2.3	Other Aspects... 64
	3.4	A New Vision of MDD.. 66
	3.5	Domain-Specific MDD 67
		3.5.1	Requirements for Domain-Specific MDD 69
		3.5.2	Non-Metamodeling Approaches to Domain-Specific MDD 70
		3.5.2.1	Class Libraries and Inheritance 71
		3.5.3	Single Metalayer Approaches 73
		3.5.3.1	Patterns 74
		3.5.3.2	Stereotypes.. 74
		3.5.4	Metamodeling Hierarchy Approaches 77
		3.5.4.1	Classical Metamodel Hierarchies 78
		3.5.4.2	Nonlinear Hierarchies 79

	3.6 Conclusions	83
4	An Analysis of the Web Application Domain	84
	4.1 Properties and Problems of Web Applications	84
	4.1.1 Technical Properties and Problems	84
	4.1.2 Usability Issues and Properties	86
	4.1.2.1 Consistency	87
	4.1.2.2 Navigability and Site Structure	87
	4.1.2.3 Visual Presentation	89
	4.1.2.4 Internationalization	90
	4.1.2.5 Accessibility	91
	4.1.2.6 User- and Domain-Related Issues	92
	4.1.3 Additional Problems	92
	4.1.4 Summary	93
	4.2 Conventional Approaches to Web Engineering	93
	4.2.1 Web Design Languages	94
	4.2.1.1 The Object-Oriented Hypermedia Design Method	96
	4.2.1.2 The Web Modeling Language	98
	4.2.1.3 Other Web Design Languages	98
	4.2.2 Web Application Frameworks	99
	4.3 MDD Approaches to Web Engineering	103
	4.3.1 Frameworks, Web Design Languages and MDD	103
	4.3.2 The Contribution of MDD to Web Engineering	103
	4.3.3 Existing Approaches	105
	4.4 Conclusions	108
5	The OMEGA Approach	109
	5.1 A Metamodel-Based Extension Mechanism for UML	109
	5.1.1 The Metamodel for OMEGA Hierarchies	111
	5.1.1.1 MetaElements and Instances	113
	5.1.1.2 Model Layers	114
	5.1.1.3 MetaClasses and MetaAttributes	116
	5.1.1.4 MetaAssociations	119
	5.1.1.5 Implementation Notes	121

5.1.1.6	Properties of the OMEGA Metamodel	121
5.1.2	The Metamodel for OMEGA/Dynamic Hierarchies	124
5.1.2.1	Instance and MetaElement	126
5.1.2.2	States and Transitions	126
5.1.2.3	MetaStates and States	128
5.1.2.4	MetaStateCharts and StateCharts	128
5.1.2.5	Properties of the OMEGA/Dynamic Metamodel	129
5.1.3	Mapping to UML Profiles	130
5.1.4	Using the Extension Mechanism for Code Generation	131
5.2	A Metamodel Hierarchy for MDD	132
5.2.1	The Static Metamodels	133
5.2.1.1	The M3 Layer: Web Application Structure	133
5.2.1.2	The M2 Layer: Content Management System Structure	135
5.2.2	The Dynamic Metamodels	137
5.2.2.1	The M3 Layer: Web Application Behavior	137
5.2.2.2	The M2 Layer: Content Management System Behavior	140
5.3	Prototypical Implementations	141
5.3.1	General Plugin Architecture	142
5.3.2	The OMEGA Modeling Tool	143
5.3.3	The OMEGA Data Structure Plugin	144
5.3.3.1	The Mapping From OMEGA to S-OMEGA	146
5.3.3.2	The Mapping From OMEGA/Dynamic to S-OMEGA	147
5.3.4	The Code Generation Module	147
5.3.4.1	Code Generation Process	147
5.3.4.2	Static Code Generation Templates	149
5.3.4.3	Dynamic Generation Templates	149
5.3.4.4	Code Generation for the Web Domain	151
5.3.5	A Brief Introduction to the COBANA Framework	151
5.3.5.1	Basic Concept	152
5.3.5.2	Framework Architecture	152
5.3.5.3	Navigation	153
5.3.5.4	Addressed Problems	154

5.4	The Digital Library Example	154
5.4.1	Submission Mechanism Variant 1	155
5.4.1.1	Static Model	156
5.4.1.2	Dynamic Model	156
5.4.2	Submission Mechanism Variant 2	157
5.4.2.1	Static Model	158
5.4.2.2	Dynamic Model	158
5.5	Summary	160
6	Conclusions and Future Work	161
6.1	Theoretical and Practical Evaluation	161
6.1.1	Evaluation Approach	161
6.1.2	Scalability and General Applicability of the Example	162
6.1.3	Quality Criteria for the Extension Mechanism	163
6.1.3.1	Assessing the Variable Costs	164
6.1.3.2	Assessing the Fixed Costs Due to Time Overhead	165
6.1.3.3	Assessing the Fixed Costs due to Initial Training	167
6.1.4	Explanations and Conclusions	168
6.2	General Assessment of the OMEGA Approach	169
6.2.1	Complexity of the Approach	169
6.2.2	The General Layout of the Model Hierarchy	169
6.2.3	Conceptual Issues	170
6.3	Open Questions and Future Work	171
6.4	Related Work	172
6.4.1	UML as a Family of Languages	172
6.4.2	Software Product Lines	173
6.4.3	MetaCASE Tools	173
6.4.4	Software Factories	174
6.5	Conclusion	174

Table of Figures

Figure 1 - Hypothetical Cost Comparison 2
Figure 2 - Semantics and Syntax of Modeling Languages 14
Figure 3 - Example MOF Elements 16
Figure 4 - Core Elements of MOF 17
Figure 5 - The Model/Metamodel Dualism 18
Figure 6 - Instantiation Semantics of Association 20
Figure 7 - Naïve Linear Hierarchy 24
Figure 8 - MOF's Layer Limitation due to its Instantiation Semantics 25
Figure 9 - Orthogonal Metamodel Hierarchy 26
Figure 10 - Violations of Strictness 33
Figure 11 - A Scenario With Relaxed Strictness 34
Figure 12 - Introducing a Persistence Metaclass in M2 35
Figure 13 - Potency of Attributes 37
Figure 14 - An Example of Recursive Metamodeling 44
Figure 15 - Inheritance as a Substitute for Instantiation 72
Figure 16 - Stereotypes 75
Figure 17 - The Classical Metamodel Hierarchy (see [160], pg. 2-3) 78
Figure 18 - A Metamodel for the Domain of Art 80
Figure 19 - Improved Artist Metamodel 80
Figure 20 - Modularity in Hierarchies 81
Figure 21 - Different Levels of Abstraction in Hierarchies 82
Figure 22 - An Overview of Different Web Application Issues 94
Figure 23 - Navigational Structures Versus Explicit Links 95
Figure 24 - Pages With Multiple Contexts 96
Figure 25 - The Elements of the Extension Mechanism 110
Figure 26 - OMEGA Metamodel Overview 112
Figure 27 - OMEGA Instantiation Concept 113
Figure 28 - OMEGA Model Layer Concept 115
Figure 29 - Examples of Frozen Layers 116
Figure 30 - OMEGA MetaClass-Class Instantiation Concept 116
Figure 31 - MetaAttributes 118
Figure 32 - Motivation for the Inclusion of Slots 119
Figure 33 - MetaAssociation-Association Instantiation Concept 120

Figure 34 - MetaAssociation and Association.. 120
Figure 35 - OMEGA Implementation and Usage.. 121
Figure 36 - OMEGA/Dynamic and OMEGA 125
Figure 37 - The OMEGA/Dynamic Linguistic Metamodel 126
Figure 38 - OMEGA/Dynamic Instance-Level Elements 127
Figure 39 - An Example for the Interpretation of Substates 127
Figure 40 - OMEGA/Dynamic State Concept... 128
Figure 41 - OMEGA/Dynamic StateChart Concept.. 129
Figure 42 - OMEGA to UML Profile Mapping 131
Figure 43 - An Example Metamodel Hierarchy for OMEGA... 132
Figure 44 - Type-Instance Relationship Notation 133
Figure 45 - The Static M3 Layer 134
Figure 46 - Replacement Pattern for DynamicView and DataSet.................................. 135
Figure 47 - The Static M2 Layer 136
Figure 48 - The Dynamic M3 Layer.. 138
Figure 49 - The Dynamic M2 Layer.. 140
Figure 50 - Prototype Plugin Structure.. 142
Figure 51 - Screenshot of the Plugin 143
Figure 52 - S-OMEGA 145
Figure 53 - OMEGA to S-OMEGA Mapping.. 146
Figure 54 - Code Generator Input.. 148
Figure 55 - Code Generation Process.. 148
Figure 56 - Code Generation Concept... 150
Figure 57 - Core Classes of COBANA 152
Figure 58 - COBANA Page Assembly Strategy 153
Figure 59 - Static Library Model (Variant 1) 156
Figure 60 - Dynamic Library Model (Variant 1)... 157
Figure 61 - Static Library Model (Variant 2) 157
Figure 62 - Dynamic Library Model (Variant 2)... 158
Figure 63 - Comparison Between a Custom and an Extended Tool 163
Figure 64 - Cost Factors 164

List of Abbreviations

AM	Agile Modeling
CASE	Computer Aided Software Engineering
CDIF	CASE Data Interchange Format
CIM	Computation Independent Model
CMS	Content Management System
COBANA	Context Based Navigation
CORBA	Common Object Request Broker Architecture
CotS	Commercial of the Shelf
CWM	Common Warehouse Metamodel
EAI	Enterprise Application Integration
EDOC	Enterprise Distributed Object Computing
EJB	Enterprise JavaBeans
J2EE	Java 2 Enterprise Edition
JMI	Java Metadata Interface
JSF	JavaServer Faces
JSP	JavaServer Pages
MDA	Model-Driven Architecture
MDD	Model-Driven Development
MDSD	Model-Driven Software Development
MOF	Meta Object Facility
MVC	Model View Controler
OMEGA	Ontological Metamodel Extension for Generative Architectures
OMG	Object Management Group
OOHDM	Object-Oriented Hypermedia Design Method

PIM	Platform-Independent Model
PSM	Platform-Specific Model
RDF	Resource Description Framework
SME	Small and Medium-sized Enterprises
UML	Unified Modeling Language
URL	Uniform Resource Locator
WebML	Web Modeling Language
WfMC	Workflow Management Coalition
WWW	World Wide Web
XMI	XML Metadata Interchange
XML	Extensible Markup Language
XSLT	Extensible Stylesheet Language Transformation

1 Introduction

The development of software is inherently difficult. Many reasons exist for this problem but those cited most often are the complexity of the task and the high level of change that occurs during the lifecycle of a software application (cf. [49] or [103]). These factors have been addressed in numerous ways and as a net result the level of abstraction found in software development has increased dramatically. Currently, few programmers have to worry about concepts such as registers, memory management, or the details of communication protocols.

Nevertheless, recent attempts to raise the level of abstraction further have generated much skepticism, which in many cases is justified. Without judging the quality of individual works, it can be said that approaches such as visual languages or Computer-Aided Software Engineering (CASE) tools have not fundamentally changed the state of the practice in software development (see for example [123]). The reasons for this failure will be explained in detail further on. Still, one of the core problems is that these solutions tend to be proprietary and "hardwired" to a single domain.

1.1 Motivation

Recently, a lot of work is being done to address these problems in order to move away from the code level and "write" programs at the level of visual models instead. Commonly grouped under acronyms such as MDD (Model-Driven Development) or MDA (Model-Driven Architecture), the approaches proposed in this context aim at making a graphical model the core artifact to use during the entire lifecycle of a software application (e.g., [137]). The Object Management Group (OMG), one of the main contributors to this field, has defined several standards to support the establishment of a uniform approach. The Extensible Markup Language (XML) based XML Metadata Interchange (XMI) format provides a common language for the exchange of model and metamodel data [169]. The Unified Modeling Language (UML) provides a domain-neutral graphical notation for software modeling ([167] and [168]). Lately, steps have been taken to define a standard for model transformations and thus, ultimately, for code generation from models.

Still, not all problems have yet been addressed. The enthusiasm for generic code generation without restriction to a specific domain has largely subsided. This does not mean that the attention should turn back to "hardwired" domain-specific solutions, as the scientific problems surrounding them have largely been solved, but towards a way of providing an infrastructure for the fast development of domain-specific development environments as is the case with the Software Factories approach [103]. Now that domain-specific tools exist and have been shown to work, it is time to provide standards-based infrastructures, which allow the quick production of these tools.

Today, domain-specific MDD tools are created without special support, resulting in increased fixed costs but decreased variable costs as opposed to traditional software development in a domain. In other words, a lot of effort is needed initially to develop a tool and train the developers in its use but due to the improved development environment, individual projects in the domain are cheaper to realize.

Both the conventional non-MDD approach (C) and the use of custom-made domain-specific tools (D1) are shown in Figure 1. Note that the Figure is purely motivational and does not represent actual values (which can be found in case studies such as the one by Macala et al. [138]). In particular, the variable cost, consisting mainly of personnel costs (cf. [23], pg. 74), is simplified to the linear case, meaning there is no cost reduction due to learning effects. The simplification is unproblematic since the variable cost aspect is not relevant for the discussion in section 6.1.3.

Regardless of exact numbers, D1 is initially more expensive than C. However, because of D1's higher level of productivity, it will be profitable compared to conventional programming after a certain number of projects (X2). An infrastructure for the fast creation of domain-specific tools (D2), as proposed in this dissertation, is expected to lower the fixed costs and as a result the number of projects required (X1), therefore increasing the savings compared to C.

One aspect, which needs improvement to attain this goal, is the extension mechanism of the UML. The current mechanism, UML Profiles, has come under criticism due to its informal, lightweight nature. While it is not hard to provide general infrastructures, which map stereotypes, the extension elements of UML Profiles, to code generation templates, there is little possibility of reusing templates in an organized fashion. In other words, each new UML extension will

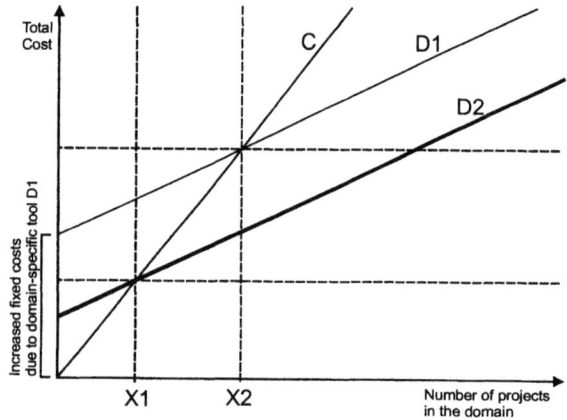

Figure 1 - Hypothetical Cost Comparison

start over again. At best, code is reused in an unplanned, opportunistic fashion, which negates many of its benefits (cf. [103] or [138]).

1.2 Objectives

The main objective of this dissertation is to provide a *hierarchical extension mechanism for UML*, which allows for a more efficient development of code generation modules for a specific domain. The mechanism should enable a description of the domain at different levels of abstraction, which can be augmented with code generation modules. In order to address the problems described in the previous section, the extension mechanism must provide concise rules for creating new domains based on previous domains and clear guidelines on how different code generation modules interact.

A secondary goal is to evaluate this mechanism by implementing a *prototypical code generation environment*, which can flexibly load hierarchical domain descriptions using the extension mechanism. The evaluation should use a problem domain for which MDD is suitable, since the goal of the evaluation is not to find out whether or not the new extension mechanism allows the application of MDD to domains, which have proven difficult so far. Rather, it should be shown that the approach integrates smoothly into the existing MDD concepts and that it will reduce the number of steps required for the realization of a new subdomain.

1.3 Chapter Overview

This dissertation is organized in the following manner. First, the *principles of metamodeling* are explained in detail and a clear terminology is established. Metamodeling will be used as a tool to create a hierarchical partitioning of a domain, giving it a central role in the development of the extension mechanism.

Next, the *model-driven development concepts* as found in the current literature are explained and illustrated by examples. The aspired goals of MDD are discussed, leading to a list of shortcomings that will be used to describe which of these goals are realistic. One of the identified shortcomings, the need for an improved extension mechanism, is further analyzed, describing existing approaches and their connection to metamodeling.

In chapter 4, the *domain of Web applications* is analyzed to serve as an example for the implementation. It is shown that the domain is not only suitable for MDD but that it will also profit from the application of model-driven techniques when compared to the current state of Web engineering.

The different threads are brought together in the main chapter by introducing a metamodel-based *hierarchical extension mechanism* for UML and creating an example hierarchy in the Web application domain. Using two models based on the hierarchy, the practical application of the extension mechanism will be explained.

The models and the applications generated from them also serve as a basis for an *evaluation*, which is described in the last chapter. By comparing the developed prototype software with a hypothetical non-hierarchical version of itself, it will be shown that the effort required for the creation of a code generator is reduced by the introduction of a hierarchy. The chapter also addresses some theoretical issues of the chosen approach and discusses related work. It ends with a short conclusion.

Throughout the text, the following *notational convention* will be used. Text in bold and italics will be used to attract attention to the key topic of a paragraph or to the introduction of new concepts. The intent of this notation is to provide orientation to the reader. Constants, class names, and model element names are printed in italics.

1.4 Scientific Contributions

This dissertation demonstrates several improvements to the current state of the art in the fields covered. Because of the need for an example domain, not all of the contributions are directly related to the extension mechanism itself.

As a contribution to the field of metamodeling, a *design space* covering the options of metamodeling hierarchy creation is proposed, which classifies and evaluates the choices available when creating a metamodel hierarchy. The options are taken mainly from existing hierarchies but also include new suggestions.

The second major contribution is the *critical analysis* of the goals as well as the state of the art of MDD as currently discussed. It is demonstrated as to which of the suggested approaches can be considered realistic, unrealistic, or outdated. Also, the precursors to MDD are briefly identified and their differences to MDD are explained. This distinction is important yet rarely made in the existing literature on MDD.

The core contribution is the definition of the *extension mechanism* based on metamodeling hierarchies, as well as its critical evaluation. The mechanism is evaluated with a prototypical code generation environment consisting of an Eclipse plugin and a Web application framework.

The final major contribution is the analysis of the Web application domain to determine the suitability of MDD to its context. Also, by comparing MDD to existing approaches in the Web context, it is shown that MDD offers advantages over the current solutions used for Web Engineering.

2 Metamodeling Hierarchies

This chapter establishes the basics of metamodeling. Briefly speaking, metamodels are models, which describe other models, i.e., provide rules for their model instances. According to Albin, every model has a metamodel, although in many cases it is just implicit ([6], Chapter 11).

Metamodeling is a wide field; therefore, this chapter focuses on those aspects relevant for the domain-specific MDD solution described in chapter 5. It starts with a short description of the motivations for the use of metamodeling followed by some of the relevant standards, which exist in this context. The first main section then describes the rules and concepts of object-oriented metamodeling, establishing a clear and consistent terminology. After that, different variants of metamodeling are presented and evaluated in the context of a newly established design space for metamodel hierarchies. The chapter ends with some conclusions.

Generally, the definitions and assumptions in this chapter are very pragmatic, especially with regard to language semantics. While formal semantics descriptions are very helpful for code generation, the topic of compiler design is considered beyond the scope of this analysis. In section 2.3.2 some arguments are given as to why a less formal approach to semantics is seen as non-problematic in this context. Also, the techniques and models described here are largely independent of specific software engineering processes, which are far too complex to be considered properly in this context.

2.1 Conventional Applications of Metamodeling

Metamodeling, especially with multiple layers (see section 2.4.2), is a complex subject. The traditional interpretation of metamodels is that of a *language definition*, or more precisely, the definition of the syntax of a language (cf. Harel and Rumpe [107], pg. 16). While there are other tools for the definition of modeling languages than metamodels such as graph grammars (see [64]), Harel and Rumpe describe metamodels as more intuitive ([107], [108]).

A metamodel, combined with a mapping to a semantic domain, is used to represent a system of real-world elements, e.g., a software system. Most modeling applications leave their users unaware of the details of the metamodel. Some users would not even know that they are implicitly using one. In section 3.5, it will be shown that there are situations where an exposure of the metamodel can be useful for the enhancement of software engineering.

There are many examples of metamodels used for a variety of modeling purposes. Common examples include the Meta Object Facility (MOF) (see section 2.2.2), the Common Warehouse Metamodel (CWM) [164], the Workflow Management Coalition's (WfMC) metamodel for workflows (see [215] for an overview), and the Unified Modeling Language (see section 2.2.1).

A metamodeling language can be either for a general purpose or it can address a specific domain. A *domain-specific modeling language* is a modeling language, which addresses "domain specific modeling requirements" (cf. Muller et al. [143]). The language usually consists of a metamodel defining a suitable syntax and a mapping to a semantic domain, which adequately describes the topic. Domain specific metamodels are sometimes called reference models. They can be interpreted as a basic decomposition of the problem domain ([6], chapter 11).

Domain specific modeling is very popular, e.g., Süß et al. propose a metamodel hierarchy for Web-based teachware with domain-specific models for different fields of teaching such as databases or music [203]. A recent example is the multimedia metamodel proposed by Obrenovic et al., which can be used for content repurposing as well as code generation for multimedia interfaces [157]. Other examples include Nordstrom et al. [155], Völter [209], Albin [6], or Deng et al. [56].

An important aspect of metamodels is that they can be considered models themselves. There are some metamodels, whose purpose is to allow the definition of other metamodels, in effect languages, which allow the description of languages. MOF is the predominant *metamodeling language*, with MOF 2.0 [170] serving as the metamodel for the UML metamodel. In the context of Model-Driven Development (see chapter 3), the ability to define customized languages has been given new impetus and the ability to provide UML-related variant languages is deemed desirable by many (e.g., Duddy [62]). The advantage of custom languages is that they can be designed to specifically address those problems that are most time consuming or difficult.

It should be mentioned that metamodeling languages are not the only way of defining custom metamodels. For those unwilling to define a completely new language, UML offers the concept of UML Profiles, which allows the inclusion of domain-specific model elements into UML diagrams. The UML Profile concept is a lightweight extension mechanism, which has several problems that will be discussed in section 3.5.3.2.

The last classical application of metamodels is as an *interoperability mechanism* between different modeling tools. Compatibility problems between different data formats are a common occurrence in the field of information technologies. In the case of applications, which operate on the same semantic domain, this incompatibility is purely a question of syntax and not of content. A standardized metamodel hierarchy allows the interchange of metamodels between applications (cp. section 3.5.4.1). The necessity of metamodel interchange was the main motivation for the birth of the CASE Data Interchange Format (CDIF) standard [41] and XMI.

2.2 Metamodeling Related Standards

In the previous section, some of the standards related to metamodeling have already been mentioned as examples. However, those standards later used in chapter 5 warrant a closer look. MOF, in particular, will be used to illustrate the examples throughout this chapter, with further explanation given where required. Other standards, such as CDIF, which are of primarily historical interest, or CWM, which serves purposes largely unrelated to this discussion, will only be mentioned in passing where they offer interesting alternatives to those standards used.

2.2.1 Unified Modeling Language

The *Unified Modeling Language* (UML) [167] is probably the most well-known modeling language in the context of software engineering. As the name implies it is the synthesis of several popular modeling languages, which has helped to promote it as a common and widely accepted standard. Also, it is the core modeling language used in the MDA context, especially the mechanism of UML Profiles, which allows users to modify the metamodel to a limited extent.

As has already been mentioned, the UML Profile extension mechanism is too lightweight for most serious applications, as will be discussed in section 3.5.3.2. Other points of criticism against UML are its linear metamodel hierarchy (see section 2.4.1) and its lack of adherence to the principle of strict metamodeling (see 2.4.4) [18].

While most of the following discussion will center on MOF, it is also applicable to UML, since MOF is for practical purposes a subset of UML. Therefore, the details of UML will not be explained here.

2.2.2 Meta Object Facility

The OMG's *Meta Object Facility* (MOF) standard [161] was originally created for the purpose of providing a foundation for model repositories, as well as for tools, which transform MOF models into code. The standard consists of a metamodel, an informal description of its semantics, and rules for a mapping to Common Object Request Broker Architecture (CORBA) Interface Definition Language (IDL) interfaces (cf. [3]). The metamodel is practically a subset of UML; a MOF model corresponds roughly to a UML class diagram. Thus, it can use the same graphical notations as UML. Many of the MOF/UML concepts, such as the recursive top level definition and the four level metamodel hierarchy, go back to the CDIF standard.

MOF is a relatively simple metamodel. According to the standard, the metamodel at the highest layer is not "a powerful modeling language for expressing a range of information models, it is not intended to be the ultimate modeling language. Instead, one intended use of the MOF is as a tool for designing and implementing more sophisticated modeling systems" ([161], chapter 1 pg. 3). One example for such a language is UML, which can (but need not) be defined in terms of the MOF metamodel. In the case of UML 2.0, MOF is not only one possible metamodel but the primary, official metamodel. CWM is another metamodel based on MOF.

According to the MOF standard, the MOF metadata architecture has several advantages over earlier metamodeling concepts. First of all, its model is object-oriented, "aligned with UML's object modeling constructs", self-describing, flexible with regard to the number of layers in the metamodel hierarchy, and does not limit its models (in the sense of a collection of metadata) to one metalevel ([161], section 2.2.2).

Two statements in this context are of particular interest, i.e., the flexibility with regard to the number of model layers, and the level-spanning nature of models. Both statements imply the suitability of MOF for extended metamodel hierarchies. However, this is not the case. As will be shown later, the instantiation semantics of MOF do not generally allow more than four layers. For the same reasons using information of more than one layer is possible but very complex.

Later in this chapter (see section 2.3.3), the MOF metamodel will be described in more detail. As has already been mentioned, a MOF model is in principle a UML class diagram. However, MOF is not a perfect submodel of UML due to some minor issues, such as the lack of properly defined semantics for details such as visibilities ([161], section 3.6.3).

Note that while the latest version of MOF is 2.0 ([166], [170]), only the concepts of MOF 1.4 will be used in the following discussion. While it is true that there are some interesting changes, the MOF has been completely redefined and there is no backwards-compatibility. The other standards based on MOF have yet to catch up with the changes, and discussion on at least one mailing list seems to indicate some dissatisfaction with the alterations. As the related standards are used for the prototypical implementations described later, there is little point in describing an architecture, which is incompatible with them.

As described above, a MOF repository was intended to be a distributed system accessible via a set of CORBA IDL interfaces. However, since the use of CORBA implies a heavy overhead for any kind of non-distributed repository, the alternative standards described in sections 2.2.3 and 2.2.4 have been developed.

2.2.3 Java Metadata Interface

The *Java Metadata Interface* (JMI) [61] is a Java-based version of the CORBA IDL interfaces defined in the MOF standard. Instead of using remote repositories, the interfaces are intended to allow access to data structures in a Java program, which describe a MOF-based model. The JMI standard is useful because it provides tailor-made Java interfaces for the manipulation of arbitrary metamodel data. This makes it an ideal infrastructure for experiments with newly defined metamodels.

There are currently three major implementations, the rather unreliable reference implementation (RI) provided by Unisys, Netbeans' MetaData Repository (MDR), and the MetaModel Repository (MMR), which is part of SAP's Netweaver[1]. At the early stages of this work, only the first two implementations existed. RI has several technical problems; a simple example model created using the RI-generated interfaces could not be reloaded by RI's own repository! MDR on the other hand is in a far better state and is actively supported by its programmers via a mailing list. Therefore, MDR was used as JMI implementation for the examples and the prototype.

2.2.4 XML Metadata Interchange

The *XML Metadata Interchange* (XMI) standard [169] is an XML-based data format for the serialization and interchange of MOF-based models. Most commonly the standard is used with UML models but other applications are also possible. For example, the JMI standard offers a method to serialize arbitrary MOF compliant model data as XMI files.

XMI documents for a particular metamodel comply with an XML Schema created based on rules found in the XMI standard. Therefore, the documents offer all the advantages inherent to XML, e.g., a universally accepted syntax and human readability. On the down side, XMI documents are overly complex, in some respects redundant, and offer too many variant notation options. Though it appears to be tempting, generating code from XMI files using Extensible Stylesheet Language Transformations (XSLT) [48] scripts becomes a difficult endeavor for these reasons.

2.3 *Core Concepts of Object-Oriented Metamodeling*

The previous sections have shown how and where metamodeling is currently used. Before metamodeling and its potential beyond the traditional applications can be discussed in detail, it is necessary to establish some core concepts and basic definitions. For this purpose, a terminology is defined in section 2.3.1. The terminology is explicitly limited to object-oriented concepts; while metamodeling also applies to other paradigms such as Entity-Relationship diagrams, these concepts are irrelevant to the discussion in this dissertation and are therefore omitted. What follows afterwards is a brief description of the semantics of models, which helps understand the intention of models and becomes important for the discussion of the role of metamodels in MDD (see 3.5.4). Finally, in section 2.3.3 a basic metamodeling concept (based on MOF and the model developed by

---

[1] See the JMI home page for details (http://java.sun.com/products/jmi/).

Atkinson [22]) is described. These basics can then be used to discuss metamodeling variants in section 2.4.

2.3.1 Definitions

When examining the advanced features of metamodeling, it is easy to become confused due to the similarity of the model layers, the recursive definitions, or one of the other problematic details, which will be described in the later sections of this chapter. Therefore, it is helpful to provide simple but meaningful definitions in the beginning. Currently, there are a wide variety of terms being used in the research community. In order to establish a basis for the understanding of the further explanations, a list of definitions primarily based on Atkinson's work (mainly [22]) and MOF is presented. Note that in this context these terms are the only ones used, therefore, if cited papers use different ones, these are briefly mentioned but are replaced with the introduced nomenclature for the sake of clarity. Also, even though most of the concepts can easily be applied to other paradigms as well (e.g., Bézivin and Lemesle [32]), object-oriented models are assumed for the sake of simplicity. The definitions are meant to be as pragmatic and technically oriented as possible; more philosophical aspects (cf. the definitions provided by Seidewitz [187]) will only be included where appropriate.

The definitions are divided into two distinct groups. The first consists of definitions, which establish the basic concepts found in the metamodeling context. The second are the core terms of metamodeling, which will be defined using the basic concepts. At the end of the section, the definitions used here will be briefly compared to some alternative ones, which deviate in more than mere terminology.

2.3.1.1 Basic Definitions

The core concept of metamodeling relies on the terms instance and type or alternatively instance and template in the terminology of Atkinson [22]. While the origin of these ideas is difficult to determine, they are related to the ontological aspects of Plato's theory of Forms (cf. [174]).

> A *type* is an abstract concept or category of things. An *instance* is a concrete occurrence of an element generically described by a type. Thus all instances are structurally and behaviorally identical. An instance is said to *instantiate* its type, the (possibly implicit) connection between the two is called an *InstanceOf relationship*.

In object-oriented modeling, types and instances usually occur in the form of objects, links, classes, associations, and metaclasses. While these concepts are likely to be familiar to the reader, a short definition is nevertheless useful to firmly establish them for the following discussion.

> An *object* encapsulates a state, represented by a set of attribute values, and a behavior, represented by a set of methods. Additionally, a unique identifier distinguishes it from all other objects. Objects

can be considered nodes in a graph. The connecting edge between two objects is called a *link*.

A *class* is a type, which has objects as instances. Its methods and attributes serve as a structural template for the methods and attribute values of its instances. A class can also be an object. Its class is then called a *metaclass*.

An *association* is a type, which has links as instances. Its properties define how many links are allowed and which objects they can connect. An association can also be a link. Its association is then called a *metaassociation*.

2.3.1.2 Metamodeling Definitions

Having established the very basic object-oriented metamodeling concepts, it is now time to look at the elements required for a more general view of metamodeling. This overall concept can be described by the terms model and metamodel.

A *model* is a collection of objects and links (called *model elements*), which describe or specify a real world or abstract system. A *metamodel* is a model, which can be used to describe other models. The models described by a metamodel are its instances, the metamodel in return is the type of these models.

The definition hints at two different applications for models. First, a model may be used to describe an existing system, to analyze it in order to postulate on its behavior. Second, it may be used to specify a system (as a sort of blueprint), which has yet to be implemented (cf. Seidewitz [187]). An interesting interpretation offered by Nordstrom et al. is that metamodels describe a modeling paradigm, which holds true for the models, which are their instances [155].

While it is possible to define additional terms such as metametamodel for metamodels, which describe other metamodels (as in done for example in the CDIF standard), it is generally better to simply number metamodel layers and exploit the fact that metamodels can also be models with regard to other metamodels. The following definitions provide the means to uniquely identify all model layers.

A *metamodel hierarchy* is a tree of models connected by *InstanceOf* relationships. The term *model layer* or *model level* describes all (meta-)models with the same distance to the root metamodel in a metamodel hierarchy. Each level is given a unique name, often containing a number.

The most common naming practice for model layers is a letter combined with a number index, e.g., M_1. The letter M is the typical choice in the MOF and UML context (cp. [161]). However, in more complex metamodel hierarchies it is useful to use different letters to identify different types of layers. An example of this practice will be shown in section 2.4.1. Also, it should be noted that most hierarchies examined in this chapter will have only one model per layer, so sometimes a model is identified by the name of its layer.

So far, the relationships between a metamodel and a model have been left intentionally generic. The reason is that these relationships can differ from hierarchy to hierarchy. For a concrete application, they have to be specified via instantiation semantics. The semantics of instantiation, which can vary widely, are defined in the following way:

> **Instantiation Semantics** are a set of rules associated with a type. All instances of the type must comply with these rules.

Instantiation semantics are rarely considered in papers on metamodeling. Atkinson and Kühne [20] were among the first to identify the concept, though without offering a formalized definition. The choices made regarding the instantiation semantics have a strong influence on the nature of the model hierarchy (see section 2.4.3). As a side note, it is debatable, whether instantiation semantics are part of the semantics or part of the syntax. This subject will be briefly discussed in section 2.3.2, however, in order to comply with already-established terminology, the term "instantiation semantics" will be used anyway.

The connection established by instantiation semantics forms a relationship between model layers. Riehle et al. introduce the term *causal connection* to describe this relationship between metalayers and layers:

> A modeling level is **causally connected** with the next higher modeling layer, if the lower layer conforms to the higher level and if the changes in the higher level lead to respective changes in the lower level [177].

Therefore, if instantiation semantics are specified, a strong and formalized causal connection is established. The causal connection is required for models to be validated and interpreted.

2.3.1.3 Comparison With Alternative Definitions

The diversity of different interpretations of metamodeling has already been mentioned. While most variations are merely of a terminological nature, there are also some approaches, which are conceptually different. Since a clear choice of definitions has already been made, these alternatives are of only minor interest. However, several examples are provided together with arguments on why they were not chosen as a basis for this work. Of particular importance are two papers by Seidewitz ([187], [188]) as they are the result of a lengthy discussion with many members of the OMG involved in the UML 2.0 proposals.

The terms *model* and, to a lesser extent, *metamodel* are used in many contexts and therefore have been defined in many different ways. Even when limiting oneself to the field of computer science, there are still many different definitions. Seidewitz defines a model as a "set of statements about some system under study" [187] and a metamodel as a "specification model for a class of [systems under study] where each [system under study] in the class is itself a valid model expressed in a certain modeling language" [187]. While the theoretical foundation provided by Seidewitz is a basis useful for some arguments in favor of certain metamodeling choices and at a superficial glance does not appear to differ from the definitions chosen for this dissertation, it is too complex to assist in understanding the basics of metamodeling theory. Also, the definitions provided in section 2.3.1 are far more pragmatic and oriented towards an implementation of data structures for handling metamodel hierarchies, whereas those of Seidewitz are wider and less tangible. As the theory described in this chapter is meant to serve as a basis for the description of the prototype in chapter 5, the provided definitions are therefore more suitable.

Albin describes a metamodel as a "set of instructions for creating an instance of a class of models", which makes a metamodel a "domain-specific, self-contained design ontology" ([6], chapter 11). This definition was not used because it closely ties metamodeling to domains and ontologies. While this view definitely has its merits, it makes the terminology more confusing, for example with regard to the distinction of ontological and linguistic metamodels in section 2.4.1.

In the previous section, the term *instantiation semantics* has been introduced. It has already been mentioned that this term is rarely used and that the concept behind it is often (but not always) implicitly assumed rather than explicitly defined, even though instantiation semantics provides a strong causal connection between the model layers. Seidewitz, however, is of the opinion that such a strong connection does not exist, stating that the "concept of 'instance_of' has meaning only *within* the theory of the metamodeling language [and] *not between a metamodeling-language element [...] and a modeling language-element*" ([187], emphasis added).

This assumption is reasonable based on the definitions Seidewitz provides and his separation between metamodel and modeling language. Naturally, Seidewitz is not opposed to a connection between the two concepts but rather believes it to be nonexistent in current versions of UML or MOF, leading to problems where its existence is implicitly assumed [187]. With regard to MOF 1.x, this statement is debatable. While it is true that in UML an "instance_of" relationship is defined, which does not exist in MOF 1.x, and that there is of course no such relationship possible between model layers (cp. 2.4.4), the MOF standard provides enough information to talk about a strong logical interdependency. In fact, the standard dedicates a whole chapter to the definition of the instantiation semantics. Seidewitz is vague in his criticism, and it is hard to understand why he views this as a deficiency.

2.3.2 Model Semantics

The importance of model semantics cannot be stressed enough. The vagueness found in the context of metamodeling terminology is even worse when it comes to the field of semantics. Some authors seem to have a rather fuzzy concept of the term semantics and, possibly for this very reason, refrain from providing an exact definition. For example, a common error is to assume that semantics is a description of a model's behavior, when, in reality, it also encompasses a description of the structure of a system (cf. [108]). To avoid potential confusion, it seems prudent to devote an extra section to the topic of semantics, despite the fact that this topic cannot be handled properly in such a small space. For a complete discussion see the articles by Harel and Rumpe ([107], [108]).

2.3.2.1 Syntax versus Semantics

As has been mentioned already, a metamodel is the definition of the *abstract syntax* of a language, i.e., the "machine's internal representation" ([107], pg. 5, also see [210]) of the model. There is also a *concrete syntax*, i.e., the visual representation of the concepts (cf. Atkinson and Kühne [19], Clark et al. [49], pg. 16, and Nordstrom et al. [155]). However, for a language to be useful, it has to have some kind of *semantics*, i.e., a set of rules for the interpretation of its elements. Figure 2 shows the relationship between the basic elements of a modeling language as described by Harel and Rumpe ([107], [108]). This arrangement in many ways resembles the one found with textual languages and many of the problems are similar. However, unlike textual languages, visual languages incur additional complications due to their non-sequential nature ([108], also see Ferrucci et al. [67], pg. 1884).

The semantics of a language, whether it is textual or visual, "assigns an unambiguous meaning to each syntactically allowed phrase in the [...] language" ([107], pg. 6). The semantics encompasses both a semantic domain and a *semantic mapping* between model elements and concepts of the semantic domain, sometimes called the *interpretation* of a model (cf. Seidewitz [187]). The *semantic domain* is "an abstraction of reality, describing the important aspects of the systems that we are interested in developing" ([107], pg. 9). Each of these three aspects, i.e., syntax, semantic domain, and semantic mapping in turn have

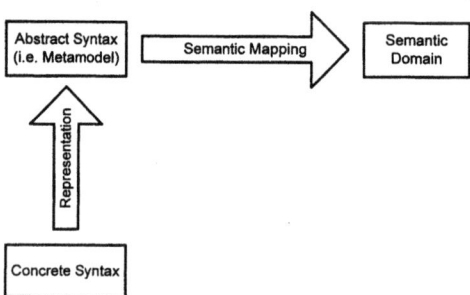

Figure 2 - Semantics and Syntax of Modeling Languages

to be described in some sort of language, leading to a cascading set of recursions.

Due to their different natures, the three aspects require different types of languages. For example, the semantic domain can use, among other things, natural language or mathematical expressions, the abstract syntax can be defined using a graphical notation, and the semantic mapping by any language, which contains the other two languages as a subset (cp. [108]).

As the semantic mapping has to provide a logical connection between all possible syntactically correct constructs and the corresponding elements in the semantic domain, defining a mapping typically is a very complex task. While it is possible to use some form of compositional semantics, i.e., to use already defined mappings as a basis for mappings involving the same syntactic elements, Harel and Rumpe state that such an approach is not always possible. For this and other reasons, many modeling languages are based on a semantic mapping, which is only informally described by giving examples and general descriptions instead of a formal definition [108].

However, in practical applications the boundary between syntax and semantics is sometimes perceived as nebulous. Harel and Rumpe complain that *context conditions*, i.e., constraints on which "sentences" are syntactically correct, are often called "semantic conditions" even though they do not define any semantics ([107]. pg. 14). The instantiation semantics as defined in the previous section also fit into this category, limiting the number of syntactically correct models but not providing any kind of meaning. Therefore, a different name would be more appropriate.

It should also be mentioned that the definition provided by Harel and Rumpe is not universally accepted and not all other approaches can be necessarily be considered false. For example, Clark et al. consider the semantics to be part of the metamodel, since a metamodel without semantics is meaningless ([49], pg. 19 and pg. 25). Also, there are other formal specification techniques for visual languages. Tortora for example proposes a formal definition of an iconic programming language as a triple of icon dictionary, grammar, and domain-specific knowledge base [206].

2.3.2.2 A Pragmatic Approach to Semantics

The explanations of the previous section illustrate the complexity inherent in the definition of a precise semantics and for these reasons no attempt is made to provide a fully-fledged semantic mapping in the context of this dissertation. The more pragmatic solution, which will be used in chapter 5, is to define semantics by mapping to a programming language (cf. Völter [210]), for example, by defining templates for each model element. This could be described as piggybacking the models onto the semantics of the programming language.

While such a "short-cut" is not an entirely satisfactory solution, it is possible to argue in favor of a less formal semantic definition in this context. According to Harel and Rumpe, the degree of formalism largely depends on the intended target audience. While tool vendors require a high degree of formalism, especially for code generation, end users will usually prefer less precise but more readily understood descriptions ([107], pp. 21-22). In the context of this dissertation, however, there is no need to provide a formal definition for a tool vendor, and such a definition is therefore considered future work.

2.3.3 Principles and Examples

Using the definitions established in the two previous sections, several examples explaining the principles of object-oriented metamodeling can be constructed. The notation chosen for all examples is the subset of UML used in the MOF standard ([161], section 3.1) with the addition of a non-standard *InstanceOf* relationship to explain the inter-layer connections.

The first two examples describe the core concepts of MOF, which bring up the problem of the model/metamodel dualism. After explaining the inherent problems of the dualism, the main elements of MOF, class and association, and their instantiation semantics are described.

2.3.3.1 Core Elements of MOF

Figure 3 shows an example MOF-based metamodel (M1) and a possible instance (M0). The types and their instances are connected by *InstanceOf* relationships. *Goya* is an instance of the class *Painter* and is connected by links to his paintings, which are in turn instances of *Painting*. The instantiation semantics conform to the general object-oriented paradigm.

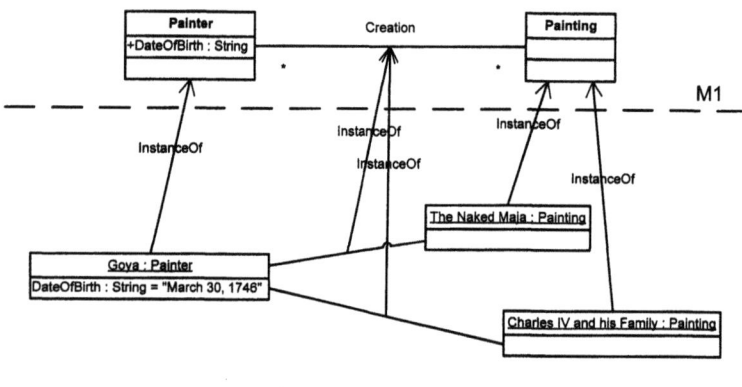

Figure 3 - Example MOF Elements

The M1 level shown in the Figure is only one example of a possible MOF-based metamodel. In other words, the metamodel M1 of M0 can also be interpreted as a model of a layer M2 (not shown), which contains the MOF metamodel.

Before moving on to the metalevel M2, it is helpful to establish the following *notational convention*: The names of classes and associations such as *Painter* or *Creation* are capitalized and written in italics. This makes it easier to distinguish between a class called *Association* and an actual association. While the necessity of this convention might be unclear at the moment, it will become obvious when looking at the next examples.

Figure 4 removes the M0 layer from the example above and instead shows the M2 layer, which contains the MOF metamodel. Two interesting facts can be discerned when combining the information found in both Figures. First, the *instantiation semantics* of an M1 element is influenced by its M2 type. A *Painter* uses the instantiation semantics of a class, because it is an instance of *Class*, *Creation* uses the instantiation semantics of an association, because it is an instance of *Association*. Second, there seems to be a mismatch between the M2 types and their M1 instances. For example, an *Association* instance must contain two *AssociationEnd* instances, however, in the M1 layer, these are not explicitly shown. This phenomenon can be attributed to the model/metamodel dualism described next.

2.3.3.2 The Model/Metamodel Dualism

The reason why the M1 level in Figure 4 does not seem to match its metamodel in layer M2 is that there are two possible views on a metamodel at any level of a MOF hierarchy. This *dualism* is one of the most complicated aspects of MOF, as it is not immediately obvious from the specification. Several researchers have

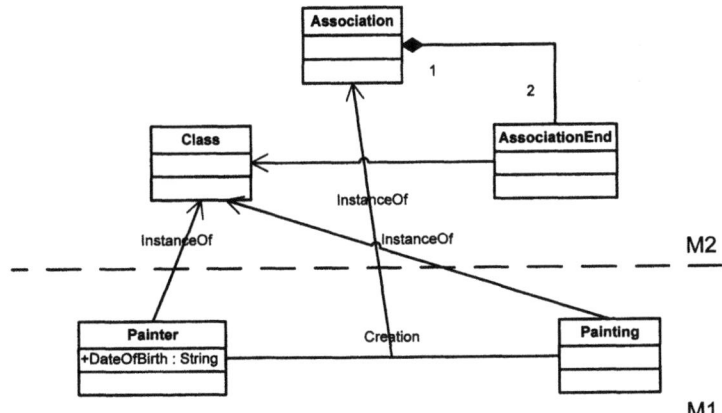

Figure 4 - Core Elements of MOF

pointed out its existence, for example, Álvarez et al. [7] and Völter in his metamodeling tutorial [209].

Figure 5 illustrates the model/metamodel dualism by showing two ways of interpreting an element of the M1 layer. Notational variant 1 interprets *Painter* as a type, in particular a class. Variant 2, on the other hand, shows *Painter* as an instance of the class named *Class* residing on layer M2. The instance data of variant 2 contains all information needed to allow the interpretation shown in variant 1.

The fact that *Painter* can be seen as an instance of *Class* suggests that *Class* has the instantiation semantics of a class. When applying the reasoning given above recursively, it is suggested that *Class* might also be an instance of some element called *Class* found at a higher level. This is the case, as MOF is defined recursively. This recursion is reflected in the definition of the instantiation semantics, which will be described next.

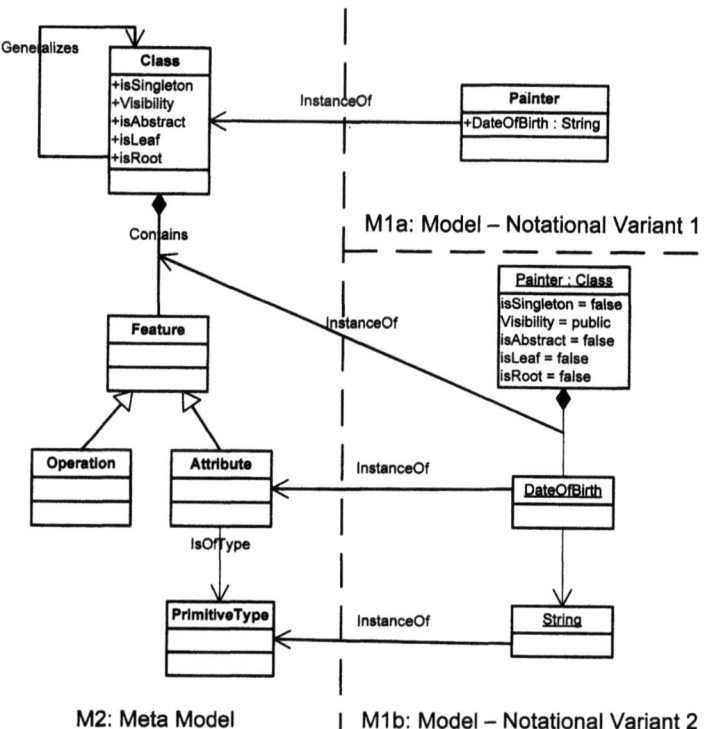

Figure 5 - The Model/Metamodel Dualism

2.3.3.3 Class Instantiation Semantics

Figure 4 and Figure 5 illustrate several examples of instantiation, some of which have already been informally discussed. An interesting aspect of MOF is that the instantiation semantics are always based on an element's type, i.e., *Painter* has the instantiation semantics of a class, because it is an instance of *Class*. In the standard the transitivity of the definition is not mentioned explicitly. The statement that an "M1-level Instance is a value, whose type is described by an M2-level Class" ([161], section 4.5), is slightly misleading. More accurately, it should be described the following way: An M1-level instance is a value, whose type is described by an M2-level instance of M3 *Class*.

The MOF *core semantics for class instantiation* (i.e., the instantiation of model elements, which in turn are instances of *Class*) can be summarized in the following way (cf. [161] sections 4.5 and 4.6):

- The instance has an object identity, which is in no way reliant on its attribute values.
- The instance belongs to the computational context known as the class extent.
- The attributes of the instance are defined by M2-level attributes. The name and type provide the basic signature for the relationship between the instance and the attribute value (often an instance of a M1 primitive data type).
- The instance can be linked to other instances via links.
- An M1 instance of an M2 *Class* cannot have instances if its *isAbstract* attribute has the value *true*.

Informally, these rules lead to the behavior of class instantiation known from the UML context. The object *Goya* in the example has an object ID (not shown), belongs to the extent of all *Painter* instances, and has a single attribute slot, which links to a string value. Its participation in links is governed by the associations defined for *Painter*.

2.3.3.4 Association Instantiation Semantics

Figure 6 shows the instantiation of an *Association*. Again, there are two ways to interpret the M1 layer shown here as variant 1 and 2. *Association* is one of the more complex and possibly sub-optimally defined elements in the MOF hierarchy. For instance, *Association*'s position in the inheritance hierarchy of MOF is counter-intuitive. Due to this poor design choice many unneeded properties, such as the participation in the *Generalizes* association or the ability to contain arbitrary elements, are inherited and have to be forcibly suppressed by constraints.

For these and other reasons, the Figure shows only a simplified form of the MOF definition, which nevertheless has the same semantics as the original. For example, many attributes are omitted as is most of the inheritance hierarchy. Since both *Class* and *Association* inherit the *Contains* relationship from *Namespace*, this association appears twice in the Figure. The *Contains* relationship for *Association* has been explicitly limited to *AssociationEnds*. In the standard the same effect is obtained by constraints.

The notational variant 2 shows us that an *Association* is defined primarily by its endpoints, i.e., instances of *AssociationEnd*. These endpoints determine such factors as navigability, aggregation, and multiplicities, which are concepts all very similar or identical to those found in UML. The "type" of the endpoint (as determined by the *IsOfType Association* instances) identifies the type of the valid nodes the link can connect to.

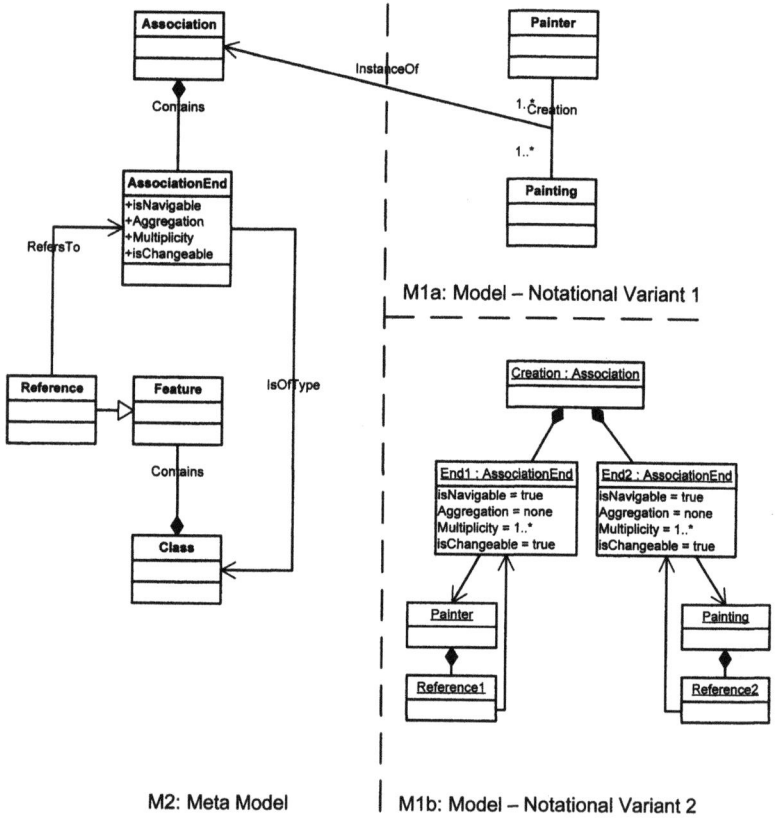

Figure 6 - Instantiation Semantics of Association

A curious fact found in the Figure is that *Association* and *AssociationEnd* are instances of *Class*. Therefore, the instantiation semantics of class introduced in the previous section are used to determine the look of notational variant 2. Instances of *Creation*, on the other hand, use the instantiation semantics of association, since their type is *Association*. It might be surprising that *AssociationEnd* uses an association to identify the allowed classes at its end. This arrangement is far from intuitive and it usually takes some time to understand the details of these design choices.

The most important aspect of the instantiation semantics, which apply to MOF *Associations* are given below (see [161], section 4.9):

- A MOF M2 level instance of *Association* defines a binary relationship between pairs of the M1-level instances of the M2 level instances of *Class*, which are allowed by its *AssociationEnds*. These relations are called **links** and are grouped in a **link set** (i.e., an extent for links). The link set is a subset of the Cartesian product of the two sets of instances of the M2 types allowed as endpoints by the two *AssociationEnds*.

- Thus a link, which is a member of the link set, can be any tuple of the form "<c1, c2>" where "c1" and "c2" are members of the two sets of allowed endpoints.

- The link set must adhere to the rules specified for multiplicities, uniqueness etc. in the *Association* instance.

To go back to the example, instances of *Creation* will be part of the link set for *Creation*, which ensures that its links do not violate the rules specified in the *AssociationEnd* instances *End1* and *End2*, which are contained in the namespace of *Creation*.

While there are other elements in the MOF metamodel, the understanding of class and association instantiation semantics is sufficient to understand the following reasoning about metamodel hierarchies and the descriptions of the prototype. In the next section, the MOF concepts are compared to other metamodeling approaches, establishing a design space for metamodel hierarchies.

2.4 A Design Space for Metamodel Hierarchies

While MOF and UML are the most commonly used metamodel hierarchies, there are also other approaches (for an overview see Atkinson [22]). Even within the group based on object-oriented modeling, there is enough deviation to prevent the definition of a universal structure underlying all metamodel hierarchies. There are several possible choices, which have different advantages and drawbacks and thus are suitable for different purposes. In this section these choices are identified by discussing several variants and extensions to the simple metamodel hierarchy described in the previous subsections, creating a **design space** of different value combinations (cf. Herbleb and Mockus [113]).

Since the design options discussed in this section result in different metamodel hierarchy properties, it is necessary to find a common frame to identify, which of the options are suitable for a specific situation. However, it is difficult to come up with a list of quality criteria without the concrete definition of a goal. Thus, an applicable yet sufficiently abstract quality concept has to be identified. Starting with the goal of *cost reduction*, it is possible by successive partitioning to eventually create the desired list of quality criteria.

There are two qualities of a metamodel hierarchy, which help reduce the cost involved in its use. These are a *general applicability of a hierarchy* and its *ease-of-use at all levels of abstraction*. While there are other aspects, which further the goal of cost reduction, good arguments can be brought forth for using these two subgoals as a basis for an evaluation of the different metamodeling variants. First of all, a metamodel hierarchy infrastructure is complex. A generally applicable solution is by far preferable to any custom-made framework because both the creation and the maintenance of complex software are costly. Second, a metamodel hierarchy has to be maintained at all of its levels at different points of time, which means that it has to be easily usable in all these contexts, otherwise more time (and money) than necessary will be required.

The next refinement step leads to the list of quality criteria used for evaluation. While it would be possible to include "obvious" technical criteria such as the existence of machine-readable formats for the models, these details are already part of all major metamodeling frameworks like MOF/JMI. Therefore, they are considered to be forming an existing infrastructure and are not discussed here. Rather, this section will focus on criteria, which better reflect the quality of different design options.

A good criterion for the ease of use of a metamodel hierarchy is its *complexity*. Generally, if the complexity of a hierarchy is high, it will not be easy to use and therefore will be more error-prone than a less complex variant. A typical sign of high complexity is the replication of concepts, which Atkinson and Kühne define in the following way:

> If a modeling element from any layer in a metamodel hierarchy is reproduced on a lower layer, the hierarchy contains a **replication of concepts** [20].

A replication of concepts negatively influences the complexity of a model in two ways. First of all, with additional elements, the model size is increased unnecessarily, making it harder to understand. Second, inconsistencies might be introduced, if the replicated concepts are accidentally implemented differently in each case (cf. Atkinson and Kühne [20]). While such a model is still "technically correct", it is harder to use, because each layer might potentially have its own "dialect".

Thus, a replication of concepts also has a negative impact on another important criterion for the ease-of-use of a metamodel hierarchy, its *consistency*. A lack of consistency will make it difficult to use the hierarchy, because of errors or the need to look up definitions in order to find the correct approach to modeling a certain aspect of the domain. Another consistency problem identified by Atkinson and Kühne is ambiguous classification:

> A metamodel hierarchy is called **ambiguously classified** or as suffering from **ambiguous classification**, if there exists an instance, which has more than one type [20].

However, not all researchers agree on the thesis that ambiguous classification poses a problem. For example, Seidewitz states that "a single modeling language might have more than one metamodel, with each expressed in a different modeling language" ([187], pg. 29). Obviously, each instance in the model must have a type in each of the metamodels, and thus it is ambiguously defined according to the definition provided above. On the other hand, the definition of ambiguous classification might be interpreted as referring to several types per metamodel, seeing the types in other metamodels as part of alternative model hierarchies. For the discussion in this section, the latter point of view is adopted and ambiguous classification is used as an indicator of inconsistency.

A third property affecting both applicability and ease-of-use of a metamodel hierarchy is its ***expressional strength***. A great expressional strength not only allows the modeling of a wide range of domains, but it also encompasses the ability to present information at different levels of abstraction. While some might argue that this criterion is in conflict with that of model complexity, it can be reasoned, based on the design decisions described in section 2.4.7, that an increase in expressional strength does not automatically increase the model complexity and vice versa.

The degree of ***extensibility*** of a metamodel hierarchy influences its applicability to a wide range of problems. Only if it is possible to add new elements, a wide range of yet unforeseen problems can be covered by the modeling language. Therefore, the extensibility forms another important evaluation criterion.

A criterion closely related to extensibility is ***robustness to change***, which reflects how much impact a genuine change as opposed to a mere extension has on the instances of the hierarchy. While it could be considered a manifestation of robustness to change, extensibility is generally easier to achieve than a general robustness to change. Therefore, the two criteria are addressed separately.

The following sub-sections will look at several options available when designing an object-oriented metamodel hierarchy. While not all quality criteria are applicable in all cases, the impact of a design decision on the overall quality of the hierarchy will be briefly discussed in each case.

2.4.1 Linear Versus Nonlinear Metamodel Hierarchies

One of the fundamental decisions in metamodeling is whether to use a traditional linear metamodel hierarchy or a more advanced nonlinear metamodel hierarchy. Since many of the other decisions, such as the number of layers or the nature of the top level depend on this choice, it is necessary to explain the two concepts in detail.

According to Atkinson and Kühne ([17], [16]), two different kinds of *InstanceOf* relationships can be distinguished; i.e., linguistic and ontological ones. **Linguistic InstanceOf relationships** describe language definition type constructs, e.g., facts like "*Painter* is an instance of *Class*" or "*Goya* is an instance of *Object*". **Ontological InstanceOf relationships**, on the other hand, describe domain-specific facts, e.g., *Goya* is a logical instance of *Painter*. While Atkinson and Kühne have coined another pair of terms, i.e., physical and logical, which they use alternatively (cf. [18]), the linguistic/ontological terminology will be used exclusively in this section, for reasons which will be discussed later. The idea to distinguish between different types of *InstanceOf* relationships has also been proposed by other authors, e.g., Bézivin and Lemesle [32] or Geisler et al. ("Intensional/Extensional Dichotomy") [82].

With two different *InstanceOf* relationships available, the question arises as to how they can be combined in a metamodel hierarchy. Based on the definitions above, it seems prudent not to mix the two types of instantiation but rather to choose one of the two for each inter-layer connection. In a naïve approach, the elements in the highest layers of a model hierarchy would connect to their instances via linguistic relationships, defining a modeling language, while the lower layers define the ontological *InstanceOf* relationships within the domain. This is in effect a *linear hierarchy* [18]. Figure 7 shows an example for such a hierarchy.

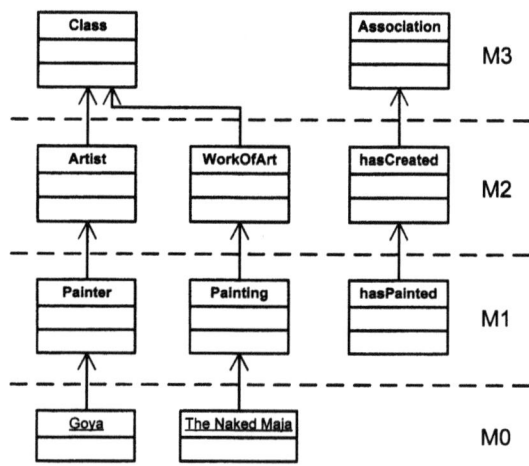

Figure 7 - Naïve Linear Hierarchy

While it might be possible to implement an infrastructure supporting hierarchies of this kind, it is not suitable for the common linear standards. For example, MOF will not allow any further instantiation of Figure 7's *Painter* due to its instantiation semantics (see section 2.3.3). The left-hand side of Figure 8 illustrates this problem. As has already been described, the type of a model element influences its instantiation semantics, i.e. *Artist* has the instantiation semantics of a *Class* for which reason *Painter*'s nature is influenced by *Class*, as shown by arrow 1. *Painter*'s instances are in turn influenced by the metaelement of *Painter* (see arrow 2). However, since MOF only defines instantiation semantics for the elements defined in the MOF metamodel, such as *Class* or *Association*, and not for other model elements such as *Artist* (which of course is not part of the official MOF metamodel) this instantiation step is not possible. Therefore, the maximum number of model layers in the existing linear hierarchy infrastructures is limited to four. When discounting the linguistic metalayers, this number is further reduced to two useable layers.

One solution to this limitation of layers is to use different instantiation semantics (see section 2.4.3). The main drawback is that instantiation semantics are not easily changed in linear hierarchies. Thus new software has to be implemented from scratch. Another solution is to enrich the model layers to supply enough information to transform the M1 layer into an alternative M2 layer. Compared to

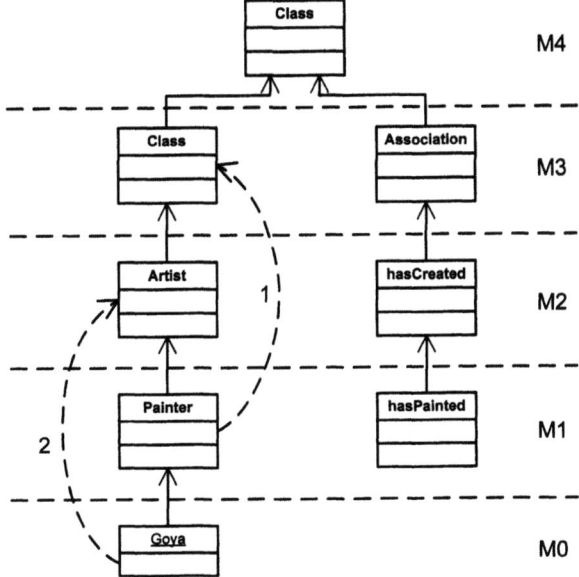

Figure 8 - MOF's Layer Limitation due to its Instantiation Semantics

other solutions this process is relatively inefficient, its details are explained by Gitzel and Schader [93].

A preferable approach is to introduce orthogonality into the model layers, creating a *nonlinear framework* [18]. There are several proposed variants for nonlinear frameworks. A typical example is the approach advocated by Atkinson and Kühne ([17], [18]), where the linguistic metamodel defines a fully functional syntax for describing metamodel hierarchies (mainly with the introduction of a linguistic association called *InstanceOf*). Figure 9 recalls the example given above, this time using a nonlinear framework. For reasons of clarity, many model elements have been omitted.

The hierarchy is now nonlinear or *orthogonal*, because the layers are no longer arranged beneath each other. Instead the *ontological layers* (i.e., layers connected by ontological instantiation) are nested within the lower of the two *linguistic layers* (which are connected by linguistic instantiation).

One important difference to the linear approach is that the two *InstanceOf* relationships now differ significantly. The linguistic *InstanceOf* relationship is an implicit "interpretation mapping from metaclass instances to [...] model elements" (cf. Seidewitz [187]). Its instantiation semantics are that of the metamodeling language used to define the linguistic metamodel, most likely MOF. The ontological *InstanceOf* relationship, on the other hand, is established by an explicit association with that name defined in L2. The instantiation semantics associated with the ontological *InstanceOf* can be defined by suitable constraints. Depending on the definition of these constraints, an arbitrary number of layers becomes possible. Since the linguistic metamodel can be defined in one of the traditional metamodeling languages such as MOF, there is no need to provide a new metamodeling infrastructure when using this approach.

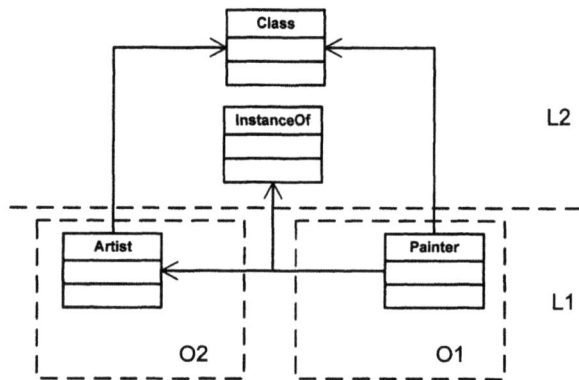

Figure 9 - Orthogonal Metamodel Hierarchy

An interesting aspect in Figure 9 is that some of the model elements seem to have two types; *Painter*, for example, is instance of *Class* and *Artist*. For this reason, in an earlier paper, Atkinson and Kühne identify ambiguous classification as a potential problem of this approach [20]. This problem is, in my opinion, a rather subtle one and depends largely on the interpretation of the model hierarchy. If a clean separation of the linguistic and ontological models exists, the linguistic classes can simply be omitted, adopting a purely ontological view of the model. With the linguistic metamodel adopting the role of a description language for the ontological hierarchy, there is no longer any ambiguity as apparent in the Figure. This view is the one used as a basis for the discussion of the nonlinear approaches later in this section.

The clear separation between linguistic and ontological concepts provided by a nonlinear hierarchy as presented so far is appealing but is not inherent to nonlinear metamodeling. For example, Riehle et al. [177] provide a comparable division between a *logical architecture* and a *physical architecture*. However, the physical architecture is very limited and the logical layer also contains elements, which are "linguistic" in the sense described above. This deviation is due to the fact the physical layer is not intended to provide the syntax for ontological metamodel hierarchies but to provide the infrastructure for a *UML virtual machine*. Thus, the complete traditional UML metamodel is reproduced on the logical level.

Álvarez et al. [7] propose to use a metamodel, which contains classes called *Class* and *Object*. These can then be used to model a *2-layered logical hierarchy*. As the upper layer of the two effectively is a metamodel, it can replicate the physical metamodel and again model a 2-layered hierarchy, **nesting the orthogonality** seen in Figure 9 several times within itself. The main drawback of this approach is that there is a massive replication of concepts, as each metamodel has to provide its own "linguistic" features. Also, the division between linguistic and ontological modeling is blurred.

In the light of these two examples, it seems advisable to refine the definitions used so far. While the concepts of ontological and linguistic instantiation can be associated with the physical and logical architectures identified by Álvarez et al., each division in my opinion emphasizes slightly different aspects. Even though they use the terms *physical/logical modeling* and *linguistic/ontological modeling* almost interchangeably (cf. [18] and [17]), Atkinson and Kühne are aware of this discrepancy. They admit the possibility of interpreting the "O_n level as defining a language to be used in O_{n-1}" [16], which "sounds linguistic" but is logical instantiation (which is seen as synonymous to ontological modeling). For the remainder of this dissertation, the concepts are separated in the following way:

> A **physical metamodel** is a metamodel, which is described in the form of program code and data structures. **Physical instances** are described by a program state but can be serialized in an appropriate

data format or, if interpreted as metamodels themselves, can be used to generate the program code required for the physical metamodels corresponding to the instances.

A good example can be found in the context of MOF or, more specifically, JMI, which uses a physical metamodel. A physical metamodel can be used to describe a logical metamodel hierarchy.

> A *logical metamodel* is a subset of the elements of the physical instance of a special physical metamodel and is therefore stored as program state. The *logical instances* are part of the same physical instance as their metamodel. A logical instance can be used as a metamodel without generating any program code by instantiating the appropriate elements of the physical metamodel.

Physical models are easier to use by programmers as they are accessible via statically typed interfaces, thus providing less of an "intellectual burden" [177]. On the other hand, they are less flexible with regard to model layers, the number of which is unconstrained only in the case of logical metamodels (cf. [18]). As an interesting side note, Atkinson and Kühne consider stereotypes (see section 3.5.3.2) "shorthand syntax for logical metamodeling" [18].

The other axis is to distinguish between different *purposes* for instantiation, either to define the syntax of a language or to describe ontological relationships. The two purposes are not completely separable and it might be argued that ontological metamodeling is a subset of linguistic metamodeling, defining domain-specific languages. However, in this context the definition of linguistic metamodeling is limited to those cases, which are not ontological, in order to provide a clear separation.

> *Linguistic metamodeling* is the technique of using a metamodel to describe a domain-neutral language syntax, which serves as a basis for the creation of ontological metamodels. *Ontological metamodeling* is the technique of using a metamodel to describe a syntax suitable for a semantic mapping to a specific domain. An ontological metamodel can be either based on a linguistic or another, more abstract ontological metamodel.

While an ontological metamodel seems to imply domain-specific semantics, it is important to point out again that a metamodel is a purely syntactical construct and therefore does not define any kind of semantics (see section 2.3.2). However, the elements in an ontological metamodel can be designed to make the semantic mapping easier and more intuitive for the human reader, due to suggestive model element names.

With the changed definitions, we can better describe the relationship between the different axes of metamodeling. A physical metamodel, for example, is almost always a language definition but can have some ontological aspects (see CWM [164] for example). Logical metamodeling is often ontological but in the case of Riehle et al. [177] and Álvarez et al. [7] as described above, it can also be linguistic.

The decision whether to use a linear or a nonlinear metamodel hierarchy is not necessarily straightforward. For the criterion of *model complexity* from the beginning of the section to be applied, two cases have to be distinguished. There are small hierarchies with few layers and larger hierarchies in which several layers are actively used on a general basis. In the context of this discussion, UML would be considered a small hierarchy, since only 2 of its layers (the model layer and the metamodel layer, which can be extended through stereotypes) are really relevant for its typical use as few people have the need to change the higher layers. Since a nonlinear hierarchy involves a certain overhead due to its linguistic metamodel, it will cause a greater model complexity than linear hierarchies for small hierarchies. In larger hierarchies, on the other hand, linear hierarchies grow exuberantly, as certain infrastructural elements have to be replicated on each layer.

Regarding the *expressional strength* of both approaches, it is hard to make a general statement. In any ontological hierarchy, the metatypes of an element can add useful information and provide a more abstract view of a model. For example, going back to Figure 7, the fact that a *Painter* is an instance of *Artist* can be used for a more abstract view, which does not distinguish between the different forms of art. On the other hand, linguistic instantiation does not benefit from this shifting of layers; the fact that *hasPainted* is a *Class* at the level M4 (not shown in the Figure) provides little useful information. Since nonlinear frameworks are more suitable for ontological hierarchies spanning multiple layers, it might be argued that the expressional strength of nonlinear approaches is higher than that of linear ones when ignoring the impact of other design choices.

Generally, the *consistency* of nonlinear hierarchies will be higher, because each ontological layer will use the same linguistic elements while each layer of a linear hierarchy involves a completely new language definition. This can lead to some bizarre situations, such as associations being instances of classes (as is the case in the MOF). While the *Association* as instance of *Class* is commonly accepted and makes sense in the context of MOF, objectively speaking such an arrangement might very well be considered an inconsistency. Also, as with any replication of concepts, inconsistencies might appear between the layers.

Linear approaches offer a good degree of *extensibility*. For example, UML can be extended using Profiles. The same applies to nonlinear hierarchies, which can easily be edited at any level. The robustness to change, however, largely depends on other factors.

Besides these criteria, it can be said that nonlinear metamodel hierarchies are helpful if more than two non-linguistic metalayers are required or non-standard instantiation semantics are to be implemented. While ontological metamodeling does not explicitly require a nonlinear hierarchy, it can benefit from this increased degree of freedom. Conversely, pure language definitions with little need for multiple metalevels can profit from the simplicity of linear hierarchies.

While in the context of current metamodeling applications, linear models seem to prevail, nonlinear metamodel hierarchies as a combination of physical and logical modeling are not as exotic as they might seem. However, logical instantiation often occurs only in the lowest layer. For example, the UML 2.0 metamodel can describe both classes (as elements of a class diagram) and objects (as elements of an object diagram) in the same layer, yet their instantiation relationship is purely logical. A similar logical instantiation relationship is proposed by Geisler et al. [82]. The benefit of such a construction is the possibility to easily describe the relationship between classes and their objects in the context of a single model as opposed to a hierarchy. This advantage also applies to cases where whole hierarchies have to be loaded, manipulated, or executed dynamically (cf. Riehle et al. [177]).

2.4.2 Number of Layers

The choice regarding the number of layers in a metamodel hierarchy is, according to Bézivin and Lemesle, "a classical problem [..] in meta-modeling" [32]. Most approaches use four layers in a fashion similar to MOF and CDIF. The classical four-layered hierarchy is usually sufficient for the conventional applications of metamodeling and for this reason is often accepted without question.

Using less than four layers in many cases is possible, if some of the benefits provided by the top-most layers are not needed. For example, if the exchange of M2 metamodels is not required for an application, the M3 layer is unnecessary. On the other hand, it is also possible not to use the lower layers, e.g., in a MOF 1.x hierarchy, an M0 layer is unnecessary, if no user data is modeled.

More layers, on the other hand, are generally only required if ontological hierarchies are to be modeled. In that case, a nonlinear metamodel hierarchy is needed, as conventional infrastructures such as MOF do not support more than 4 layers, despite claims to the contrary, and use up two layers for linguistic definitions.

The number of model layers influences the *complexity* of a model to a certain degree as each additional layer means additional complexity. For instance, when using a linear hierarchy (see section 2.4.1), a great number of replications of concepts are likely to occur as can be seen in the MOF hierarchy. A replication of concepts might also have a negative impact on the *consistency* of the hierarchy, if deviating definitions are provided for the replicated elements in different layers. In the case of ontological hierarchies, a high number of layers can increase the *expressional strength*, as each layer adds additional information to the model elements of the instances. If the number of layers is kept flexible, it is even possible to add new layers, which implies an increased *extensibility*.

That being said, the drawbacks and advantages of a specific number of model layers depend largely on the application they are used for. In section 3.5, a detailed analysis of different numbers of model layers is provided in the context of model-driven development.

2.4.3 General Instantiation Semantics

An aspect easily taken for granted in metamodel hierarchies is the *instantiation semantics*, which comprises the rules by which a type influences the make-up of its instances. In the MOF standard for example, the definition of this semantics (see [161] chapter 4) is vague and therefore to some extent open to interpretation. The decision on instantiation semantics is not an easy one and there are more options than can be discussed here. While the decisions on strictness (see 2.4.4) and shallow vs. deep instantiation (see 2.4.5) can be considered aspects of it, instantiation semantics comprises far more than that. In this section, an attempt will be made to at least look at some possible design decisions beyond the examples given in sections 2.3.3.3 and 2.3.3.4 and to briefly comment on them.

One central question is whether the same, *uniform instantiation semantics* should apply between all layers or whether each instantiation step should have its own instantiation semantics. In most cases, the uniform instantiation approach seems to make more sense. For one, the model hierarchy is easier to understand, because the set of rules is kept to a minimum. Also, a universal definition allows for the arbitrary addition of new model layers without the need to specify new instantiation semantics and thus potentially reduces replication of concepts. Atkinson provides an example for uniform instantiation semantics in [22].

While all arguments seem to be in favor of uniform instantiation semantics, there exist examples of *nonuniform instantiation semantics*. One is the JMI implementation MDR. MDR interprets the references to model layers in MOF's description of its instantiation semantics as absolute values and thus the instance of a class *Association* on the M1 layer will be an object, which cannot be further instantiated. Only a class *Association* on layer M2 produces instances, which are associations and can be instantiated by links.

The choice of general instantiation semantics has substantial impact on the quality of a metamodel hierarchy. Since type-instance relationships form an integral part of any hierarchy, a poor choice can negatively influence the *complexity* as well as the *consistency*. In both contexts, a uniform instantiation semantics is preferable, since it avoids a replication of similar instantiation rules for replicated or similar elements on different layers. Also, as the instantiation semantics generally stays in the background, nonuniform approaches are likely to lead to confusion and false assumptions, which are both symptoms of high complexity and inconsistency. Therefore, while nonuniform instantiation semantics offer more potential for *extensibility*, there are rarely cases where an extension of the instantiation semantics is desirable and the cost of the increased complexity is too high to be offset by the meager benefits.

2.4.4 Strictness Definition

Strictness is a concept that provides order to the model layers in a metamodel hierarchy. It is often taken for granted (probably without knowing the term), particularly when using architectures such as MOF where it is an integral aspect. Atkinson and Kühne define *strictness* for metamodeling in the following way:

> **Strictness:** In an n-level modeling architecture, M_0, M_1, ..., M_{n-1}, every element of an M_m-level model must be an instance of exactly one element of an M_{m+1}-level model, for all $0 \leq m < n-1$, and any relationship other than the *InstanceOf* relationship between two elements X and Y implies that level(X) = level(Y) [18].

This definition states that model elements should generally only have relationships within their own layer and not between layers, with the exception of the possibly implicit *InstanceOf* relationship, which represents the connection between the different layers. Another restriction introduced by this definition is that any elements in a model layer can only instantiate elements of its immediate parent layer.

There are strong arguments in favor of strictness. Atkinson, for example, claims that without strictness, the metamodel hierarchy would eventually collapse into a ***single super layer*** containing all model information with the layers becoming little more than ***packages*** [22], especially when associations other than *InstanceOf* are able to cross layer boundaries [18]. This must not be confused with linguistic metamodeling (see section 2.4.1), where, with the help of rigid constraints, the inaccuracy implied by the package scenario can be avoided. The problem described by Atkinson only occurs if relationships other than *InstanceOf* are allowed to cross model layer boundaries.

Another argument in favor of strictness given by Atkinson and Kühne is that without it, it is impossible to understand a model completely within the context of its metamodel without the ***influence of higher layers*** [18]. While the limitation to a single higher layer is helpful in the context of linguistic metamodels, even there the instantiation semantics often requires a transitive look at higher levels (see sections 2.3.3.3 and 2.3.3.4). This requirement is even stronger in ontological hierarchies, where model information is meant to be spread out over several layers. However, this view is strongly colored by the applications, which will be described later, so other opinions might be equally valid.

In the context of these two arguments, the limitation on relationships can be intuitively accepted. The statements made with regard to instantiation are less intuitive and require some thought. Figure 10 shows some examples where the strictness definition is violated with regard to instantiation limitations. It should be mentioned that, while the definition of strictness includes a layer M0, M0 is usually interpreted as the user data or real world layer and therefore the Figure starts at M1. However, this simplification is inconsequential for this discussion.

The instantiation labeled *Case 1* is part of a situation were a class is an instance of itself. While at first glance the definition seems to forbid such a design, it is important to realize that it actually allows *self-instantiation* but only at the topmost level n-1 (M3 in the example), which is useful for recursive definitions of the highest layer as described later (see section 2.4.8). On all other layers and therefore in the example, self-instantiation is not allowed. *Case 2* is an instantiation in the *wrong direction*, i.e., an element of M3 instantiates an element of M2. This makes little sense and is therefore also forbidden by the definition.

The instantiation called *Case 3*, on the other hand, requires some careful attention, especially if instantiation is interpreted as being transitive. It performs the instantiation of a model element, which is in a higher layer but not in the layer directly above the instance level. Again, the definition forbids this, even though at the first glance, there is little reason why this should be so. To analyze the matter further, the following variant definition, a *relaxation* of the original strictness definition as provided above, is proposed (also see Gitzel and Merz [91]):

> **Strictness:** In an n-level modeling architecture, $M_0, M_1, ..., M_{n-1}$, every element of an M_m-level model must be an instance of exactly one element of an M_z-*level model*, for all $0 \leq m < n-1$ with $m < z \leq n-1$, and any relationship other than the *InstanceOf* relationship between two elements X and Y implies that level(X) = level(Y).

A similar relaxation, although with a slightly different motivation, is proposed by Álvarez et al. The need for the relaxation arises from the use of nested layers. A layer M_i is a linguistic model for layers M_{i-1} and M_{i-2} [7]. If one subscribes to

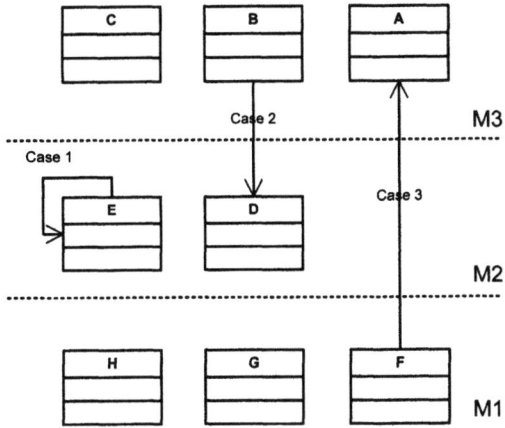

Figure 10 - Violations of Strictness

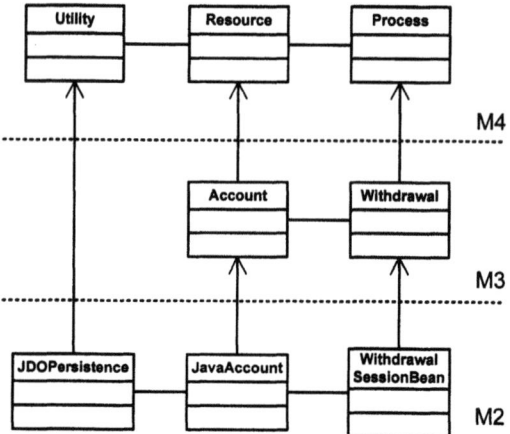

Figure 11 - A Scenario With Relaxed Strictness

the view that ontological and linguistic metamodeling are completely orthogonal (see section 2.4.1), no violation of strictness takes place. Thus, the arguments given in their paper are different from the ones found in this section and address a different problem. Albin gives an example for a metamodel hierarchy in his book, where a relaxed hierarchy is implied (see [6], chapter 11, as well as the example below). However, the text never explicitly mentions strictness and is generally vague with regard to the metamodeling semantics used.

When using a model hierarchy for code generation, the ability to instantiate a model element on any of the lower layers can be quite useful, in particular to avoid a *replication of concepts* (cf. section 2.4). Figure 11 shows an example metamodel hierarchy with three layers. The top layer, called *ontology layer*, describes a business ontology as used by Albin ([6], chapter 11), which is based on the *Convergent Architecture* architectural model proposed by Hubert [118]. There is a metaclass for *Processes* and a metaclass for *Resources*, which can be used to model domain-specific metamodels such as the banking domain described by the layer labeled M2 in the Figure. There is also a class called *Utility* in the M3 layer, which describes all kinds of elements, which support the *Processes* and *Resources*. The lowest layer in this scenario is a technical model. Its classes describe the technologies used to realize the domain concepts, e.g., the *JavaAccount* class denotes that the concept of an account should be implemented in Java (not necessarily as a single class though).

A Java Data Objects (JDO) persistence mechanism, as seen in layer M1 of the Figure and the details of which are not relevant in this context, is a *Utility* in the sense of the element defined on the ontology layer. Since the *Utility* metaclass is defined in the M3 layer, it cannot be instantiated on the M1 layer in the case of strict instantiation. One solution is to *replicate Utility* in the M2 layer (e.g., by

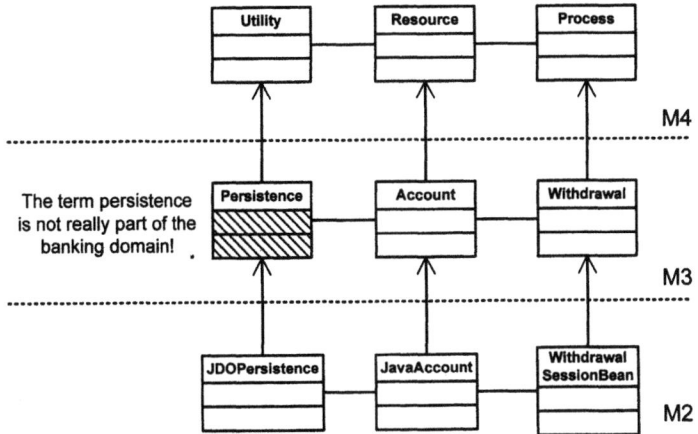

Figure 12 - Introducing a Persistence Metaclass in M2

having a metaclass called *Utility*, which instantiates M3's *Utility*). However, this leads to a replication of concepts, which should be avoided for reasons already described. Another alternative is to define a class *Persistence* in the M2 layer (see Figure 12). At first, this seems to be a good solution (solving the replication issue) but is not really consistent with the interpretation of M2 as a domain-specific layer of the banking domain.

The example above leads to two conclusions. First of all, there are scenarios where a ***relaxed strictness definition*** can be useful. Second, while there is often a technical way to avoid the need for the relaxation, i.e., by introducing a class in the middle layer(s), this can lead to problems with regard to the semantics of the model layers, especially in the case of domain-specific modeling.

Still, within the context of the example above, one could argue that the need for a relaxed strictness definition is the result of poor modeling, i.e., that a more suitable hierarchy would not require such drastic changes to the basic concepts of metamodeling. However, in a metamodel hierarchy, especially one with domain-specific layers, it is sometimes not possible to access all layers for changes, for example, the M3 layer in Figure 11 serves as a basis for all its M2 layers and changes to this metamodel negate many of the advantages described in section 2.1.

Having discussed the various advantages and disadvantages of strictness, relaxed strictness, and the absence of strictness, it is now possible to apply the quality criteria defined in the beginning. Since strictness can lead to a replication of concepts, it can negatively affect both the ***complexity*** and ***consistency*** of a model hierarchy as explained before. Relaxed strictness, on the other hand, can reduce the problem of replication. Nevertheless, some might argue that a relaxed strictness is more complex, as all higher layers have to be considered. Therefore, the degree of perceived complexity may vary. Not using any kind of strictness definition will have a negative impact on the complexity of the model, since many of the scenarios presented in Figure 10 are hard to interpret or lead to circular dependencies.

A relaxation of strictness has other effects as well, for example, it improves the *extensibility* of a hierarchy. This improvement is caused by the fact that the options for the extension of a specific model layer are not tied to the immediate parent layer but can use any model element in a higher layer as metaelement. As Figure 12 shows, this is not merely a theoretical advantage but one that can be quite useful in the context of ontological hierarchies.

The *robustness to change* of hierarchies with relaxed strictness is difficult to determine. On the one hand, the coupling between the layers is increased and therefore a change in a high layer can possibly affect all lower layers and not just the immediate child. On the other hand, if only the immediate child is changed, it is still possible, and even likely, that the resulting changes in the child will in turn cause changes in its child and so on, causing the same problem. Speaking from personal experience, in most cases a change that affects the direct child will cascade to all of its descendants, regardless of the strictness definition.

As a final remark, it should be noted that a relaxed strictness can affect other aspects of a hierarchy. For example, if the concept of *potency* is used, its definition should probably be relaxed as well to obtain a consistent result (see the next section).

2.4.5 Shallow Versus Deep Instantiation

The possibility of choosing different instantiation semantics has already been described in the previous discussion, and the decision on depth of instantiation is an important aspect of this choice. This section explains the concepts of shallow and deep instantiation and describes how the other aspects of a metamodel hierarchy influence them.

A metamodel hierarchy supports *deep instantiation*, if it is possible for a class to make statements about its instances and their instances transitively. If a class can only affect its direct subclass, the system only supports *shallow instantiation*. The boundaries between the two are not clear-cut. MOF, for example, could be considered to have deep instantiation as the instantiation semantics always depends on the metaelement of the element to be instantiated as has been illustrated in Figure 8 through the arrows. However, it makes more sense to classify MOF as supporting only shallow instantiation, because the only factor of influence from the higher layers is the name of the metametaelement, which in other words is the type of the direct metaelement. Model elements have no other possibility to influence the nature of their transitive instances, such as through their attribute values.

In a *linear metamodel hierarchy*, there are several situations where *problems* due to *shallow instantiation* occur. For example, all core modeling concepts (such as classes, attributes, and associations) have to be defined in the highest layer M_m. This means that they can only be used at the level M_{m-1} and not in lower layers, unless they are redefined in M_{m-1}. Clearly, this scenario is unsatisfactory, as it necessitates a replication of concepts. In a *nonlinear metamodel hierarchy* on the other hand, layer-spanning linguistic concepts can be defined as part of the physical metamodel, negating the disadvantages described.

Deep instantiation offers the advantage that concepts can be defined at a relatively high level to hold true for all sublayers without having to replicate this information on every layer. Atkinson and Kühne ([18], [20]) propose the concept of *potency* for attributes as an implementation of deep instantiation, which is illustrated in Figure 13. The potency P of an attribute A is an integer value, which denotes the influence on instances of the class C that contains the attribute. An attribute with potency 0 is really an *attribute slot* of C and has to be assigned a value. In this case, instances of C are unaffected by the existence of A. On the other hand, if A's potency P is 1 or higher, A requires that the instance of C contains an attribute, presumably of the same name as A, with a potency P'=P-1. The two instantiation hierarchies shown to the left of Figure 13 illustrate the potency mechanism. The number behind the name of the attributes indicates its potency value. In both cases the potencies decrease by one for each layer and result in slots as soon as the potency 0 is reached.

If an attribute (or field as it is called in [20]) is defined as being *dual*, it can also be assigned values if the potency is still above zero, yet is still reproduced in the lower layers. This can be used to model attributes occurring on several or all model layers such as the name of a model element. The third hierarchy in the Figure shows an example for dual attributes in the form of *Name*.

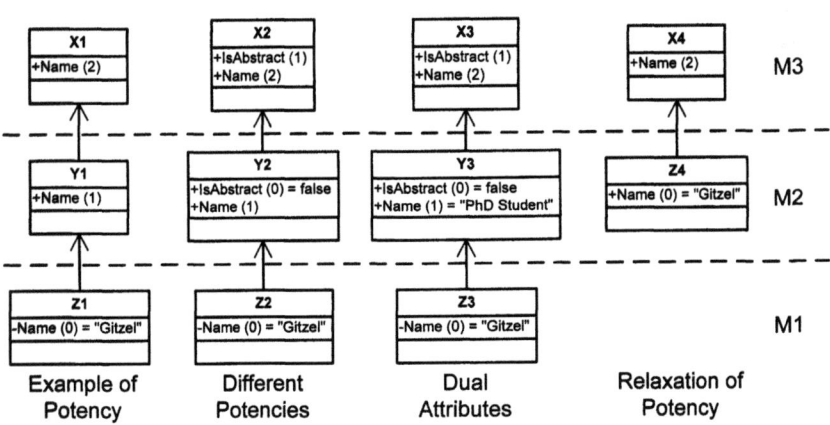

Figure 13 - Potency of Attributes

The simple and elegant potency approach has few *disadvantages*, the most important of which is the fact that it cannot be easily incorporated into existing metamodeling APIs. Also, when using attributes with potency, there is little room for changes to the *number of layers*. For example in the first hierarchy of Figure 13, it is clear that the *Name* attribute slot must occur 2 layers below X1. However, this problem is of only minor importance, as it is always possible to adapt the potencies if a new layer is incorporated.

An interesting scenario occurs when combining potency with a *relaxation of strictness* (see section 2.4.4). The central question in this case is whether potency should be reduced by one for each instantiation or by one for each layer boundary crossed. In any event, a potency value of greater than one imposes a minimum distance on instantiation, e.g., the Z1 instance of X1 could not occur on level M2, because the potency value has to be reduced to 0 first in order to allow the assignment of a value. Using a dual attribute to solve this problem has the disadvantage that some attributes might still have potency even though they are interpreted as slots. For example, in the last hierarchy of Figure 13, a further occurrence of the *Name* attribute in lower instances might be unwanted but with the normal potency rules would still be possible. A solution to this problem is to introduce a relaxation on potency as well, i.e., allowing the value of the potency to be lowered by 1 or more for each instantiation as is done for X4.

Another question to answer when implementing a potency-based hierarchy is whether *type, multiplicity, and name* of the attribute should be immutably tied to those defined by its topmost definition or not. On the one hand, it might be useful to be able to define types early on, yet on the other hand, some applications might want to leave types open to define them later on.

While deep instantiation in the form of potency works reasonably well, it is not necessarily needed for a metamodel hierarchy. It has already been mentioned that nonlinear hierarchies can define many layer-spanning concepts in their physical metamodel. In combination with a relaxed strictness definition, the same modeling power provided by potency is achieved without the need to implement a new mechanism. On the other hand, if potency is an existing concept in a modeling language, it is easier to use than this alternative.

The final question, which arises in the context of deep and shallow instantiation, is that of *instantiation transitivity*. While traditionally instantiation is not considered transitive (e.g., in the MOF standard or in discussions such as [21]), there are also benefits to adopting a pro-transitive view. In particular, ontological metamodel hierarchies can profit from transitivity. For example, the hierarchy shown in Figure 7, where instances of *Painter* are also (transitive) instances of *Artist*, introduces several levels of abstraction. The transitive form of instantiation is preferable to *inheritance*, another transitive relation, because of the larger amount of control a type has over its instances as opposed to a superclass over its subclasses. Additionally, ontological hierarchies shown in the literature that are not transitive seem to be largely proof-of-concept, thus failing to provide a practical value (e.g., the dog example in [17]). Since transitive instantiation refers to layers other than the immediate parent layer, it can be considered an aspect of deep instantiation.

Nevertheless, personal discussion has given me the impression that not everybody considers transitivity a valid option for instantiation, the main argument being that it is the primary factor, which distinguishes inheritance from instantiation. However, I adopt a different view, considering transitivity an interpretation of a hierarchy and thus part of the realm of semantics that has only peripheral influence on a metamodel, which is a pure syntax definition (see 2.3.2). Since transitive metamodel hierarchies can prove useful for code generation (as illustrated in chapter 5), it is considered a valid option for metamodel hierarchies.

With regard to the quality criteria identified for metamodel hierarchies, the arguments in the deep versus shallow instantiation discussion generally seem to be in favor of the former. Deep instantiation is a useful tool to reduce the *complexity* of a metamodel hierarchy by allowing for the definition of certain fundamental aspects in the higher layers, reducing replication. A single point of definition also helps to improve *consistency*. Additionally, it also increases the *expressional strength* of the metalayers by giving them the power to influence layers beyond their immediate instance.

On the other hand, some people, especially those working mostly with a single layer of the hierarchy, might feel that constructs such as potency increase *complexity* for them. Also, it has been mentioned that unrelaxed potency will limit the maximum number of layers in the hierarchy, thus slightly reducing the *extensibility*.

2.4.6 Explicit or Implicit Real World Level

According to the definition provided in section 2.3.1, models are a representation of systems in the real world. Therefore, a mapping between model elements and elements in the real world exists at least implicitly. In section 2.3.2 the concept of semantics was described for this kind of mapping. However, in the light of the confusion surrounding this subject, it is hardly surprising that many different views on the problem of real world mapping exist.

Opinions on how this mapping should be represented in the context of the model hierarchy vary widely. Atkinson and Kühne claim that in MOF 2.0 and UML 2.0, the real world elements are assumed to reside on the M0 level of the metamodel hierarchy, i.e., they are, in a way, instances of the model elements describing them [17]. However, it is hard to find out on which statements in the standard this claim is based and there is at least one occasion where the standard explicitly contradicts this view (cf. [168], pg. 28). Presumably, an earlier draft version is referenced.

Whatever be the case, the benefits of such an *explicit real world level* are not immediately obvious. A problem of this interpretation is that the metamodel elements have no influence on this mapping if instantiation is shallow (see section 2.4.5). On the other hand, especially in ontological metamodels, all elements of the same type should be mapped to the same class of real-world elements.

Therefore, if a solid definition of the language semantics exists, there is little need for any additional mappings to real world elements. Even more, reducing the concept of semantics to a mapping from elements of the lowest model layer to real-world entities leaves many elements undefined. With regard to the quality criteria, the decision for or against an explicit real world level has little influence. It seems doubtful as to whether the *consistency* of the hierarchy is improved by an explicit real world layer, whereas the *complexity* is definitely increased. Since the real world mapping occurs at the single layer, the overall *expressional strength of the metalayers* remains unchanged. Finally, the *extensibility* and the *robustness to change* are unaffected as well. Overall, the inclusion of a real world level seems to be of little use in most metamodel hierarchies, even though it is discussed in the literature.

2.4.7 Linguistic Model Element Definitions

The linguistic model elements defined for a metamodel hierarchy heavily influence its nature. In a *linear hierarchy*, these elements are normally defined in the topmost layer, and it is prudent to use one of the established standards such as MOF or UML for this layer. A *nonlinear framework*, on the other hand, generally has to provide more linguistic elements than a linear one. The exact nature of these elements is one of the design choices available during the creation of a metamodel hierarchy infrastructure; a few examples are provided below. Since the linguistic metamodel of MOF has already been described in detail, it is omitted from the discussion below. Also, the discussion is limited to class diagrams, even though the design space is suitable for any kind of metamodel hierarchy (see section 5.1.2).

A naïve approach for nonlinear cases (as described and criticized by Atkinson and Kühne [18]) is to have one class for each layer. The drawback of this approach is that the number of layers will be fixed by the number of model elements defined. For example, if the model elements *metametaclass*, *metaclass*, *class*, and *object* were defined, the number of layers would be limited to 4. Clearly, this is a poor solution, which would also be quite confusing in more complex cases with many layers.

On the other end of the scale is a solution offered by Atkinson and Kühne that has but a single element called *modelelement*, which contains a level attribute that identifies the level the element is found on, making it a class, object, or metaclass [18]. A problematic aspect of this approach is the mixing of different concepts in a single element, causing it to be more difficult to use.

A third variant, again proposed by Atkinson, can be found somewhere in the middle between the two other propositions. It consists of the model elements (*meta*)*class*, *clabject*, and *object*. A (meta)class is a type for an object or a clabject and has no type itself. A clabject, on the other hand, is both an instance and a type, combining the properties of both object and (meta)class. Thus, it has links as well as associations, attributes, and attribute slots [22]. A model hierarchy based on these elements would have a clear top level and clear termination at the bottom. It is interesting to note that this structure implies an axiomatic top level (see section 2.4.8). While this solution remedies the problem of the previous approach, the clabject concept feels like an artificial construct, at the very least due to its name.

Another solution, proposed in chapter 5, is a form of compromise between the single model and the clabject approach. There are three main elements, *class*, *metaclass*, and *model layer*, ignoring any classes representing associations for the moment. Instead of identifying an element's layer by an attribute value, the element is associated with a model layer by containment. This approach has the advantage that it allows the relatively easy introduction of new model layers at the bottom or in between, without having to change the value of the layer attribute in many or even all elements. Also, it allows for the inclusion of information about a layer, which affects all its elements and can be used to check compliance to domain-specific constraints. Effectively, a metaclass has all the properties of a clabject and a metaclass as proposed above. This simplification reduces the number of model elements but in my opinion does not reduce the power or quality of the model. Note that the inclusion of an *object* class is also possible but adds little to the power of the modeling hierarchy, especially when using the models in an MDD context.

A further question is whether to include *methods* or *operations* in the model hierarchy or not. While UML makes extensive use of methods, they are less useful in higher model layers or when no direct one-to-one mapping to code is intended. Atkinson shares this view, claiming that "[i]n practice the operations and methods are unimportant for meta-modeling purposes" ([22], pg. 97). Yet, Geisler et al. criticize this view, pointing out the contribution of methods to the "description of system dynamics and evolution" ([82], pg. 18). One possibility is to have methods at the metalevels to support the enforcement of constraints, for example by providing derived information via methods such as *allSupertypes()* found in *GeneralizableElement* of MOF. With arguments existing for both opinions, the decision whether to include methods or not is largely situation-dependent.

With the typical object-oriented model being a graph, it is also important to include several *static and dynamic relationships* to describe the interdependencies (represented by edges) of the model elements (represented by nodes). Atkinson [22] provides such definitions, which are used as a basis for the following description. The minimum set of required relationships contains *associations* and *links*. Associations are types of edges and links are their instances. However, associations may also be instances of other associations. An association is called a ***dynamic relationship***, because it can be instantiated. A link, which cannot be instantiated, is called a *static relationship*, even though this terminology is usually only applied to those links, which do not occur in the lowest model layer. In effect, an association is not so different from a metaclass or class, and alternative definitions similar to those described so far in this section can be found. Also, some instantiation semantics will make association an instance of class (cp. section 2.3.3.4), although this is less likely in the logical (as opposed to the physical) part of a nonlinear hierarchy.

A typical example for a static relationship is a ***generalization***. It is static, because a generalization cannot have instances. Generalization implies that all features found in the so-called superclass are also included in the subclass. This mechanism is generally useful but there are several variants, which have to be considered. Typical questions with regard to this topic are the inclusion of multiple inheritance or inheritance (with specialized semantics) for associations (as found in a certain way in CDIF).

Far more interesting is the question of whether classes, which are instances of a metaclass A, can inherit from classes, which instantiate another metaclass B. If so, what are the implications, and how is it interpreted in terms real world analogues? Should there be different types of generalization associations (possibly with different semantics) to connect different metaclasses?

While it seems easier to disallow inheritance across metaclass borders, there are examples for its usefulness. Consider the ***Java concept of interfaces***, which effectively serve as a superclass for classes, which *implement* them. ***Implementation*** in this sense is a specialized generalization between interfaces and classes with standard inheritance rules but enough conceptual difference to warrant the introduction of a new language keyword. In a more general context, concepts such as ***power types***, classifiers, whose instances are also subclasses of another classifier [158], or their prototypical concept pattern variant [20] depend on "inter-type" inheritance, providing another example for its usefulness.

There are other kinds of associations, which can be included into a modeling language. A ***containment*** association, for example, denotes an aggregation. Similar to generalization, containment can be defined in several ways. For example, in MOF, it has the effect that the aggregated elements' instances will be a physical part of the aggregating element's instance when the layer is interpreted as a metamodel (see section 2.3.3.3 for an explanation of this dualism). For example, *Attribute* model elements contained by a *Class* are not seen as individual elements but rather as attributes of the class.

Having described just a few of the endless options available in this context, it is difficult to make a general statement about the impact of the choice of model elements on the quality criteria. The ***complexity*** is influenced by the number of linguistic elements as well as by their design. For example, adding methods will increase the complexity of a hierarchy. However, in general, the addition of carefully chosen new model elements will reduce the complexity. This is the case with the addition of a generalization link, which helps avoid the need to define attributes redundantly.

Also, a limited number of elements might reduce the *expressional strength* of the metalayers, since many instances will have the same metaclass. Therefore, the choice of metaclass does not convey a lot of information about the instance. For example, when trying to provide a simplified look at the hierarchy by using the metaelements, a lot of information will be lost.

The *consistency* of a hierarchy is also strongly influenced by the choice of its linguistic model elements. For example, overlapping responsibilities should be avoided since they easily lead to inconsistencies.

Generally speaking, the most expensive changes to a metamodel hierarchy are those made to its linguistic elements, since they mostly reside in the higher layers of the hierarchy or, in the case of some nonlinear hierarchies, they directly affect all ontological layers. If linguistic metaelements are identified, which can cover a wide range of ontological instances, changes to the ontological model layers are unlikely to require a change at the linguistic level, which implies a certain *robustness to change*. Similarly, an intelligent choice of elements positively influences the *extensibility*.

Due to the fact that the choice of linguistic model elements has a great impact on the quality criteria, it is of vital importance and requires careful planning. On the other hand, no general rule of thumb can be provided and applied to all cases.

2.4.8 Axiomatic Versus Recursive Top Level

In a strict metamodel hierarchy all elements in a layer M_i are defined by the metaelements in M_{i+1}, the obvious exception being the top-most layer. The top-most layer can take two forms. It can be a *recursively defined layer* or an *axiomatic layer*. MOF is an example for a recursive top level, as is CDIF. Riehle et al. [177] give an example for a logical metamodel, which is recursive at the top. On the other hand, some researchers, such as Seidewitz [187] or Geisler et al. [82], are opposed to the recursive top level concept.

In the case of a *recursive top level metamodel*, the metamodel is self-describing. Figure 14 shows an example taken from the MOF metamodel, reduced to the *Class*, *Association*, and *AssociationEnd* elements. For reasons of clarity, the Figure shows the top level twice; theoretically, a recursive definition can be resolved by introducing an identical copy of the recursively defined layer. In the following explanations, when elements are interpreted as metaelements, they are part of the virtual copy and are marked with the prefix VC.

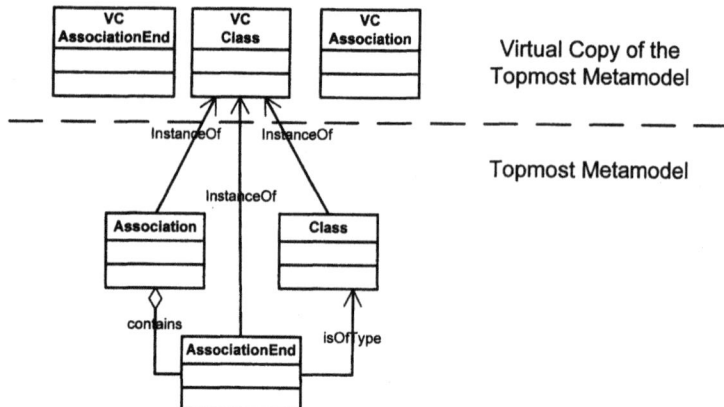

Figure 14 - An Example of Recursive Metamodeling

All elements of the metamodel, which have properties such as a name, are described by VC *Classes* and their relationships are modeled with VC *Associations*. For example, an *Association* is an instance of VC *Class* as it is clearly an element, which has properties such as a name and a visibility (see section 2.3.3.4 of this document as well as section 3.4.21 of [161]). It also participates in relationships with its *AssociationEnds*, which in turn have a relationship with the *Class* at the endpoint. These relationships are themselves instances of VC *Association*, which contain instances of VC *AssociationEnd* (these instantiations are not shown in the Figure).

An *axiomatic top level metamodel*, on the other hand, does not rely on itself as a metalayer but uses another language to describe the top level metamodel. The simplest example is specifying the metamodel in natural language or some formal language. For example, the simplified metamodel in Figure 14 would require about a page of colloquial explanations.

The discussion about whether an axiomatic or a recursive metamodel is preferable is a convoluted one. The **main advantage** of a *recursive top level* is that the model hierarchy is **self-defining**, a fact used in the definition of the MOF hierarchy. Harel and Rumpe consider this solution to be "elegant" and useful "from a pragmatic point of view" ([107], pg. 17), as users are probably already familiar with the language by the time they look at the metamodel and are therefore spared from having to learn another language. However, they also point out that the recursive metamodel is not self-sufficient and must be supplemented with alternative definitions ([107], pg. 17).

The potential **problems** of a recursive top level described in the literature are hard to grasp. For instance, according to Atkinson, it is difficult to understand a definition with information "coming from thin air" [22]. While recursive definitions also exist in areas such as mathematics and are not considered problematic in that context, the situation is different with metamodels. While a mathematical definition has a recursion base, which breaks the infinite loop, there is no such thing in the context of recursive language definitions. Thus a *recursive definition is not self-sufficient* (cf. [107], pg. 17) but needs to be supported by some other form of definition at least for a subset of its elements.

Seidewitz also criticizes recursive (or in his terms "reflexive") metamodels. As has been shown in Figure 14, the recursion can be resolved by duplicating the metamodel. These duplicate metamodels need less different types of model elements (i.e., only a subset is required for the self-specification) but still become increasingly complex with regard to the number of instances. For example, an *Association* in MOF, when seen as an instance of the MOF metamodel, consists of three objects and several relationships. All these instances have to correspond to the metamodel. Repeating this step for the metamodel again in order to check its validity in turn leads to increasingly complex models if done repetitively (cf. [187], [188]). However, the purpose of resolving the recursion in such a way is left unclear. Therefore, this argument is only considered to be of minor importance in this context.

The concept of an *axiomatic top level definition*, on the other hand, is far easier to grasp than a recursive one. Geisler et al., for example, propose the use of a formal metalanguage to avoid "self-referencing problems" ([82], pg. 5). Note that in the context of *nonlinear metamodel hierarchies* (see section 2.4.1), the highest ontological layer can easily be seen as axiomatic with the linguistic metamodel taking the part of the metalanguage. However, axiomatic top level definitions are criticized as well and suffer from a few *drawbacks* that are not shared by the recursive version. Atkinson [22] finds an axiomatic top level problematic, because its top level elements cannot be treated as objects, however gives no example when such an interpretation would be useful. Albin even indirectly negates the possible existence of axiomatic metamodels by saying that "every model has a metamodel that describes it, although the metamodel may be implicit" ([6], chapter 11). Since many metalanguages, such as natural language, are also recursively defined, it might seem questionable to some why they should be preferable to a recursive top level model. On the other hand, for the purposes of most applications, the natural language part can be safely ignored and be seen as a purely philosophical issue.

The decision between an axiomatic and recursive definition has some influence on the quality of a hierarchy, but based on the various statements made in this context, it will be hard to come up with an evaluation, which gives equal recognition to all the opinions described above. For example, while some see a recursive definition as a tool for reducing *complexity*, others feel exactly the opposite way. If a recursive definition can really be considered self-sufficient, the former opinion is probably correct. On the other hand, when designing a new recursive top level, there is a great danger of introducing mistakes, i.e., the task of creating the hierarchy is very complex.

The same arguments can be applied to the *consistency* of a model. If self-sufficient, a recursive definition avoids the need of a replicated metamodel definition in another language and thus reduces the risk of inconsistencies.

The criteria of *extensibility* and *expressional strength* of the metalayers are largely unaffected by the decision with regard to the topmost layer. However, some might argue that by resolving the recursion, additional layers can be added to the hierarchy, which can then be extended with additional metaelements.

Whether this reasoning is correct or not, the most prominent real world examples tend to have a recursive top level. In my opinion, in a linear hierarchy, a recursive metamodel, augmented with natural language clarifications, is preferable to a purely axiomatic approach. However, it is even better to have a recursive metamodel and its explanations offered as an alternative to an existing formal definition, as is proposed by Harel and Rumpe [107]. In a nonlinear hierarchy, the highest ontological layer can be considered axiomatic as it is defined in terms of the linguistic metamodel, which are beyond the scope of the ontological aspects. In this case, the addition of a recursion in the logical part only adds additional complexity as the linguistic metamodel already exists.

2.4.9 Evaluation of a Metamodel Hierarchy

Given the countless number of choices described above, it is hard to form a solid opinion on what constitutes a good metamodel hierarchy with regard to the goals of general applicability and ease of use at all levels of abstraction. Even with the criteria of complexity, consistency, expressional strength, extensibility, and robustness to change, this decision is difficult, especially since the emphasis between these criteria can vary for individual projects.

Still, tendencies can be identified, especially when looking at those design options, which are limited to a finite number of choices or whose possible values can at least be grouped into categories. Table 1 shows the tangible design options for metamodel hierarchies in an overview, assigning each of the possible choices a rating where applicable.

With the help of the Table, several conclusions can be drawn. First of all, the real world level discussion seems to be largely pointless, at least in the light of the defined criteria, and thus, an explicit real-world level is not worth the effort. The discussion regarding whether an axiomatic or recursive top level model is the better choice, on the other hand, cannot be solved, because the interpretation of its impact depends largely on one's standpoint. Thus, no recommendation can be given.

Another interesting fact is that there are quite a few values where the contribution towards a specific criterion depends on the right circumstances. For example, a wide range of linguistic model elements can lead to less complex models, however, without effort, a very complex but wide-ranged metamodel can be designed, for example, by adding useless elements.

Impact of Design Options on the Quality of a Metamodel Hierarchy	Complexity	Consistency & Precision	Expressional Strength	Extensibility	Robustness to Change
Linearity					
Linear	-	0	0	+	0
Nonlinear	+	++	+	+	0
Number of Layers					
Less than 4 Layers	0	0	0	0	0
4 Layers (cf. MOF)	(-)	(-)	0	0	0
More than 4 Layers	(-)	(-)	+	(+)	-
Real World Level Explicitness					
Explicit	-	(+)	0	0	0
Implicit	0	0	0	0	0
Top-Level Definition					
Axiomatic	+/-	+/-	0	0	0
Recursive	+/-	+/-	0	0	0
Strictness Definition					
Strict	-	-	0	0	0
Relaxed	(-)	0	0	+	0
None	+	--	--	+	0
Instantiation Depth					
Deep	++	++	+	0	0
Shallow	-	-	0	0	0
Instantiation Semantics					
Uniform	(+)	(+)	0	-	-
Layer-dependent	--	-	0	+	+
Scope of Linguistic Model					
Wide	(+)	0	0	(+)	(+)
Medium	(+)	0	0	(+)	(+)
Narrow	(-)	0	(-)	(+)	(+)
Legend: -- to ++ (more or less pos./neg. influence, with -- being unacceptable), 0 (no influence on this criterion) +/- (depending on standpoint), (_) (under certain circumstances)					

Table 1 - Design Space Options and Their Impact on Quality (cf. [87])

Finally, there are some choices where a clear, situation-independent statement can be made. For example, a nonlinear hierarchy is required to allow choices such as relaxed strictness to be realized. Besides nonlinearity, there are some other choices where a general (but not universal) recommendation can be offered. For instance, relaxed strictness is a preferable choice when possible, avoiding many of the problems caused by traditional strictness. Also, the linguistic model, if carefully designed, can provide a number of improvements in nearly all categories. On the other hand, a layer-dependent instantiation semantics should be avoided at all costs, increasing the complexity to an unacceptable degree, unless there are only a few layers.

2.5 Conclusion

In this section, a robust set of definitions has been created from a selection of conflicting opinions on the subject matter. Using these definitions, the principles of metamodeling have been explained with examples based on the MOF standard. Also, options available to the designer of a metamodel hierarchy have been analyzed and evaluated by applying several quality criteria derived from the goal of creating a highly reusable and easy-to-use hierarchy. Based on the definitions and the design options for metamodels, the benefits of metamodeling for Model-Driven Development can be explained in detail in the next chapter.

3 Model-Driven Development

According to Denning, the misconception that "Computer Science equals programming" is a major problem, which led to the software crisis in the sixties. It causes problems even today as it leads to a neglect of other important aspects, such as the engineering of systems and modeling [57]. Bézivin even goes so far as to talk of a second software crisis due to increasing complexity caused, among other things by massive technological heterogeneity ([31], pg. 7). *Model-driven development (MDD) approaches* aim at putting the model at the center of attention, making it the most important artifact for the whole software lifecycle. With the help of code generators applied to these models, software engineering takes a step away from programming. The focus on models is meant to increase the level of abstraction involved in the creation and alteration of software and to reduce a product's vulnerability to change during its whole lifecycle. Its supporters see it as a next step in the evolution of software development akin to the *introduction of compilers* (e.g., [142], chapter 1, pg. 3) and its opponents as big hype with little substance that will basically amount to a recycling of ideas that have already failed in the past. A derisive term often quoted in this context is *"cocktail party myth"* (e.g., [101]).

In order to provide a foundation for reasoning, both for and against the concepts of MDD, its goals and fundamentals will be briefly described, at first without differentiating between realistic visions and marketing hype. This abstract overview will be illustrated by describing the state of the art and further examining the OMG's MDA concept and the Executable UML approach. After that, the advantages and disadvantages as described by various authors will be discussed. It will be shown that domain-specific approaches are a solution to MDD's shortcomings, and the role metamodeling can play in realizing such approaches will be described.

3.1 Goals and Aspired Benefits of MDD

While there are many different interpretations of what the benefits of MDD are or will be, it is possible to identify two central goals, which are often cited. One of these goals, in the words of Atkinson and Kühne, is to "reduce [the primary software artifacts'] *sensitivity to the inevitable changes* that affect a software system" [19]. This quotation forms a roof for a catalogue of sub-goals and benefits resulting from the aspired robustness. The second goal, identified by authors such as Mellor and Balcer [140], Bézivin [31], Selic [191], or Booch et al. [35], is an *increase of abstraction*, allowing to better deal with the problem of *complexity*. While it would be going too far to see change and complexity as the only difficulties in software engineering, they can be considered two of its core problems (cf. [103], [39]). Thus, any approach addressing these two problems will ultimately result in a *reduction of cost*, which is the main selling argument given by MDD proponents [142]. However, the cost reduction depends on whether the model-driven concept lives up to its stated goals.

3.1.1 Resistance to Change

According to Greenfield et al., software development is the process of implementing a mapping between a problem and a solution domain, with the final software product being an element of the latter ([103], pp. 90). Based on this abstract point of view, it becomes obvious that there are two areas of change, which must both be considered. Besides the expected changes to the *solution domain* (e.g., the addition of new solutions due to new technological platforms), changes can also occur in the *problem domain* (e.g., the addition of new business processes) ([103], pp. 99). In order to achieve resistance to change both types must be considered.

Greenfield et al. identify several *software aging problems*, which are caused by multiple modifications in a software system. These problems can manifest regardless of whether the change occurred in the problem or the solution domain. The first one, called *stagnation*, increases with the amount of required changes, which have been deferred to the future. A high level of stagnation can eventually render the required changes impossible. *Fatigue* covers all problems caused by suboptimal changes to the software, e.g., due to the addition of new features, which the original architecture did not foresee and is unable to appropriately support. *Brittleness* is a measure of how well software can take additional changes and is likely to increase over time unless countermeasures are taken. Finally, *redundancy* describes the level of data and code duplication in a system or the whole organization ([103], pp. 88).

While other views on the subject are possible as well, the above analysis of the problem of change is a good basis for describing how MDD can potentially address its challenges. According to its proponents, the MDD approach introduces resistance to change in several ways, as described below.

Many discussions of MDD focus on *changes in the solution domain*, seeing the technological platform as a prime source of change. By focusing on a model, which is in synch with the software artifacts at all times, MDD supporters hope to achieve a *separation of business requirements and technology* ([110], [142]) and therefore a *platform independence* of sorts ([190], [142]). Platform independence implies the ability to quickly react to changing technological backgrounds ([190], [208]), provides *improved portability* ([54], [142], [140], pg. 11), and supports *interoperability* ([142], chapter 1, pg. 2).

However, the ability to react to *changes in the problem domain* is also improved by keeping the model as the central artifact during all stages of a software project's lifecycle. Such a model not only greatly aids the understanding of the system but can also be used to quickly implement business level updates, thus providing the potential for *improved maintainability* [54] [137]. Maintenance, which is not limited to error correction but rather focuses on the addition of new business level features, is an important factor in software engineering that is neglected by many approaches (cf. Glass [95]). Support for alterations to the software at any time of the lifecycle is a major advantage of using model-centric approaches. Also, the in-synch model could be useful for other neglected tasks such as *project retrospectives* to avoid what Glass calls "making the same mistakes on project after project" [99]. For Haywood the proper *emphasis on modeling and design* seems to be the most important benefit of model-centricity, as he doubts that the resistance to change will be as great as generally assumed by most MDD advocates [110].

The expected advantages of MDD increase the resistance to change, because they better address most of the *software aging problems* described above as opposed to the general state of the practice (cf. [103], pp. 101). First of all, the easier maintenance becomes, the less danger exists that stagnation will occur. Brittleness is currently reduced by the use of encapsulation and adaptive design (i.e., anticipating changes and providing a modular structure, which allows easy replacement of components). Reduced to its smallest common denominator, MDD offers no special potential here. On the other hand, fatigue can be avoided, as it is now easier to refactor systems based on the model, which reflects the system's architecture rather than its implementation details. Finally, data redundancy at an organizational level can be reduced due to MDD's contribution to interoperability.

In summary, MDD as a concept addresses many but not all of the problems associated with change (as shown in Table 2). Thus, if MDD lives up to its potential and if software really is prone to the types of change described here, MDD represents an improvement over the current state of software engineering. The arguments found in this context will be discussed in section 3.3.

3.1.2 Increased Level of Abstraction

As has already been mentioned, many researchers, such as Mellor and Balcer, see a *higher level of abstraction* as the main goal of MDD, which addresses the problem of complexity. Again, it seems prudent to come up with a definition of the problem first and then describe how MDD intends to address its aspects.

Problem	Theoretical MDD Contribution (from *None* to ++)
Problem Domain Change	+
Solution Domain Change	++
Stagnation	++
Fatigue	++
Brittleness	None
Redundancy	+

Table 2 - Potential Benefits of MDD for the Resistance to Change

Complexity can be defined as a "measure of the difficulty of solving a given problem" ([103], pg. 35). According to Brooks, it can be divided into essential and accidental complexity. *Accidental complexity* describes complications, which are not part of the actual problem, e.g., difficulties, which can be ignored when raising the level of abstraction without significantly changing the behavior of the system. *Essential complexity*, on the other hand, covers those aspects, which cannot be ignored safely as part of an abstraction, in other words, the essential parts of the problem, as the name implies [39].

Thus, only the accidental complexity can be reduced by increasing the level of abstraction. While Greenfield et al. see a lot of accidental complexity in modern systems such as the Java 2 Enterprise Edition (J2EE) [192] (cf. [103], pg. 36), Brooks sees it as a minor aspect and fears that too much abstraction will lead to "a tool-mastery burden that increases, not reduces, the intellectual task of the user, who rarely uses the esoteric constructs" [39].

Greenfield et al. identify feature delocalization as a typical accidental complexity factor. *Feature delocalization* occurs if an object in the problem domain is addressed by several objects in the solution domain, often due to technical requirements regarding persistence etc. The delocalization makes it difficult to find out which solution elements correspond to which problem elements, leading to a *traceability problem* (cf. [103], pp. 36). Feature delocalization is the focus of attention of aspect-oriented programming (cf. [103], pp. 71).

In order to overcome the problem of accidental complexity as described, Mellor and Balcer hope to achieve a higher level of abstraction by using an executable variant of UML (see section 3.2.2.3). The increase in abstraction is an advantage of MDD also cited by Booch et al. [35], Kühne [137], Selic [191], and Muller et al. [143]. Cook and Booch et al. see the introduction of *domain-specific lan-*

guages, as opposed to technology-oriented conglomerates of different programming languages, as the main reason for this new level of abstraction ([52], [35]). Since the abstraction from programming-level issues makes the integration of domain experts easier (see Völter [210]), possibly by providing several different views on the same system (cf. Kent [132]), MDD might be considered related to or maybe even a subcategory of the field of End-User Development (see Stutcliffe and Mehandjiev [204]), another well-known approach to reducing complexity.

The technical foundation, allowing the increased level of abstraction, consists of code generators of various types, which convert business models into platform-specific code ([110], [140], and [142]). The reduction in complexity caused by the use of *code generation* is expected to lead to improved *software quality* ([54], [110], [137], [35], [210]). It can also result in high *reusability* ([137], [190]) and therefore *increased productivity* ([54], [110], and [210]) as well as *rapid development* ([110], [35]), by deferring many of the less intellectually challenging aspects of programming to the code generator [35].

Some MDD-proponents see great potential in *aspect oriented programming*, believing that the introduction of aspects is possible and will help to reach the goals of MDD ([31], [110], [137], [140], pg. 39, [210]). While it is never mentioned in these terms, the problem of feature dislocation can thus be solved within the context of MDD.

Complexity is a somewhat intangible term, making it hard to assess solutions to this problem. The general opinion among its supporters seems to be that MDD has a lot to offer in this context, providing a wide range of advantages related to this subject. However, as we will see below, this view depends a lot on how much of software's complexity is accidental and how much is essential.

3.2 MDD Origins and State of the Art

Whether proposed under the name **Model-Driven Development**, **Model-Driven Software Development** (MDSD) [210], **Model-Driven Engineering** (MDE) [31], or mistakenly under the trademarked label **Model Driven Architecture** [142] (cf. Cook [52]), the model-driven approach is considered to herald a new era of software development. Just as the advent of compilers introduced a new abstraction layer on top of the machine code layer in use at that time, the goal of MDD approaches is to achieve further simplification by using design models and code generators ([190], [208]). Jacobson, one of the architects of UML, is convinced that Executable UML models will be possible, first for "a small stereotypical class of systems" and in the long run for "the majority of software development" ([140], pg. xxiv).

3.2.1 Origins of MDD

It is hard to discern the *origins of MDD* due to the typical terminological confusion. Early MDD approaches (cf. [198]) seem to be based on ideas described by Zachman [216]. At that time, code generation was not yet an important issue; however, certain fundamental concepts such as the separation of technical and domain-specific aspects were already defined. More commonly, *CASE tools* (see [46]) and *visual programming languages* (see [67]) are seen as the early forms of MDD and some interpret MDD as nothing more than a reincarnation of these old ideas. However, while many of the goals and ideas of these approaches are also present in MDD, it goes beyond its predecessors, learning from the mistakes made in the past.

Briefly speaking, there were several differences between the work of the CASE and the visual programming movement and the ideals of MDD. First of all, the pre-MDD approaches suffered from a general *lack of standards*, leading to a lot of effort being put into "infrastructural" developments (cf. Selic [190]). For example, an abundance of different modeling languages existed instead of today's UML, making it more difficult to learn how to use a tool. Furthermore, several other standards important for MDD, such as XMI and MOF, were not yet available. This lack of support for standards made it risky to create a model or visual program in a proprietary modeling language of a tool provider, who might not be able to give long-term support ([103], pg. 118, also cf. Booch et al. [35], Guttman [104], and Selic [190]). While the CDIF standard represents one attempt to solve this problem for CASE tools, only the introduction of a widely accepted metamodeling language such as MOF and a data format standard such as XMI enable a genuine universal exchange.

After the initial enthusiasm had faded, several other problems of CASE tools were identified. One of the main pitfalls not present in the concepts of MDD is the fact that many CASE tool proposals were tied to specific *methodologies* (cf. [123]). Ironically, the latter fact was initially seen as an advantage of CASE tools, as it allowed developers to adopt the then-newly-introduced software development methodologies more easily by providing a tailored development environment (cf. [46]).

Other problems, which were identified but are not integral to the concepts of CASE, were the generally *weak code generation*, which produced low-quality code and had poor synchronization between code and models, despite being elaborationist ([103], pp. 118). Also, the code generation of the CASE area was brute force, creating massive amounts of code instead of only providing key fragments complemented by a suitable framework ([103], pp. 144). Since these problems are not inherent to CASE tools, they might also apply to MDD tools and will thus be addressed in the discussion below.

Unfortunately, especially in the Web context (see section 4), there are many researchers, who merely use the label MDD (or, even worse, MDA) for their old

CASE tools. While these are not necessarily of a low quality, they do not conform to the ideas at the basis of MDD and thus the accusation of re-use is not entirely unfounded in some cases. Ironically, the same problem was identified at the height of the CASE movement (see [46]).

3.2.2 MDD State of the Art

According to Selic, design models describing the system under development are the central artifact in any MDD approach. These models accompany the software that is built from them throughout the whole lifecycle, i.e., not only do they support the initial implementation, but they are also used for later modifications, for maintenance, deployment, and operation of the software. MDA, for instance, aims at machine-readable application and data models to be used for implementation, application integration, maintenance, tests, and simulations [190].

By cleverly choosing the level of abstraction for the model, MDD approaches might provide conceptual views of the systems to be developed. Separation of business concerns and technical concerns not only enables developers to concentrate on the business logic of the system but also facilitates the automatic generation of different implementations from the same model, leading to the advantages described above.

While countless MDD approaches are currently proposed at conferences and in various forms of publications, it can be said that the OMG's MDA architectural framework is the one most commonly used as a basis for the different papers, making it a good candidate for a description of the state of the art. After a brief description of the concepts of MDA, two approaches of rather different outlook based on MDA, the Executable UML and the ArcStyler tool, will be described.

3.2.2.1 The Model-Driven Architecture

The Model-Driven Architecture (MDA), conceived in 2001, is the OMG's architectural framework meant to address the issues of *software maintenance* and *data integration/application interoperability*, two key problems of software development today. Thus, its declared *goals* are portability, interoperability, and reusability ([142], pg. 2-2, also cf. [214]), and its *aspired benefits* are easy migration to new technologies, automatic production of integration bridges, support for maintenance, and facilities for early testing and simulation, all based on machine-readable application and data models ([142], chapter 1, pp. 1-2). The MDA is based on several OMG standards such as UML, MOF, and XMI and can be used with domain-specific extensions such as CWM or the UML Profile for Enterprise Distributed Object Computing (EDOC) [172].

Being an *architectural framework*, the MDA does not describe a specific approach to MDD but rather a family of approaches centering on model transformations between different viewpoints on the system to be developed. It does not propose any particular software development process, a fact, which, though criticized by Kent [132], helps MDA to avoid the core problem of CASE (see section 3.2.1). Kleppe et al. provide a short list of possible processes and their suitability for MDA ([134], pp. 40-42).

Typically, the designers start with the creation of a *Computation-Independent Model (CIM)*, a domain model, which describes the problem independently from the implementation in the vocabulary of the domain's practitioners. This model serves as an informal basis for the design of the *Platform-Independent Model (PIM)*. The PIM is a technology-neutral description of the system, ideally described as a program for a generic virtual machine. This neutral model, when combined with a *Platform Model*, i.e., a description of the technical concepts and services of a specific platform, can be transformed into the corresponding *Platform-Specific Model (PSM)*. The PSM in turn may be used as the starting point for subsequent transformations, which eventually lead to the generation of source code. The output of a transformation can also include a *record of transformation*, which can be used to synchronize the PIM and PSM in the case of changes in either model ([142], chapter 2).

The MDA is somewhat open in its definitions and *offers several alternatives* for the nature of the models and the transformations. In the most advanced scenario, the PIM is semantically rich enough to not require additional annotations and can be transformed to code directly. The PSM can still be generated, of course, but mostly serves debugging purposes. On the other end of the scale are transformation approaches where the model elements in the input model are marked with annotations, for example UML stereotypes, which allow mapping rules for the automatic (or manual!) generation of the output model ([142], chapters 3 and 4).

A single input model may also be submitted to several different transformations, e.g., generating the application in variants for different platforms. In a more involved scenario, different components of the system are generated for different platforms, and bridges are automatically provided as part of the transformation ([142], chapter 5).

While the MDA has raised the interest in MDD approaches and offers several intriguing ideas, it is generally too theoretical and abstract to assess its feasibility. These problems along with the intentionally high degree of freedom for its instances have led to a wide range of different implementations. According to Haywood, MDA-based approaches can be separated into two distinct, even competing, branches he calls the *elaborationists* and the *translationists*. In an elaborationist approach, the static aspects of an application are described by PIMs. Additional information is then added by annotating the PIMs to create PSMs. However, the behavior of the modeled system is mainly described by code added to the generated files, limiting code generation to about 50-60%. *ArcStyler*, a tool by IO-Software falls into this category [120]. Translationists, on the other hand, aim at 100% code generation, specifying behavior by using statecharts and an action language compliant to the Precise Action Semantics of

UML [163], generally eschewing the use of PSMs. As an example for the translationist approach Haywood cites the *Executable UML* [110]. In the following two subsections, both schools of thought are illustrated by their corresponding example.

3.2.2.2 ArcStyler

As has already been mentioned, an example for the *elaborationist approach* is the ArcStyler tool by IO-Software [120]. While there are similar tools such as AndroMDA [2], ArcStyler was chosen as an example, because it is one of the most well-known commercial products in the MDA context. It is advertised as addressing "real world needs of system developers" ([121], pg. 3) and as the "only fully cross-platform and cross-vendor MDA solution on the market" ([121], pg. 3).

ArcStyler is oriented very much towards programmers, helping with the generation of code for the technical infrastructure but leaving protected sections in it for developers to add their code. The level of abstraction is relatively low, as can be seen in the "Hello World" example provided by IO-Software (see [119]). The modeler is able to configure every single aspect of the target platform in the code generation modules. On the other hand, the tool does support several key features of the MDA such as platform independence or support for standards such as UML and XMI. The development process is tightened thanks to the integration of tools for all steps. Another feature seen a major selling point by IO-Software is the automatic generation of documentation ([121], pg. 9).

Overall, ArcStyler appears to be more of a support tool for traditional software development than a new level of raised abstraction. Given the purpose of the tool, i.e., generating useable code of high performance, and the fact that a tool based on a completely different paradigm is probably hard to sell, this conservative stance is understandable and a good choice. However, other approaches such as Executable UML are of greater interest in the context of this dissertation and therefore ArcStyler is not discussed in further detail.

3.2.2.3 Executable UML

Executable UML, a descendant of the Shlaer-Mellor approach [194], can form the core of an MDA-based software engineering methodology and is a good example for a *translationist approach*. It is described by Mellor and Balcer ([140], for a summary see Mellor [141]).

Executable UML uses a *subset of UML* with slight changes to the semantics in order to ensure that the models are executable. According to Mellor, it is "a profile of UML that allows you ... to define the behavior of a single subject matter in sufficient detail that it can be executed"; still, the models provide a higher level of abstraction than code, because "there is no point in writing 'code' in UML just to rewrite it in Java or C++" ([140], pg. xxvii). The *higher level of abstraction* is achieved by not modeling such aspects as distribution, transactions, or specific concurrency algorithms. Therefore, Executable UML is not just a visual programming language ([140], pg. 9, however, cf. the description of diagrammatic visual programming languages in [67], pg. 1868). As a consequence, a specific model compiler is needed for each platform, a "one-size-fits-all" solution being too complex to realize ([140], pg. 10). The choice of compiler depends on the user's specific requirements with regard to performance, distribution etc. ([140], pp. 299). Existing model compilers cover platforms such as embedded systems (e.g., with the Bridgepoint tool [1]). A Java/Enterprise JavaBeans (EJB) [58] model compiler or similar solutions are not yet fully realized ([140], pg. 10). The generated code will not be optimal ([140], pg. 11) but with modern systems that is an acceptable trade-off.

The core models for Executable UML are class diagrams and statechart diagrams with procedures made up of actions. Other models can be included but are not part of the executable model ([140], pp. 6-7). As an initial step, the application to be modeled is modularized and for each model a *class diagram* is devised. Afterwards, *statechart diagrams* are defined for all relevant classes. These diagrams include procedures made up of actions defined in an *action language* compliant with the Precise Action Semantics for UML. The actions in the procedures can access the data in an object of the class they are defined for, in order to read or alter it, and can be used to send *signals* to other objects, causing instance creation, destruction, or state changes with associated procedure executions. As a final step, the different models are integrated using *bridges*, i.e., amongst other things, external actors in one module are mapped to elements in another module. It should be mentioned that the approach does not distinguish between a PIM and PSM, using the models described here directly as a basis for code generation.

Executable UML is a realistic down-to-earth approach to MDA, which does not promise magical results, but rather raises the level of abstraction in a reasonable way by sacrificing degrees of freedom in order to hide technology-specific details. It also requires choosing the right model compiler based on a requirements analysis ([140], chapter 18.3). The case study in [140] illustrates the power of this approach. According to Mellor, the Executable UML is also a good foundation for agile methods [141].

3.3 A Critical Evaluation of MDD Approaches

The previous two sections have described the goals of MDD as well as existing implementations, which aim at reaching these goals. However, not everyone agrees with the visions of the various proponents of MDD. Neither are the claims and marketing slogans made by the vendors of existing solutions regarding the state of the art as well as the future potentials universally accepted. There are some rather exaggerated claims, which Frankel feels are responsible for much of the criticism brought forward against MDD [73]. Before looking at the shortcomings of MDD though, the open questions found in its context will be discussed.

3.3.1 Open Questions

As can be seen in the division into translationist and elaborationist camps as well as the large number of MDD variants currently existing, there are still several questions, which have yet to be answered satisfactorily, in order to avoid the fragmentation, which led to the downfall of earlier approaches. In particular, Selic feels that a lot of research is still needed to find out what MDD can and cannot do. Until then any amount of "hype" and associated over-expectations will only do harm to the idea of MDD [191]. It should be noted that the view on open questions adopted in this section is purely technical and deliberately ignores such problems as the concrete division of responsibility between various organizations as mentioned by Bézivin ([31], pg. 46).

One central problem of MDD is choosing the most suitable *abstraction level*. While some metamodels such as the workflow models by Breton and Bézivin [37] reside on a high level of abstraction, UML's Action Semantics constructs are very concrete and fine-grained. It appears that works with a main focus on code generation prefer the increase in the abstraction level to be as low as possible (cf. [140], [111], [34]), whereas works with a main focus on users and usability favor strong abstraction in order to allow business experts and other non software developers to build models (cf. [37], [191]). It is possible to reconcile both approaches using refinement processes, but the question for adequate abstraction levels still remains (even though it has been identified some time ago, for example by Harel and Gery [106]). OMG's MDA defines three levels, characterized as being "computation independent", "platform independent", and "platform-specific", respectively [142]. Which level or levels are reasonable, expedient, and at the same time feasible represents an interesting research topic.

However, multiple levels of abstraction lead to another problem, the need for *model transformations*. Currently, there is no standard for these transformations yet, however, eight different propositions have been made for the OMG's Query/Views/Transformations RFP [162], which are summarized by Gardner et al. [77].

While the OMG seems determined to incorporate model transformations into its MDA approach, many researchers question whether it makes sense to perform a model transformation between a platform-independent and a platform-specific model before code generation, especially translationists such as Mellor and Balcer [140]. If the transformation rules are transitive, the value of intermediate steps can at least be questioned, unless modifications are made to the transformation output. These modifications, however, lead to the same problems inherent to all elaborationist approaches. Some proposals ([137], [75]) suggest even more modeling levels, involving manual refinement activities between those levels. Kent goes even further, feeling that a division between PIMs and PSMs describes only one dimension of model categories, suggesting adding others such as different subject areas (e.g. an order processing subsystem), which would lead to several models requiring additional transformations [132]. An alternative described later is the use of metamodel hierarchies.

If a system is specified by several models presenting different views, it becomes inevitable to integrate them in some way in order to show *interdependencies between modeling elements*. One proposal to this end is an integration model as described in [37]. The Executable UML addresses this problem with a so-called domain chart (cf. [140]). However, both of these solutions are tailored towards specific needs and are therefore not universal.

An *open problem for the translationists* is the creation of a universally applicable model compiler in order to realize the *compiler metaphor* frequently mentioned ([140], [190], [208], [210]). Not only must the code generator produce complete, self-contained source code that does not need to be extended or modified, but it must also be possible to recover compile-time and runtime errors directly in the models, not only in the generated code. Similar to source code, the models have to be verified when they are built, transformed, and used for code generation (cf. [190]). Currently, such a "model compiler" does not yet exist, at least not for a general case and the complex issues around it are yet to be resolved. *Elaborationists*, on the other hand, have different issues to address, for example, the question of whether and how to incorporate *round-trip engineering*, which is difficult due to the different levels of abstraction (cp. Völter [210]).

Other problems of equal importance are the maintenance (as opposed to integration) of *legacy systems* and whether or not to consider them in the context of MDD, *versioning* and administration tools for models [210] and templates [110], and the realization of a *unified standard for transformation and code generation languages* [210].

3.3.2 Problems in the Context of MDD and Potential Solutions

Critics of MDD and others, who are skeptical about the claims made regarding the state of the art, identify several problems of model-driven approaches. In the following sections the most common and convincing arguments are presented along with an analysis of the problem and potential solutions.

3.3.2.1 Platform Independence

One of the marketing arguments for MDA, the achievement of *platform independence* and thus *improved portability*, is contested by several authors. Fowler, for example, believes that if a platform is defined as a specific programming language such as Java as opposed to a specific hardware/OS combination, it is wrong to claim that the introduction of a new language, even a modeling language, offers platform independence [71]. In a similar vein, Haywood criticizes that many MDD solutions are vendor specific, introducing a new platform dependency of a different kind [110], clearly a step back to the age of CASE tools.

Haywood also questions the *usefulness of platform independence*, claiming that platforms, especially enterprise systems and Web Services [212], are far more stable than the business aspects of systems. Therefore, there is no real advantage to being platform independent. Also, Haywood doubts that MDA tools would help to keep up to date all the time, citing the fact that the transformation rules (and therefore code generation templates) for each platform are a *cost factor* that is not to be neglected. Finally, he criticizes that many of the current commercial MDA tools cannot be used for arbitrary MOF metamodels so far and are unlikely to have this feature in the future, factors, which also limit platform independence [110]. Cook mentions **reduced performance** and **compromises in platform integration** as additional problems, which he feels were the "primary downfall of many [platform independent] products in the past" [52].

The arguments against platform independence are, in my opinion, a quite realistic assessment, however, other authors disagree. For example, Ambler, an opponent of MDD (cf. [208]), identifies the constantly ***changing technologies*** and more specifically the focus of education on technologies, as opposed to the common concepts behind them, as a major problem of today's software development practice, because it keeps the level of skill in software development low ([8], chapter 1). With platform independence, this problem could be solved, providing a counter-argument against claims that platform independence is not required.

Regarding the cost factor, an interesting proposal how general platform independence can be realized is offered by Bézivin. He envisions that in the future the market will punish those ***platform providers***, who do not include standard templates with their products ([31], pg. 10). Thus, it will not be necessary to put a lot of effort into the in-house development of templates, reducing the cost factor. Yet, whether such a scenario is applicable or not remains to be seen. It only seems realistic if MDD becomes wide-spread and its templates standardized, e.g., with the introduction of a common transformation language.

Nevertheless, it is true that the platform independence concept is the primary weak point of model-driven development, because it will be expensive to come up with new templates for new platforms, regardless of whether they are bought or custom-made. In addition, if it is true that the problem domain is more likely to change than the solution domain or if a more conservative investment policy reduces the number of platform changes, the usefulness of platform independence is greatly diminished.

Regardless of its value in general, I do believe that, on a smaller scale, platform independence can be achieved, for example for the ***user interface***, generating code for different clients such as Web browsers or mobile phones. Within a strictly limited and easily tested field, changes would not be as costly, thus allowing the software designers to keep up with the current developments in key areas. Similarly, it might be useful to support several platforms, which are suitable for different system complexities (cf. the discussion in [85]) and to support minimal platform independence for the creation of bridges to ensure interoperability.

3.3.2.2 Code Generation

Another heavily contested aspect of MDD is *code generation*. Glass, for example, assumes that those, who argue in favor of code generation, typically "vendors selling automation tools" and "gurus promoting 'breakthrough' concepts", believe that "software work ... is easy, is automatable, and can be done by anyone" while it actually is "the most complex undertaking humanity has ever tried", requiring a level of creativity, which can not be provided by a machine ([100], also cf. Steinmann and Kühne [200]). Many people doubt that the problems involved in code generation will eventually be overcome, at least in the near future, due to the fact that most of software development's complexity is essential rather than accidental (see section 3.1.2).

One of the fundamental arguments is that code generation approaches have already failed in the past with CASE tools (cf. Cook [52], Steinmann and Kühne [200], and Uhl and Ambler [208]). Particularly, existing tools are therefore judged to be insufficient with regard to the holistic view of "generative MDD" [208] by critics such as Ambler.

Often arguments against code generation target the *intended input format*, i.e., graphical modeling languages, as *insufficient for code generation*. Many researchers complain about the expressional weaknesses of UML and other existing modeling languages and therefore consider them to be an inadequate starting basis for automatic code generation ([103], pp. 116, [208]). However, adding additional expressiveness harbors the problem that models will become too complex [200]. Glass and, to some extent, Cook share these sentiments, considering it a major mistake to see models as a formal analysis, preferring an interpretation of *models as sketches* used to facilitate the communication between domain experts and developers (cf. [97], [52]). As a related problem, some researchers feel that a graphical environment will not be beneficial to software development with too much effort required for the graphical modeling aspects (cf. [71], [199], [200]).

Some authors identify the fact that *behavior is difficult to model* as a reason for the shortcomings of models as code generation input (cf. Haywood [110], Steinmann and Kühne [200]). Giving UML as an example, Haywood points out that interaction diagrams describe only example cases as opposed to a general behavior and that approaches based on the UML's Object Constraint Language (OCL) are too complex for the average modeler, resulting in complex and difficult-to-understand code. The alternative solution, using action semantic languages as advocated by the translationists, also has some problems. While the translationists undeniably enjoyed some success, their approaches are largely confined to real time or embedded systems and with vendor-specific metamodels, introducing a new compatibility problem [110].

Code insertion sections in the generated code as promoted by elaborationists, on the other hand, avoid these problems but remove the responsibility from the model and negate the term model-centric [110]. Also, when using code insertion, pitfalls such as the overwriting of hand-written code during new generation runs or debugging problems due to cryptic generated code have to be avoided (cp. Kent [133]).

Even though these arguments are plausible, there are several counterarguments that can be brought forth in favor of code generation. The argument that programming is *creative work* and that there is too little accidental complexity must be seriously doubted in light of the abstractions proposed by the Executable UML or the programming overhead inherent to J2EE. While only an empirical study could provide concrete numbers, these examples strongly suggest a great amount of accidental complexity in currently used systems, which can be avoided through code generation. Indeed, Selic feels that a rejection only stems from the fact that many of the arguments against using models as a basis for code generation are based on a misunderstanding regarding what a model described in a modern modeling language really means [191].

The argument that *past approaches* to code generation have failed has an interesting connotation to it as it seems to suggest that one should try to solve only problems where the solution is already known. However, it seems natural to focus one's research efforts on problems that have not been solved yet, trying to learn from the factors, which led to the earlier failure. It is true that there are those, who repeat past mistakes, but most serious MDD approaches try to avoid the problems of CASE and, as has been described in section 3.2.1, both the goals and the premises of MDD differ in some core aspects from those of CASE. Thus, MDD cannot be equated with CASE or other early approaches, exhibiting enough differences to justify continued research in this field.

The argument that *models as input format* are unsuitable cannot be denied outright when considering the currently existing modeling languages. However, these problems should not be insurmountable. For example, the Precise UML Group is currently working to reduce the ambiguity of the UML [175], allowing a clear mapping from models to code. It remains to be seen whether this endeavor will be successful or not.

The argument that it is difficult or impossible to model *behavior* is one that I feel is based on a misunderstanding. Obviously, a sketch-like model is a high-level abstraction that removes a lot of the essential complexity and is thus useless for code generation purposes. A more realistic increase in abstraction has to use some sort of action language (see for example the recently added UML Action Semantics). The examples found in the context of Executable UML show that the resulting complexity is still lower than in source code.

Overall, it seems that the arguments brought forth against code generation address existing problems but are often too pessimistic or counter some outrageous marketing claim. With a translationist solution within reach, elaborationist attempts to me seem impractical and of limited use when compared to tools such as XDoclet, even though their pitfalls can be overcome by treating the models as part of the code, i.e., making them subject to versioning (cf. [133]).

There are, however, two problems in code generation not identified elsewhere, which should be addressed by the MDD community. First, the claim that generated code will constitute *software of better quality* is, in my opinion, questionable. While it is often supported by reasonable arguments why such a quality improvement would be the case, and there are studies in related fields (e.g. software reuse for product lines [138]), which circumstantiate these statements, there is still room for doubts. In particular, if code generation facilities are assembled from different vendors' products, or if the platform and therefore the template are changed frequently, it can at least be doubted that the resulting code would be better than hand-written one. More importantly, while it has been shown that code can be generated from models, the question remains whether the new level of abstraction is improvement enough to justify the *paradigm change* involved in moving away from code and using models instead.

3.3.2.3 Other Aspects

While not arguing against model-centric approaches in general, Spinellis feels that using graphical models a great deal of the time (which the typical MDD approach implies) will *decrease productivity*. Spinellis states that while a graphical representation is far easier to understand than a textual one, the "tedious and time consuming" ([199], pg. 96) task of properly arranging the classes detracts attention from the important design decisions. Also, Spinellis fears the inherent danger that major refactoring will be avoided in order to not to have to rearrange the classes to accommodate the alterations. In his opinion, it is far better to model declaratively in the form of text and to generate graphical views automatically for visual representation [199]. This sentiment is shared to some extent by Fowler [71], Kent [133], and Steinmann and Kühne [200], who fear that UML will become a visual programming language of low abstraction and are not convinced that this will offer any improvements over current programming techniques.

While the arguments given against graphical modeling are reasonable, it is my opinion that models will appeal to different people than programming languages do. While detailed research in this respect is beyond the scope of this work, I am convinced that some people are better at working with text and others are more adept at thinking in pictures. Different people will excel at different tasks and graphically oriented people would be able realize the potential of MDD without suffering from the problems described above.

Haywood criticizes that MDD is not as *model-centric* as often claimed, but that there are still several different places where changes are required. For elaborationist approaches there are up to four points, i.e., PIM, PSM, code, and transformations where a system might have to be changed for maintenance. While the translationist approaches have only two points, i.e., PIM and transformation templates, the promise of having only the model to change is not kept. Changes to the transformations are of particular interest, requiring intelligent versioning to avoid problems [110]. Thus, the promise of *improved maintainability* might not be fulfilled by an MDD approach, especially if MDA-based.

These arguments are interesting because they are hard to deny. Finding a solution, which helps to avoid problems due to the changes in the code transformation templates is a major challenge. However, as stated before, frequent changes of platform and thus alterations to the code templates are not worthwhile. Therefore, if platform independence is discarded, it is possible to establish the model as the single point for changes. For example, maintenance-heavy projects or software products, which need to be heavily customized for each instance (i.e., *software product lines* to use the term in a general sense) belong to this category. In these cases, the same code generation templates can be used many times, because change will be confined to the business logic. MDD as a help for *software maintenance* is a very attractive proposition; the shortage of tools for maintenance is seen as a major problem by members of the software engineering community (e.g., Glass [95]).

Another problem with MDD is the *hidden initial cost*. Haywood states that the development and debugging of transformations will clearly be an intensive process and therefore be costly. The cost will be particularly high if changes to the transformations have to be made, something very likely for a solution that requires new software rather than a "Commercial of the Shelf" (CotS) solution [110]. Völter identifies the same difficulty but believes that MDD will pay off in the long run if used for the right kinds of problems such as the implementation of *software system families* (SFF), i.e., applications, which share enough common properties to warrant the creation and maintenance of code templates [210]. The extension mechanism proposed in this dissertation also aims at reducing the initial cost by providing a formalized framework for the reuse of templates (see section 6.1.3).

As a last point of criticism, some researchers fear that there will be problems on an *organizational and personal level* ([110], [210]). Haywood believes that organizations, which did not show any interest into models such as logical and physical data models so far, are unlikely to develop the discipline to work with PIMs. He also feels that the deep structural changes required by switching to MDA, i.e., the shift from programming skill requirements to modeling, will be difficult to perform [110]. However, Völter believes that a gradual change can alleviate these problems [210].

3.4 A New Vision of MDD

In the previous sections, the goals and promises of MDD were critically analyzed, showing that there are certain potential shortcomings with regard to platform independence and code generation. However, by reducing the stakes, it is possible to overcome these problems and possibly lay the foundations for further progress in the field of MDD. In particular, the following issues with regard to MDD should be critically evaluated:

- *Platform independence* is an alluring but costly property, which is most likely not needed to the extent promised by the OMG
- The *increase in abstraction*, when using today's inexpressive modeling languages as opposed to programming languages, is not as spectacular as often claimed.

The first issue is one that probably cannot be resolved on a grand scale but this is not really necessary as, according to Fowler, the lack found in the "platform independent argument" does not mean that "MDA is a waste of time" [71]. On the one hand, platform independence can still be used in critical but limited areas such as user interfaces and possibly to implement bridges between systems. On the other hand, there are many additional benefits of MDD such as faster development, which are still desirable and attainable. In essence, the computer takes over the routine work [210], the existence of which even those, who see software development as a highly creative process, have to admit (cf. Glass [100]).

The second issue, however, must be resolved in order to make the use of MDD appealing. While there is no general solution to this problem yet, there are many approaches, which work in small and well-understood domains such as embedded systems, telecommunication protocols, or real-time programming (see Booch et al. [35], Mellor and Balcer [140], and as a concrete example National Instruments' LabVIEW [145]). While there are also some examples from Enterprise Computing, these seem to be elaborationist approaches and are therefore not considered here ([120], [210]). It is interesting to note that apparently those domains, which have clearly defined interaction points for input and output, are most suited for MDD approaches.

Many of the translationist examples predate the MDA initiative of the OMG and are sometimes considered to be visual programming languages (cf. Ferucci et al. [67]). However, even if applied to specific domains, MDD aims at going beyond such niche solutions, offering an infrastructure for domain-specific solutions instead of a single isolated domain-specific code generation tool, which means re-inventing the wheel over and over again. Based on the experiences gained with the precursors of MDD, it should be possible to come up with highly reusable solutions. In the next section, the problems associated with domain-specific MDD will be discussed.

3.5 Domain-Specific MDD

Domain-specific MDD focuses on maximizing the increase in abstraction by using the semantics of a domain. Many MDD supporters see domain-specific approaches as the "low hanging fruits" [73] of model-centric development being the easiest option for complete code generation (see [35], [52], [73], [210], and to some extent [140]).

While there are some success stories for *domain-specific MDD* cited in the previous section, these are difficult and time-consuming to verify for somebody who does not have at least basic knowledge of their corresponding domains. For this reason, a more general rationale in favor of domain-specific MDD might be helpful at this point. Domains such as compiler-compilers, databases, or Enterprise Resource Planning (ERP) systems are all homogenous enough to allow a solution to their associated problems with standard software (see Glass [101]). While there are still domains, which are not covered by a CotS solution, it can be argued that many of these domains are homogenous enough to at least allow the introduction of domain-specific modeling languages, which can generate software for the various instances in the domain. Additionally, domain-specific approaches will be able to better address the intrinsic differences in various software domains. Glass, an avid critic of MDD in general, speaks out in favor of tailored domain-specific solutions (cf. [96], [98]):

"Let's acknowledge the diversity of application domains and realize that different domains require different techniques. ... [A]dvocates of every new concept to come along ... have claimed that it's universally applicable. Those claims are, almost without exception, wrong" ([98], pg. 103).

Domain-specific metamodels allow for better modeling of behavior for two reasons. First of all, the *problem domain is far smaller* and thus there are far less problem variants than in a general case. More importantly, however, as Booch et al. point out, the model-to-code mapping will "make assumptions about the domain to greatly reduce the size of the specification by exploiting regularities" ([35], also see [103], pg. 59), thus also reducing the number of allowed mappings from problem to solution domain. For example, a domain-specific language for Web applications will not allow the modeling of database details. Instead, the model compiler will make these choices based on heuristics. Similarly, the definition of the physical presentation will probably be part of the model and is therefore likely to be limited in some way. This *degree of freedom vs. level of abstraction tradeoff* is in parallel to the one made with the introduction of compilers as opposed to machine code. Presumably, it is for this very reason that so far code generation has been most successfully used in areas where there is only a limited degree of freedom to begin with, for example embedded systems or window-based GUIs, which are heavily dominated by the operating system's style guide.

Another view on domain-specific MDD is that it is a *hybrid between a generic CotS application and a custom implementation*, trying to combine the advantages of both, i.e., the fast availability with the ability to customize. Obviously, this is not entirely possible and the result might not suit the needs of a particular customer. On the other hand, there is a vast potential for cost reduction. To make a bold statement, it seems possible that a customer, when faced with the fact that a seemingly minor but really specific change to a Web site's appearance, e.g., the inclusion of a three-dimensional pie chart to replace an existing 2D solution, causes a significant increase in price, it might lose a lot of its urgency. The decision regarding whether customization or cost reduction takes precedence for a particular project depends on the circumstances. A similar opinion is expressed by Steinmann and Kühne, who see a shift from programming to "configuration" as an important aspect of MDD [200].

But domain-specific modeling is more than a workaround for MDD problems. It actively contributes to the goal of *increased abstraction*. For example, Booch et al. identify a *semantic gap* between domain and technology concepts and see a reduction "of the semantic distance between problem domain and representation" as an enabler for "more accurate designs and increased productivity" [35]. In other words, by removing technical aspects from the modeling language, the domain specialists will be able to focus on the actual problem instead of tedious technological details. Without these technological distractions, there is a potential to build better software, but not because of the high quality of the templates as suggested by some (see section 3.3.2.2) but because of the reduction of accidental complexity due to the removal of technological aspects.

It has already been hinted at that MDD can be seen as a descendent of *visual programming languages* in some respects. These existing domain-specific metamodels/visual programming languages differ widely in their level of abstraction and basic structure, therefore most require unique software tools to support them. The added benefit of MDD, besides the claim of platform independence, is that all domain-specific languages are "dialects" of the same language, adhere to the same principles, and are supported by the same infrastructure. Not only does this mean that learning languages for new domains is fast and simple, thereby addressing one of the problems of domain-specific languages (cf. [85]), it also implies that new domain-specific metamodels can be introduced relatively quickly and that exiting dialects are easy to modify and, more importantly, easy to extend (cf. Steinmann and Kühne [200]).

There are several different ways to realize this vision of domain-specific MDD, among them well-known lightweight solutions such as class libraries or stereotypes. In the following sections, the requirements for a domain-specific MDD environment are identified and the different possible solutions will be analyzed in the lights of these requirements.

3.5.1 Requirements for Domain-Specific MDD

As has been mentioned before, the core concept of MDD is to raise the level of abstraction by focusing on the model as central artifact. A detailed analysis has shown that not all of MDD's goals are realistic but that a domain-specific approach might help to achieve the remaining goals. The following requirements are identified in the literature as crucial for the realization of a domain-specific MDD environment:

- The environment must provide a *language/metamodel definition* for each relevant domain with both syntax and semantics (i.e., a precise mapping to real world elements). This encompasses an abstract syntax, which describes the concepts available, a concrete syntax, which provides the elements for the graphical notation (and which can be interchangeable), and mappings from model elements to real-world artifacts including code [19]. This mapping can be considered a set of model interpretation rules ([156], pg. 18). The *level of abstraction* of the language must be raised significantly as opposed to the programming languages used in code generation but must still be meaningful, to avoid the problems identified by Ambler [208] and Haywood [110].
- The environment should have a high degree of *modularity* ([82], pg. 26), i.e., a *dynamic extension* in the form of new languages and code generation modules must be possible without major effort ([19], [156], pg. 7, [82], pg. 26). The implementation of new domain-specific "dialects" should allow the *reuse* of already existing concepts to a high degree and changes to existing languages should affect as few elements as possible. Ideally, different domain-specific languages can be *integrated* with each other [210].
- Mappings for the *interchange of models* between different tools ([19], [156], pg. 7) should be feasible to avoid a new kind of platform dependence.
- The facilities to perform *formal analyses and simulations* of models ([156], pg. 7) must be incorporated.
- *Compiler-like behavior* ([140], [190], [208]) with error messages that identify problems in the models and not within the generated source code is helpful. This includes validation support ([82], pg. 26).

While these requirements are particular to domain-specific MDD, they are also related to the general goals and benefits defined for MDD in general. Table 3 shows the relationship between the criteria described above and the goals discussed in sections 3.1 and 3.3.

The next sections give a presentation of concepts for domain-specific MDD with and without metamodels (cf. Gitzel and Korthaus [88] for an earlier version of this analysis). The approaches are evaluated based on the list of requirements described above. Of particular interest is the criterion of modularity and dynamic extensibility, since the goal of this dissertation is to provide an improved *extension mechanism* and thus it is crucial to identify the proper technological basis. It is important to realize that domain-specific MDD tools, which do not provide such a mechanism, are a step back to the era of early visual programming languages. While the possible modeling paradigms are boundless, it seems prudent to limit the discussion to object-oriented models and assume a visual means of modeling. According to Atkinson and Kühne, this combination is very suitable to cover the requirements of the list given above [17].

3.5.2 Non-Metamodeling Approaches to Domain-Specific MDD

While users of domain-specific MDD tools might think otherwise, there is little potential in non-metamodeling approaches. This is due to the fact that any kind

Requirements	Goals/Benefits
Language (metamodel) definition and mappings	• raised level of abstraction • automatic code generation • separation of concerns • increased productivity • emphasis on modeling and design • partial platform independence
Modularity and dynamic extensibility	• improved maintenance • support for different domains • improved reusability
Model interchange	• improved reusability • improved maintenance • improved portability
Formal analyses and simulations	• improved software quality
Compiler-like behavior	• rapid development • improved software quality

Table 3 - Requirements for Domain-Specific MDD

of modeling language definition implies a metamodel. Therefore, if an MDD approach makes no mention of a metamodel, it nevertheless exists implicitly; otherwise there would be neither an abstract nor a concrete syntax.

However, it is possible that tools *limit the role of the metamodel* to a pure language definition inaccessible to the user, which exists only implicitly and is "hard-coded" into the MDD software. Such a metamodel does not have to be formally defined and will be largely ignored. In light of the requirements list for domain-specific approaches provided above, this has to be considered highly problematic. While the *compiler-like behavior* and *simulations* can be realized, the other requirements are not so easily met.

First of all, *model interchange* is difficult without an explicit metamodel. While it is possible to come up with bridges, which transform models from one format into another one, problems arise as soon as the metamodels are not equivalent, and in the context of domain-specific models such a situation is not unlikely. A better strategy is not to transform the models but to import a suitable metamodel along with the model into other tools. Nordstrom for example argues that a metamodel is in this case not only helpful but required ([156], pg. 14). This exchange is not possible if the metamodel is only implicit.

Additionally, the non-metamodeling approach lacks major *extensibility potential*. While a *mapping to code* is possible without a known metamodel, user defined mappings are going to be difficult, as elements of the model are usually mapped to code based on their type, i.e., which element of the metamodel they instantiate. As a simple example, consider a code generation rule, which maps UML classes to Java classes. Without access to a metamodel such a rule cannot be defined, because which elements in a model are to be considered "UML classes" is defined in the metamodel. Similarly, *user extensions to the syntax* are quite difficult without access to the metamodel, which represents the language definition unless one uses class libraries as described below.

3.5.2.1 Class Libraries and Inheritance

The *easiest domain-specific extension* of a model, and the only one that can be used without explicit access to the metamodel, is to introduce domain-specific classes and use them as a basis for modeling by using generalization. While the classes do not form a language, class libraries can, to a certain extent, provide the same information as domain-specific language elements and can be used to describe user-defined domains. Since both inheritance and instantiation relationships are sometimes colloquially called "is-a" relationships, there is clearly some kind of conceptual overlap between the two concepts.

The technique is illustrated by an example from the domain of art, which will be used throughout this section. The domain contains the concepts *Artist* and *WorkOfArt*. *Artists* can be representatives of one or several *Styles* and be associated with one or more *Regions*. Each *WorkOfArt* also belongs to a *Style*. The

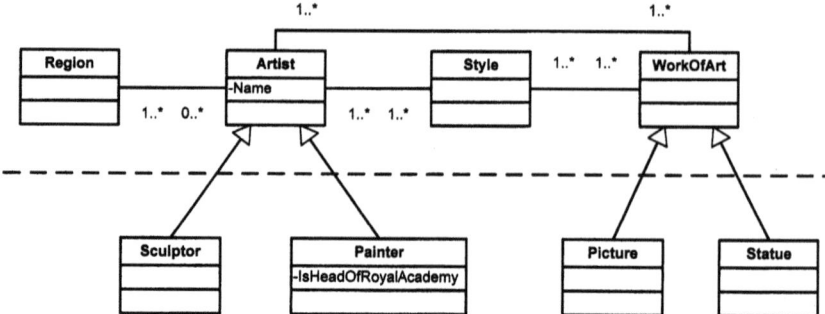

Figure 15 - Inheritance as a Substitute for Instantiation

concepts are assumed to carry a strongly defined meaning, which can help in code generation.

Figure 15 shows an example, where the domain extension is realized with inheritance. *Artists* of all kinds can be associated with *Styles* and *Regions*. *WorksOfArt* (both *Pictures* and *Statues*) can also be associated with a *Style*. The model is kept simple and a genius like Michelangelo, who was both *Painter* and *Sculptor*, would not fit into this schema unless multiple inheritance is used.

One advantage of using inheritance is the relatively **low complexity** (compared to ontological metamodel hierarchies as described in section 3.5.4.2). Also, the classes defined in the class library are not only available as superclasses for user-defined classes but can also be used directly in the user's model. The latter is possible due to a relatively weak separation between the superclasses and the subclasses as opposed to that between types and their instances (see the strictness discussion in section 2.4.4 for further details). Whether this **lack of separation** is an advantage or a disadvantage depends on individual interpretation.

However, there are also other disadvantages. For example, the model in Figure 15 in no way forbids objects of *Painter* to have a link to a *Statue* object, even though this restriction was probably intended, thus introducing the opportunity for **domain violations** in the model. Extensive use of constraints can address this problem but reduces or negates the simplicity advantage of inheritance and does not scale well with larger models as the constraints are required for every class. Removing the association between *Artist* and *WorkOfArt* and replacing it with individual sub-associations solves the problem of false links but removes an important aspect of the model, which is the information that artists are somehow related to works of art.

Another disadvantage is the **lack of control over the subclasses**. Modelers, who receive the classes above the parting line in Figure 15 as a class library, have little if any guidance how to define their own classes. Due to the syntax of inheritance, the new classes can have arbitrary attributes, even ones that do not make any sense in the domain. Some people might not think of this liberty as a drawback, but it can be argued that it is an advantage to prohibit invalid cases instead of having undefined behavior.

A more serious drawback of this liberty is that the new attributes and new associations that are introduced do not depend on the class library in any way. This means that no information whatsoever exists about their *domain-specific semantics*. However, for code generation and model validation such information is very helpful if not mandatory.

To recapitulate, inheritance and class libraries can be used to provide user defined metamodel extensions but are generally too unrestrictive to convey the full meaning of the newly introduced concepts. Thus, class libraries are only partially suitable for dynamic extensions as well as domain-specific MDD environments in general.

3.5.3 Single Metalayer Approaches

Even when looking at conventional approaches, metamodeling takes a very central role in domain-specific MDD. According to Atkinson and Kühne it is even "an essential foundation" of MDD in general [17]. While this claim is debatable, primarily from the point of view of the users of MDD tools, many researchers try to improve existing MDD concepts by enhancing their metamodeling aspects (e.g., Atkinson and Kühne [17], Nordstrom [155], or the various works of the Precise UML Group [175]). However, metamodeling is complex, so restricting oneself to a *single metalayer* seems appealing. In one of his earlier works, Atkinson provides an argument against multi-level metamodeling, citing the fact that many of the concepts at the M2 level are often replicated at the M3 level and that it is possible to limit oneself to a single metalayer and still have the same modeling power [22]. While it is true that an end user is not interested in any higher modeling layers, for example, many UML users are probably unaware of the existence and nature of its metamodels, the advantages of metamodeling are generally seen in other directions as will be shown later on (see section 3.5.4). Single metalayer approaches cannot meet all of the requirements as described above.

While the single metalayer approach is well-suited for the traditional "role of defining languages" [19] and can provide model *simulation* and *compiler-like behavior*, it is not sufficient for the other requirements. The first problem occurs with *model tool interoperability*, which profits from a metalevel above the concrete metamodels (cf. [19], [156] pg. 14). Just as M1 models can be loaded by tools based on the same M2 metamodel, serialized M2 metamodels can be used by tools, which use the same M3 metamodel in which the M2 metamodels are defined. After dynamically loading a metamodel, models based on this metamodel can be created or manipulated. The CDIF metamodel hierarchy was created for specifically this application. Without these additional metalayers, metamodels cannot be loaded; there simply exists no common format for the metamodels!

The question of whether *user-defined metamodel extensions* can be realized with a single metalayer is not easily answered, even though some researchers are convinced of it (cf. [74]). There are several ways to allow the extension of metamodels, without allowing the user explicitly to metamodel, such as patterns or stereotypes as well as the class library approach described in the previous section. The following sub-sections provide a look at patterns and stereotypes and their suitability as domain-specific extension mechanisms.

3.5.3.1 Patterns

According to Albin, design patterns are similar to metamodels, as both describe working principles, which influence the structure of the code implementing the concepts of the model ([6], chapter 11). It is not unreasonable to imagine patterns, which describe elements of a metamodel in such a way as to make them obsolete. For example, instead of defining a metamodel with elements such as model, view, and controller, the Model View Controller (MVC) pattern (see [76]) could be applied to generic classes. Thus, a pattern can easily take the role of metamodel elements and a catalogue of patterns could serve as a domain-specific model extension.

Overall, metamodels have far more structure and provide more consistency to their instances than patterns do. Albin states that metamodels are more generic than patterns, as there need not be a one-to-one correspondence between its concepts and elements within the source code of corresponding software. He also cites the fact that patterns can also be used in the context of metamodel hierarchies ([6], chapter 11). Thus, the advantages of patterns and metamodel hierarchies can easily be combined. Since the pattern approach is little more than a *variant on the stereotype concept*, it will not be discussed in detail.

3.5.3.2 Stereotypes

Stereotypes are a *lightweight metamodel extension mechanism*. Instead of introducing new metamodel layers, the existing metamodel is extended. By changing only the immediate metamodel layer, there is no need for users to understand or be aware of the metamodel hierarchy. In the following discussion, the UML 2.0 Profile concept of stereotypes is used (see [168], pp. 164-178). UML 2.0 stereotypes are considered lightweight, because they only allow adding new elements to the metamodel but not to remove or alter already existing elements.

In UML, a stereotype is defined on the M2 layer of the linear UML metamodel hierarchy. While it can be argued that this makes stereotypes a multiple layer approach, the higher layers are transparent to the user of the tool and therefore stereotypes are included in this section. To define which model elements a particular stereotype can be applied to, an instance of *Extension* is used to connect the stereotype to an M2 layer element such as *Class* or *Association*. For example, if a stereotype called <<*Entity*>> is connected to *Class* by an instance of *Extension*, instances of <<*Entity*>> can only be applied to classes (i.e., instances of *Class*).

Generally, a model element may have more than one stereotype. A stereotype defines a number of attributes, which are assigned values on the M1 level, and it can be given constraints, which will affect its instances. Due to the reference the stereotype has on the model element it is attached to, it can also apply constraints on the model element itself and all elements transitively reachable. The stereotype's attributes are sometimes called *tagged values* for historical reasons. However, this terminology is officially no longer used.

To identify the advantages and disadvantages of the stereotype approach, the artist model extension used before is this time modeled with the use of stereotypes as shown in Figure 16. The upper part shows the *UML Profile*, which is a collection of stereotypes. The classes below the line show the actual model that uses the stereotypes. In the example, the profile represents the domain-specific model extension.

The model created using the Profile is simple and intuitive. However, it is interesting to note that the stereotypes as shown in the Figure exercise little control over the classes. Therefore, there is not really a rule, which dictates that the *Painter* and the *Sculptor* class have to have an attribute *Name*. The associations are also not regulated in any way, i.e., there is no rule, which indicates that a *Painter* cannot be associated with a *Sculpture*. Even if the modeler "plays by the rules", this situation is very unsatisfactory as in larger models, some of the required associations are easily forgotten, and there is no way to formally validate these implicit rules, reducing the potential for *formal analyses*. Also, there is no longer a causal connection between associations of the same kind unless they are also stereotyped.

However, as has been mentioned, stereotypes in UML 2.0 can contain constraints. Also, while the notation does not make it clear, stereotypes are linked to

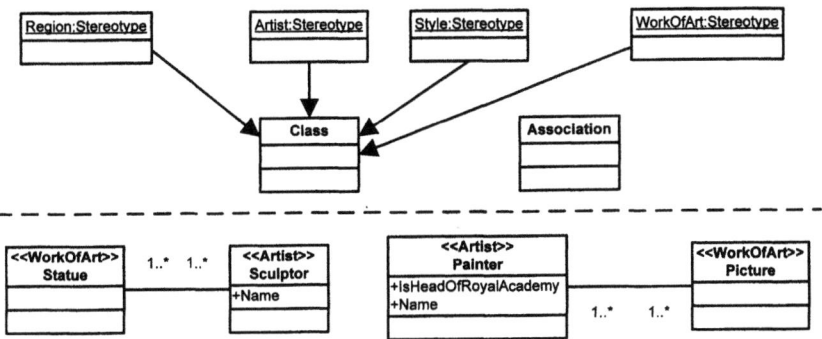

Figure 16 - Stereotypes

their model elements via an instance of the *Extensions* (i.e., the arrows shown in the Figure). Due to this navigable association, the stereotype is able to influence the instances (i.e., model-level classes) its own instances are attached to. While the shortcomings described above can all be avoided this way, the addition of many very similar, but still slightly distinct, constraints counteracts the simplicity of the stereotype concept.

The advantages of stereotypes are twofold. First, they are relatively *easy to use*. Second, they are *easy to implement* in MDD tools, even if those tools do not use a fully-fledged metamodel internally (see [18]). One of their drawbacks (as identified by Atkinson and Kühne) is that they are easily abused to make statements about an object instead of a class, leading to many unnecessary singleton classes in a model, which are only distinguished by the attributes of the stereotype [18]. Another problem is that they exercise little control over the classes they are attached to unless constraints are provided by the user. Cook holds a similar view, feeling that UML profiles offer only a "very limited level of extensibility" [52], which might be explained by the fact that, while the stereotype mechanism allows almost arbitrary extensions, it does not provide any mechanisms to define their meaning, i.e., *language support for a semantic description* (cf. Harel and Rumpe [107], [108]). However, the same argument might be applied to the other extension approaches described in this section, so it is not relevant for the comparison at hand. Nevertheless, it should be noted that people with metamodeling experience seem to dislike stereotypes. Völter, for example, sees the use of UML Profiles as less "conceptually clean" [209] than the use of fully fledged metamodels.

Overall, the quality of the stereotype approach depends a lot on personal preference. UML Profiles are very lightweight but can be fleshed out by adding constraints. This means that, if the metamodel is very generic or a lot of information is provided in the form of natural language, stereotypes are advantageous. If, on the other hand, the metamodel should carry a lot of semantic information, stereotypes will produce hard-to-maintain results due to the addition of many constraints. As domain-specific MDD environments need semantic information for code generation, stereotypes are not a good solution.

Pragmatics might point out in this context that UML Profiles, and therefore stereotypes, are *widely accepted* and apparently sufficient for practical use. Kent in particular points out their great flexibility [132]. However, this view is only partially correct. Duddy, for example, states that many of the UML Profiles designed so far go beyond this simple extension mechanism. He claims that the Enterprise Application Integration (EAI) UML Profile [171] really uses its own metamodel, which does not reuse UML, and cites the EDOC Profile as another example where an originally fully-fledged metamodel was "shoehorned" into the UML Profile context ([62], also see Kent's view on EAI and EDOC in [132]). If these claims are true, they provide a strong argument for the insufficiency of stereotypes as well as showing that stereotypes can be used as a "front end" for more complex extension mechanisms.

3.5.4 Metamodeling Hierarchy Approaches

As discussed in the previous section, the common single metalayer approaches are not very suitable for model exchange, and their domain-specific extensibility has problems with providing sufficient levels of semantics. Metamodel hierarchies not only offer all the advantages provided by single metalayer approaches but also address these open problems.

The fact that metamodel hierarchies offer a solution for *model interchange* between tools has already been mentioned, the most common examples being CDIF and MOF. They also provide a good platform for *dynamic extension mechanisms*. Völter states that metamodeling supports several key aspects of MDD, namely architecture-centric modeling, tool adaptation, model validation, model transformation, and code generation. A metamodel also facilitates domain-specific modeling by providing an infrastructure to define new modeling languages [209]. Given a generic "metametamodel", it is possible to use the same infrastructure to design models for domains, which have vastly different or even contradictory semantics (cf. Cook [51]). A custom metamodel can be used with all the benefits a specialized modeling language offers within a known tool framework. Duddy proposes a vision for MDA where models based on custom metamodels can be designed and then transformed to a PSM common to all metamodels to use for code generation [62]. This vision of UML as a "family of languages" [62] is also advocated in other forms by Atkinson and Kühne [18], Völter [209], Nordstrom ([155], [156]), Frankel [73], Kent [132], Clark et al. [49] and many others. A metamodel hierarchy not only allows the creation of new domain models but also the maintenance of existing ones to incorporate possible changes (cf. Nordstrom [156], pg. 3).

A very interesting interpretation of metamodel hierarchies is given by Albin, who sees a possible parallel to *knowledge management* ([6], chapter 11). A similar opinion is expressed by Chandrasekaran et al., who see a gradual convergence between ontologies and what they call "object systems", i.e., OO-models [45] and also by Obrenovic et al. [157] and Bézivin ([31], pp. 41, 54, and 64). Another indicator is the OMG's request for proposal regarding a metamodel for ontologies called Ontology Definition Metamodel (ODM) [165]. While this similarity cannot be discussed in detail here, it should be noted that the parallel could possibly be exploited to use artificial intelligence to enhance code generation from models.

There are at least two types of metamodeling hierarchies, which are of interest for domain-specific MDD. The first is the classical metamodel hierarchy with four layers, as introduced by CDIF and adopted by MOF. While it has certain shortcomings, it is well-established and has found its way into OMG's MDA approach. The other type of metamodel hierarchy relevant in this context is a nonlinear hierarchy with a focus on ontological metamodeling.

3.5.4.1 Classical Metamodel Hierarchies

The classical metamodel hierarchy is the four layered MOF pyramid, which exists in very similar form in UML and CDIF. The MOF-type hierarchy has several advantages, the MOF standard mentions some such as the easy definition of new languages and model interchange already described above (cp. [161], section 2.2.2). Figure 17 shows the MOF metamodel hierarchy. As can be seen, UML can be interpreted as an M2 metamodel instance of the MOF metamodel (M3).

While MDA-based approaches commonly use this metamodel hierarchy and thus meet the requirements for domain-specific MDD as defined above, there is still room for further improvement.

While the existence of levels beyond M1 is a necessity for ***dynamic extensions***, the *fixed number of layers* (see Figure 8) makes it difficult to introduce new concepts in a modular way. If for example a domain-specific modeling language was created, it could only be placed at level M2 (as is done in the case of the Common Warehouse Metamodel). Therefore, only linguistic and no ontological concepts are available to define the new language, as one is limited to the elements of the MOF metamodel. The inherent disadvantage here is that ***concepts*** common to many domains ***will have to be replicated*** in different M2 metamodels, which is a critical issue as, according to Kent, the acceptance of MDD approaches will depend on the avoidance of spending too many resources on building domain-specific tools (cf. [132]). For example, a metamodel for online shopping applications and a metamodel for Content Management Systems (CMS) have a large conceptual intersection, which could be represented by a shared metamodel, but this is impossible with a fixed number of layers. In this

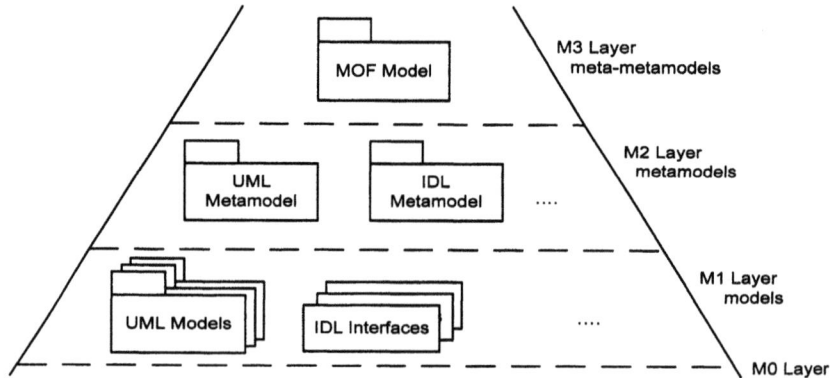

Figure 17 - The Classical Metamodel Hierarchy (see [161], pg. 2-3)

context, Atkinson and Kühne criticize that there is no distinction between "ontological" and "linguistic" instantiation [17]. Clearly, ontological/logical instantiation would provide a mechanism to introduce further model layers (see section 2.4.1 for details).

Atkinson and Kühne see the concepts behind the classical metamodel hierarchy as an "unbalanced view" due to which the "evolution of MDA technology will be stifled and the full potential of metamodeling will not be fulfilled" [16]. While this statement is probably intended to be a hyperbole, it is true insofar as nonlinear metamodel hierarchies offer additional possibilities with regard to user extensions as will be described in the next section.

3.5.4.2 Nonlinear Hierarchies

The concept of nonlinear metamodel hierarchies and their connection to ontological metamodeling has already been described in detail in section 2.4.1. The key advantage of nonlinear metamodeling hierarchies lies in the ability to customize the modeling language in a modular way, something all other approaches mentioned so far have problems with. Linguistic customization is one aspect but the real strength lies in the ability to provide languages for domain-specific modeling. According to Atkinson and Kühne, ontological metamodeling fulfills the requirement for *dynamic extensions* to the model as mentioned in the requirements list [17]. Also, a parallel to Operations Research and Decision Theory can be suggested. Schneeweiss identifies *constructional hierarchies* as a means of making the solution of a problem easier by creating a hierarchy of different levels of abstraction based on the problem. The solution to the simplified problem can then be used to solve the whole problem at the higher level ([183], pg. 9 and Fig. 1.3 (d) and (e)). Similarly, a hierarchy of ever more limited domains can be seen as a hierarchy of ever-simpler problems (due to a smaller solution space), whose solution can be in turn used for solving the more complex problem. While the two applications of hierarchical thinking are not entirely the same, similar principles are behind both. In order to allow the reader a direct comparison with the modeling techniques described in section 3.5.3, the example from the domain of art is used again.

Figure 18 shows an ontological metamodel, which describes the domain of artists and works of art with the instantiation relationships of the associations to their metaassociations omitted for clarity. At a first glance it looks similar to Figure 15 but is slightly more complex in the lower part. A more thorough comparison reveals several interesting differences. First of all, the metamodel provides far more *structure* to the model than a class library would. Unlike in Figure 15, instances of the *Painter* class shown above can only be connected to instances of *Picture* but never to other *WorkOfArt* instances. Depending on the nature of the linguistic metamodel, even the multiplicities of the associations could be controlled (see section 5.1.1).

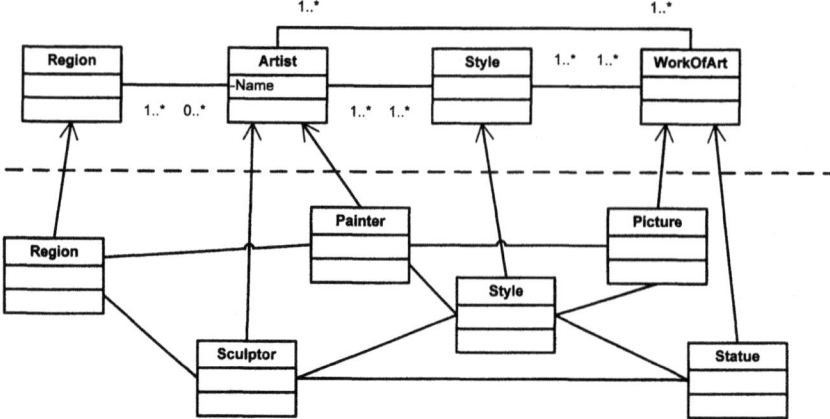

Figure 18 - A Metamodel for the Domain of Art

Second, the model in Figure 18 seems to have a ***higher complexity*** than the model in Figure 15. While it is true that a metamodeling approach is in principle more complex than an inheritance approach, it is less complex than an inheritance approach, which offers the same kind of structural information. In other words, a class library, which enforces a behavior that mimics that of Figure 18, is far more complex than the metamodel because it contains many constraints. The metamodel, on the other hand, provides a common set of rules that make these constraints unnecessary. Also, as Frankel points out, using some meta-

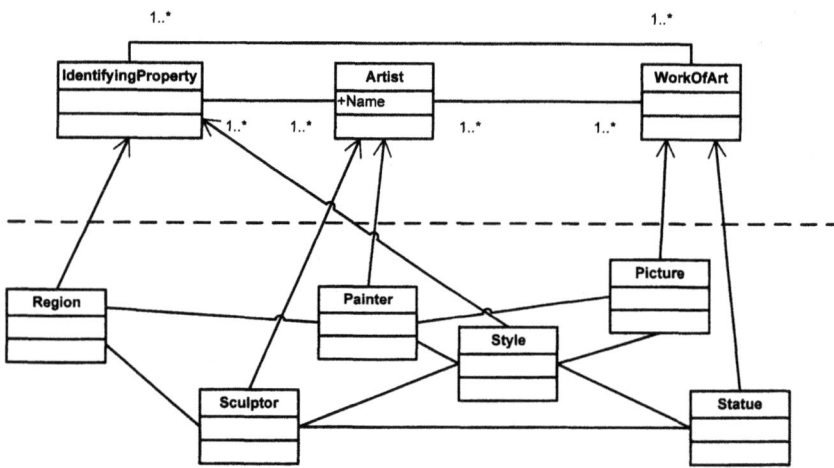

Figure 19 - Improved Artist Metamodel

modeling language does not require the end users to be familiar with it, but rather only the "tool builders" [73].

Another problem besides complexity that sometimes occurs with ontological metamodels is a ***replication of concepts***. Both *Style* and *Region* in Figure 18 exist on both the top and the bottom layer, an unpleasant occurrence that should be avoided if possible (cp. section 2.4). However, in many cases this replication is the result of poor modeling and can be avoided, as shown in Figure 19. By increasing the level of abstraction, both *Region* and *Style* now have the same base-class without limiting the model at the lower level. Yet, it should also be noted that such a change is not always desirable in the context of the domain model.

The main advantage of nonlinear hierarchies is the ability to ***define modular model extensions***. Figure 20 illustrates this property. On the left side of the Figure, the *Artist-Painter* instantiation discussed before is shown. It is possible to introduce another metaclass called *Person*, which defines rules for the modeling of persons of different kinds. The concept is similar to inheritance hierarchies but does not have the specific drawbacks as described in section 3.5.2.1. However, it should be noted that, unlike inheritance, instantiation is not always transitive (see [17]). While non-transitivity makes sense in the context of linguistic definitions, the example in Figure 20 should make clear that transitivity is useful in the case of ontological hierarchies. Thus, in the context of this work, ontological instantiation is generally considered to be transitive in accordance to the design space options defined.

If a new domain, e.g. the domain of science, were to be introduced, the common infrastructure defined by the *Person* metaclass could be reused leading to what Hubert calls ***conceptual isomorphism*** and defines as a condition where "a concept can be learned once and applied similarly in many situations" ([118], pg. 36). In other words, a generic solution can be provided to be reused at all levels.

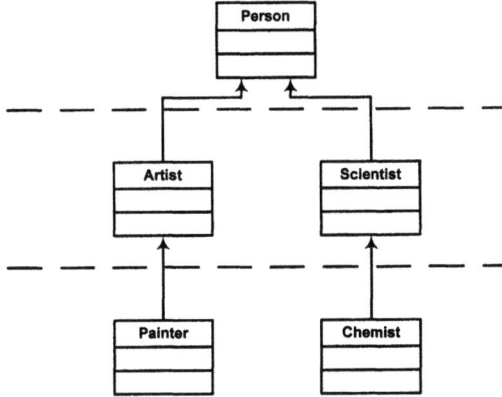

Figure 20 - Modularity in Hierarchies

Two advantages of such a solution are an *improved learning curve* for and better understanding of models and tools ([118], pg. 36). Also, code generation tools can provide *generic solutions for abstract concepts* and augment them at lower levels. If the higher level models are independent of the underlying domains, they provide a suitable platform to describe domain-specific models, which are easy to modify and extend (cp. Süß et al. [203]). In this example, code templates for *People* could provide basic Java classes with a *Name* attribute and *Artist* templates could provide additional data elements such as *Style* etc. By intelligently defining rather abstract domains, the design of new domain-specific metamodels can be vastly simplified.

Not only does the modular approach of nonlinear hierarchies allow reuse of concepts, it also provides several views on a problem at different *levels of abstraction*. Consider the small example given in Figure 21, which expands the example from Figure 18. Due to the transitive instantiation semantics, *Goya* can be seen as a *Painter*, an *Artist*, or a *Person*.

There are several advantages associated with these levels of abstraction. For example, if the semantics of M2 and below are unknown, it is still possible to argue about *Goya* and *The Naked Maja* on a more abstract level as it is known that one is a *Person* and the other an *Artifact* and that both are in some way connected. Also, even if all semantics are known, it is sometimes not desirable to distinguish between different kinds of *Artists*. This way, a common behavior for all transitive instances of *Artist* can be defined. Transitive instantiation in meta-

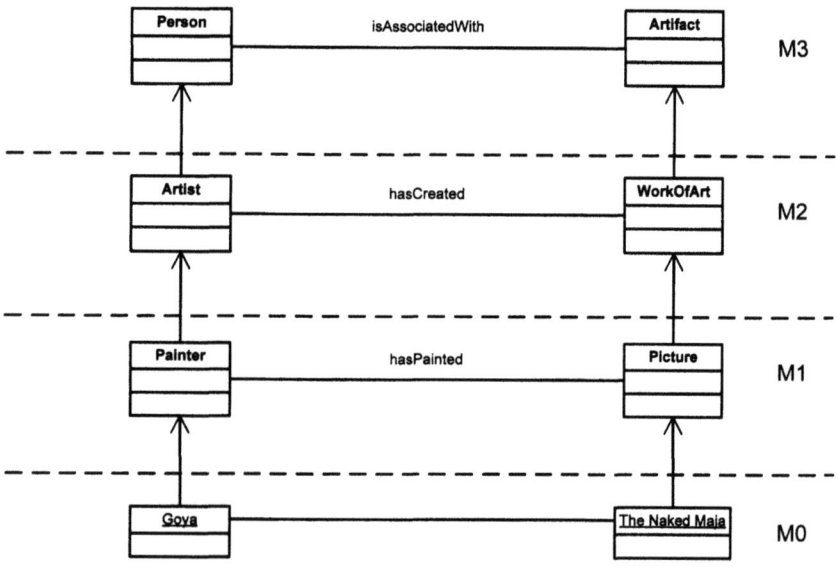

Figure 21 - Different Levels of Abstraction in Hierarchies

model hierarchies seems to combine the advantages of instantiation and inheritance.

3.6 Conclusions

In this chapter, the benefits and problems of MDD were briefly discussed. In the light of all arguments, it seems reasonable to say there is a great amount of hype blurring the vision of MDD, but also that a number of serious and realistic goals can be defined, which are attainable with domain-specific approaches. The most notable among these is the increase in abstraction similar to that achieved by compilers many years ago (cf. Bézivin [31], Selic [190] for a further discussion of the hype and reality of MDD). The following statement by Bézivin nicely describes the potential of MDD/MDA:

"MDA is not going to solve *all* the problems in IT. But it is going to allow *some* solutions with better efficiency than other technologies" ([31], pg. 52, emphasis added).

It has been shown that domain-specific MDD shows the most promise regarding this goal, but that a domain-specific tool has to be able to handle different domains by providing a suitable extension mechanism for which several alternatives exist. In the next section, the domain of Web applications will be introduced as an example for a rather active field of MDD research, along with several examples of existing approaches. After that, there is a sufficient base to showcase the proposed model extension mechanism using a domain suitable for MDD.

4 An Analysis of the Web Application Domain

In the previous chapter, the general concept of MDD was introduced and after a thorough analysis, it became obvious that domain-specific approaches in well-specified domains are one of the best starting points for MDD. Web application design and implementation is an area, which seems to be a popular target for current MDD research, possibly due to the great maturity of Web design methodologies, which can, with some effort, be adapted to include dynamic behavior. MDD approaches also profit from the use of frameworks (cf. Völter [210]), another field where Web engineering has a lot to offer.

This chapter (which further elaborates on the arguments provided by Gitzel et al. [90]) starts with a brief discussion of Web applications and their unique properties as opposed to general software, leading to a list of specific problems that must be addressed. In turn, several conventional approaches for the realization of Web applications will be examined, as well as how each of them helps with solving the domain's inherent problems. In section 4.3, an analysis is conducted as to how MDD can both incorporate the existing approaches and address the open issues of the field. The chapter ends with a summary and conclusion.

4.1 Properties and Problems of Web Applications

The World Wide Web (WWW) has revolutionized the life of modern society. From its roots as a largely text-based collection of information to its current incarnation as a worldwide multimedia-capable client-server application, the technology behind the WWW has undergone vast changes without abandoning its basic paradigm. It is for this reason that *"Web projects"* tend to differ from other software projects, giving rise to some doubt about the suitability of standard software engineering processes for this field (cf. Glass [98], Deshpande and Hansen [59]). Regardless of whether this objection is true or not, the unique aspects of Web applications should be analyzed and taken into consideration by any domain-specific approach in this field.

The *advantages of Web applications* are the introduction of a *standard client*, which reduces both the required training for users and the cost to create an application's interface ([59], [136], chapter 3), the ability to perform all *updates* in one place (i.e., at the server) ([136], chapter 3), and increased application *portability* ([136], chapter 3). On the other hand, there are also new kinds of problems, some of which are technical and some of which are social or human-computer interaction issues.

4.1.1 Technical Properties and Problems

The unique paradigm of Web application development leads to a couple of technical problems that need to be addressed in order to avoid complications during the development of the software and its maintenance. Some of the key features of Web applications are the reliance on the *Hypertext Transfer Protocol*

(HTTP) and *Hypertext Markup Language (HTML)* for communication and the *inhomogeneous client-side environment*, whose exact range of properties, both technical and human-related, is most likely unknown due to a great number of different browsers, plugins, and platforms as well as the global nature of the Web (cf. [59], [136], chapter 3). Offut identifies a similar *heterogeneity on the server side* due to the distributed use of various technologies [160]. Another interesting difference to traditional software is the fact that it is technically trivial to *switch to another server* providing the same service without significant loss of time or money ([98], [152], pg. 10, [160]). These unique properties lead to several problems that have to be addressed in order to produce successful Web applications.

The *lack of state* incurred by the use of HTTP is the reason for some of the most fundamental problems of Web engineering. Originally, the Web was intended for the display and intelligent linking of text. When one considers that the Web is a hypertext system, the concept of which goes back to Vannevar Bush's hypothetical MEMEX machine for storing and rearranging information from printed books in the 1930s (see [131]), it is not surprising to experience a vast conceptual gap to modern Web applications (cf. [81]). While the basics of the lack of state issue have been addressed by using cookies or Uniform Resource Locator (URL) extensions (cf. [136], chapter 3), there are still some problems to address in individual implementations. For example, *flow control* is complicated because back buttons, caching, and stored URLs allow virtually any state transition ([136], chapter 3, [152], pg. 25).

Many researchers describe *compatibility issues* due to the varying capability of the clients in dealing with the information transmitted from the server side. Besides the different browser versions with varying script and HTML interpretations, screen resolutions and color settings may vary. Of even greater impact are variations in the capability of the hardware, for example with regard to bandwidth and the quality of the output devices, which can range from small mobile phones supporting the Wireless Application Protocol (WAP) to non-visual output media, such as screen readers for the blind (cf. [59], [81], [136], chapter 3, [195], pg. 42-44). As a consequence, *software tests* are a lot harder to perform than in the case of traditional software ([59], [98]).

Even though testing is more difficult, it still makes sense, even from a business standpoint, to go through this additional effort. *Reliability* is a major factor in Web site quality, the reason being that users can easily switch to other Web sites ([28], [81], [160]). Given the unstable technological foundation of Web applications, reliability is more difficult to achieve than in some other fields of software engineering, where fewer changes occur [160].

A related problem is *performance*, as people are unwilling to wait long for pages to load. While Offut points out that this is not so much a problem on the server side, as the bottleneck is the bandwidth [160], the latter is hard to anticipate. Therefore, Web pages should be designed to load in reasonable time, regardless of the network capabilities and the performance of the client ([59], [150], [152], pp. 27-35, also cf. [28]). On the other hand, more complex applications might very well have server-side performance problems when serving a large number of clients, at which point the issue of *scalability* has to be considered, even if only as a basis for future expansions ([81], [136], chapter 3, [160]).

Due to the importance of uninterrupted reliability, performance, and scalability, Web applications undergo *constant maintenance* instead of fixes being grouped in release packages ([81], [98], [147], [160]). Besides added workload, compatibility issues have to be considered [160] and the user interface should be designed in a way to accommodate frequent changes [147]. Also, maintenance should not reduce the availability of the page. Any down time will lead to revenue losses, since people cannot use the site during that time and are likely to look elsewhere [160].

Security issues are of particular importance when developing Web applications ([28], [59], [81], [160]), because the loss of customer information can lead to loss of credibility, legal problems, repair cost, and revenue losses (cf. Offut [160]). Lack of security is not only a danger to the site itself but also to the internet as a whole, making the internet one of most important problem areas connected to information technology today (cf. Neumann [146]).

4.1.2 Usability Issues and Properties

While usability problems definitely exist on the Web (and there are many papers and Web sites identifying them), there is a high level of disagreement on the *level of abstraction* and the required *scientific foundation* to use for their diagnosis. For example, some sources see the problems in the details (e.g., Nielsen [150], [151], [152], [153], and [154]), while others believe in guidelines situated at a higher level (e.g., Shneiderman [195], pg. 65). In addition, some sources are opposed to generic guidelines at all, demanding rigorous empirical study (cf. Ivory et al. [125]), while others indicate that guidelines can be given if backed up by empirical testing (cf. Catarci and Little [40], Neuwirth and Regli [147], Nielsen [152], pp. 10-11, and the metrics given in [126]). An extreme position is held by Paolini, who questions the value of empirical studies for Web usability on the ground that, due to the global nature of the Web, it is impossible to find representative users of the application [173]. However, such discussions are beyond the scope of this work and the usability issues considered are those most commonly identified in the literature.

It should be noted that the focus of the following information is on issues particular to a Web environment and that it is likely that some of these goals are conflicting with external conditions. For example, Becker and Mottay point out that the *strategic goals* of an organization might place less value on some proposition or the other, in particular, if time-to-market is deemed an important success factor ([28], [29]).

4.1.2.1 Consistency

An important and maybe even the central factor for a Web site's usability is its *consistency* in visual design and behavior, both by itself and with regard to the Web as a whole ([28], [79], [195], pg. 65). Without consistency, one of the main advantages of the Web, the uniform client interface, is partially or completely negated. While the desire to stand out of the crowd and to attract customers is a legitimate one, it should not be achieved by reducing the usability of the site. A consistent Web site supports a high degree of *predictability*, enhancing the user's ability to foretell what results the interaction with the Web page will yield ([195], pg. 65, [79]).

Internal homogeneity is achieved by giving the pages of a Web site the same theme and by establishing conventions such as creating a common layout or using the same icon for the same purpose every time [36]. As a rule of thumb, Garzotto et al. advise treating "conceptually similar elements in a similar fashion and conceptually different elements differently" [79]. Since many organizations have established precise guidelines for a "corporate identity", at least a consistent look can currently be considered standard in professional Web pages.

Consistency with the other sites on the Web is also important, because few users are willing to learn how to use a Web application, which differs from what they are used to. For this reason, it is a bad idea to deviate from *"Web conventions"* by using different link colors [150] and introducing unexpected link behavior such as pop-up windows [153]. Also, there is currently a wide range of established *"design standards"* such as a common layout [28] including a logo and a navigation sidebar [151] or naming conventions [28] such as calling the main page of a site the "homepage".

4.1.2.2 Navigability and Site Structure

The ability to reach the intended target page is a major factor for usability and many researchers identify navigation and site structure as two of the main usability concerns in Web applications (cf. Becker and Berkemeyer [28], Nielsen [152], and Paolini [173]). Nevertheless, many Web sites still suffer from problems in this context, although the establishment of the "Web conventions" mentioned above has helped to make this problem less pronounced.

The purpose of navigation tools such as a sidebar with links is to give the user the required *sense of orientation*, not only identifying pages he can reach but also the current position within the Web site ([152], pg. 188). Without a solid concept of the *structure of a Web site*, users will quickly become lost due to the additional dimensions of movement as opposed to the forward and back in traditional text ([205], [207]).

Nielsen identifies several types of Web site structures such as *trees* and *tables*, both of which are commonly encountered on the Web. While a tree-based navigation will lead users deeper into increasingly concrete categories, table-like structures define categories based on the values of the table's attributes. A *linear structure*, which is similar to that of traditional media, is considered to be useful only in exceptional cases ([152], pp. 15, 200-207). Regardless of the structure, a good *homepage*, as the starting point for most users, is important and should give a good overview of the site ([152], pg. 166). The purpose of a Web application should be immediately obvious to an incoming user ([154], [205]).

The *categories* needed for the establishment of a navigational structure are not always easy to define. Nielsen proposes the use of aggregations, summaries, filtering, or an example-based presentation ([152], pp. 221). However, it might also be useful to allow the users to dynamically define their own categories for navigation [154]. The opinion on the proper number of categories differs. Shneiderman believes that it is better to create *shallow trees* rather than deep ones to allow users to reach their intended goal with minimal effort ([195], pg. 67). Similarly, Garzotto et al. identify the *richness* of an application, i.e. the abundance of information items and multiple ways to reach them as a good feature [79]. On the other hand, Borges et al. state that there should not be too many links on a single page to avoid cluttering [36], which necessarily leads to deeper trees.

Once a Web site has been designed, it is important to consider how to make its structure visible to the user by establishing a *navigational structure* that mirrors the internal one. This goal cannot be reached by including arbitrary links. Rather, the links should be organized in a way that emphasizes the structure, using *navigational patterns* such as site maps [150], indices [105], or guided tours [105]. However, not all links are used for structural navigation within the site. Other link types identified by Nielsen are associative links, which lead to pages containing additional information on a certain topic, and reference links ([152], pg. 51). These external links add to the quality of the page but they must be chosen carefully (cf. [152], pg. 67 and pg. 70).

In addition, the *design and realization of individual links* can also incur problems if not done properly. Generally, the name of the *link* should be concise and hint at where it leads to [36], giving the application what Garzotto et al. call *self-evidence* [79]. On the other hand, there should be no explanatory comments near the links [36]. Typical problems are pages that link to themselves [154], orphan pages (i.e. pages, whose parent Web site cannot be identified by those, who arrive there from a search engine) [154], and broken links.

Based on these insights, it is possible to come up with a recommendation similar to that of Theng, who suggests designing pages with meaningful headers and footers with origin, date, copyright info etc. (also cf. [36]), text-labeled navigation aids, making heavy use of indices, and other *landmarks* [205]. Nielsen, on the other hand, considers navigation more of a *necessary evil*, thus feeling that the links should not take up too much room on a page ([152], pg. 18). Also, about half the users prefer to use the search function rather than navigate so the search interface should be easily reachable from any page ([152], pp. 224).

4.1.2.3 Visual Presentation

The visual presentation is a very important aspect of usability ([28], [50], [152]), covering not so much aesthetic quality but rather how supportive the visual design is for solving the problems the interface was designed for. In fact, Constantine and Lockwood claim that if the aesthetic design is considered more important than usability, the site quality will suffer for it [50]. The same can be said about a focus on technological innovation, which often implies the addition of new multimedia features as opposed to quality content and service, particularly if this focus leads to errors or problems for the user ([150], [151]). When looking at problems of visual presentation, psychological aspects play an important role and a lot of literature exists on how to properly design the visual presentation for all kinds of media. However, these complex issues are beyond the scope of this work and only a few general examples will be given.

It has already been mentioned in section 4.1.1 and the introduction of 4.1 that the *performance* of a Web application is directly influenced by the graphical opulence of a Web page. Another aspect, which should be taken into account when designing the visual presentation, is the heterogeneous nature of the clients. It is prudent to choose a design for Web pages suitable for a wide variety of *heterogeneous client technologies*. This design strategy can be pursued by using generically applicable Web pages, which have properties such as scalable fonts [153], or by dynamically creating different versions, including printable versions for different paper formats ([152], pp. 93), using some form of style sheets ([152], pp. 27-36 and pg. 77).

Besides these more technical issues, the visual design should **support the intended task of the user of a page**. For example, the use of high contrast and the avoidance of distractions such as animations can help improve readability ([116], [150], [152], pp. 126, 143). Ivory et al. even claim "good pages have relatively fewer graphics" [125]. On the other hand, Horton points out that by using interactive animations, the advantages of computer applications over traditional paper media can be fully realized [116]. These positions are not necessarily mutually exclusive. It seems prudent to use graphics sparingly and activate animations only when the user is interacting with a graphic.

Besides graphical presentation, pages are also often inconvenient with regard to *"what-if support"*. Nielsen feels that many users would benefit from being able to compare products listed in a table but mentions that many sites will only display a single product at a time. For example, many airline sites only allow choosing a specific date for a flight instead of a range [154].

Generally, a Web page's *text* should be written in such a way that it allows the reader to skim over it and easily identify the parts relevant for him. This can be done by keeping the text short and dividing it into easily graspable chunks. The highlighting of keywords, clear categories and terms, as well as the limitation to one idea per paragraph, are additional measures to improve readability ([152], pp. 101-111, also cf. [36]). Usability is also improved by avoiding scrolling ([150], [153]) and eliminating headers that take up too much room [36].

4.1.2.4 Internationalization

Given the global nature of the Web, internationalization is a major concern for those Web sites intended for a multi-cultural and heterogeneous audience. However, internationalization is not limited to language translations but also includes a consideration of the cultural background of potential users [205]. A lot of work has been done in the field of internationalization already. For example, Becker and Mottay cite global marketing strategies such as those of McDonald's and Coca Cola as good examples for successful localization. The principles of these strategies in turn offer a good basis for Web localization [29]. Marcus and Gould propose using cultural dimensions such as those identified by Hofstede [114] as a basis for guidelines [139].

Rosson and Carroll identify two approaches to internationalization, i.e., standardization and localization. *Standardization* helps facilitate the design process by offering standard solutions and best practices and makes it easier for users to adapt to new systems. However, the variations of design are constrained and innovations possibly blocked ([179], chapter 10.2.1). *Localization* on the other hand strengthens cultural diversity but is more expensive than a global interface. While avoiding culturally offensive symbols and terminology is also possible for standardized user interfaces, other issues such as language, as well as formats for things such as date and currency are not so easily addressed ([179], chapter 10.2.2).

A similar distinction into two internationalization approaches is also proposed by Nielsen ([152], pp. 315). Becker and Mottay offer three solutions for localization. The first, a common design for all sites, is very similar to standardization as described above, except for the adaptation of the site language. Becker and Mottay also suggest a custom design for each site and a hybrid solution where only parts of the Web application are customized [29].

An effort to provide internationalization incurs several problems. The most obvious ones are the *added workload*, *redundancy*, and as a result additional costs [29]. Concrete *design problems* include the cultural influence on page layout, colors, and terminology (cf. [29], [139]). For example, Arabian or Hebrew applications will have a *layout*, which reflects the different direction of reading[2] (cf. [29], [55], pg. 235). The choice of *color* reflects the cultural background as well, e.g. the color red acts as a warning signal in Western cultures but not in Asian ones (cf. [29], [115], [116]). Similarly, certain *symbols* such as hand ges-

---

[2] For an example see Al Jazeera (http://www.aljazeera.net/)

tures used in icons can be highly offensive in some cultures ([55], pg. 235, [116]). A special consideration of *terminology* is required because literal translations sometimes sound archaic or are inappropriate in the context where they are used [29]. The locally applicable measurement units and formats for time and date should be used as well as the time zones considered if events are announced ([44], [152], pg. 318, [179], chapter 10.2.2). Finally, certain *processes* might vary from country to country, such as the point of time when taxes are added to a price and how they are presented in a bill [44].

While most cultural influences on Web page design stem from cultural symbolism or local customs, it is also possible to classify cultures according to certain criteria, or *cultural dimensions*, and use this information to further localize the interface. Marcus and Gould propose to use information on factors such as the role of the individual as opposed to the collective, or a culture's tendency towards strong hierarchies as a basis for Web design. For example, a culture with strong hierarchies would be more likely to dedicate part of a site to information on the leaders of a Web site's organization (cf. [139]).

Other cultural issues include different ethical values such as privacy concerns or local laws, which should be addressed appropriately, for example by displaying the proper disclaimer messages [44]. Also, there are regional differences in available technology that should be taken into account. Becker and Mottay suggest enhancing user profiles with regional and cultural information, including information on the typical bandwidth available in the user's region [29].

4.1.2.5 Accessibility

Increasingly, *accessibility* has become an important issue, and many researchers worldwide identify barriers to accessibility as key usability problems (e.g. Becker and Berkemeyer [28], Deshpande and Hansen [59], Ginige and Murugesan [81], Rosson and Carroll [179], and Shneiderman [195], pg. 42). Accessibility helps limit the problem of the *digital divide* [179], which is particularly important in contexts such as e-government ([195], pg. 38). However, accessibility also makes sense from an economic point of view, as it draws customers, who are likely to stay with a site that caters to their specific needs ([152], pp. 298, [195], pg. 42).

Many aspects of accessibility are technical, e.g., there might be a need for special hardware for physically challenged persons (see section 4.1.1). However, accessibility is also a usability problem, because the *Web page design* has to specifically support special output devices, e.g., by providing useful and short ALT text for pictures in order to allow the efficient use of so-called screen readers for the blind [154]. Other helpful properties in Web pages are dynamic enlargement, larger fonts, greater contrast, and larger mouse targets [179]. Additionally, Nielsen feels that a focus on content rather than presentation can also help accessibility ([152], pp. 298).

Shneiderman points out two interesting aspects, which suggest addressing accessibility issues from the early design stages forward. As many of the accessibility guidelines intersect with those for general usability, an accessible Web site can also *benefit non-challenged users*. Also, accessibility touches some core aspects of a Web application's code. Thus, *adding accessibility at later stages* is going to be far more expensive than incorporating it from the beginning ([195], pg. 42).

4.1.2.6 User- and Domain-Related Issues

According to several researchers, it is beneficial if information can be presented in different ways to accommodate the different skill levels and personalities of readers, possibly as part of a *personalization* feature ([68], [195], pg. 44, also see [28]), with the goal focused on making applications easy to use [79]. Becker and Mottay claim that a user's perception of usability depends on his or her profile, which includes not only the skill level but also traits such as gender or age [29]. Personalization means that an adaptation of the Web pages sent to the client is based on the personal parameters of the user. The simplest example is addressing the user by his personal name. More sophisticated examples include added shortcuts for professional users.

Of equal importance is the influence of the *domain* (cf. [125], [180]). According to Roth et al. "considerations of the users and the tasks they will be performing [...] should be central drivers for system design specification" ([180], pg. 164). The goals and constraints in the application domain play a central role [180]. In a similar vein, Rosson and Carroll state that "user interface design issues depend on the context of use" ([179], chapter 10.2.1). By incorporating domain-specific constraints, a Web application can achieve a high degree of *goal-orientation* [68], focusing on the user's tasks instead of the structure of the Web site's parent organization ([152], pp. 15 and 380).

4.1.3 Additional Problems

While technical and usability problems form the core challenges of Web application design, additional problems are also identified. Many researchers see *ethical and legal problems* as an important issue (e.g. [146], [205], [59]). Problems of this kind, which have to be considered during the design phase, include intellectual property ([205], [146], [59]), measures towards the protection of privacy ([146], [59]), accountability [146], responsibility for the content [205], and regard for liabilities for damages caused [205]. Some of these questions can become quite difficult, for example, Nielsen wonders whether there might be potential copyright problems when using frames to display content from other Web sites ([152], pg. 91).

Problems are also incurred by the *content* of Web sites. Becker and Berkemeyer identify information content and customer service as major quality factors [28]. Outdated information [150] should be avoided because it reduces trust, however, it must not be confused with archives, which are an important feature [151]. Another problem is the lack of immediate access to important information. There are many Web pages where important information, such as the prices for different flights, is difficult to obtain, requiring many steps even though the information could easily be displayed on a single page in a table [153].

The unknown nature of the users is also a problem during the design process, as Web applications have a strong focus on the "user experience" [50]. According to Deshpande and Hansen, conventional software engineering processes are based on an *analysis of user requirements*, which is hard to conduct without knowing the desires of the potentially global users [59]. On the other hand, CotS software products for a mass market such as word processing applications are also created for an unknown user, yet they reasonably match most people's requirements.

Finally, Nielsen considers the *credibility* of a Web site to be very important and achievable by appropriate Web page design. He suggests using a professional appearance and a user-friendly information policy on the pages ([152], pp. 91).

At first glance, it seems that these questions are beyond the scope of this analysis, the goal of which is to identify how suitable MDD is for the Web domain. However, these issues should be kept in mind because the solution to many of them can at least be supported by technical or design features. The best example for this is accessibility, which is in essence an ethical problem (cf. Theng [205], Shneiderman [195], pg. 42) but has many general design solutions.

4.1.4 Summary

As has been shown, Web applications can suffer from a wide range of problems due to their unique nature. The main categories (summarized in Figure 22) are technical and usability issues, as well as some other problems such as legal problems. The arrows in the Figure indicate relationships between the problems, and it is interesting to note that these connections can cross the borders between categories. Based on the analysis above, it is now possible to evaluate the quality of existing approaches and to identify goals for the design of a Web application metamodel.

4.2 Conventional Approaches to Web Engineering

In order to identify the potential of MDD for Web applications, it is important to look at conventional approaches to Web engineering in order to grasp their strengths and weaknesses. Ginige and Murugesan see Web engineering not as a subset of software engineering but rather as a holistic and *multidisciplinary approach*, which includes contributions from areas such as graphic design and process engineering [81]. However, the focus of the following discussion is limited to technical aspects, also specifically ignoring any kind of process models.

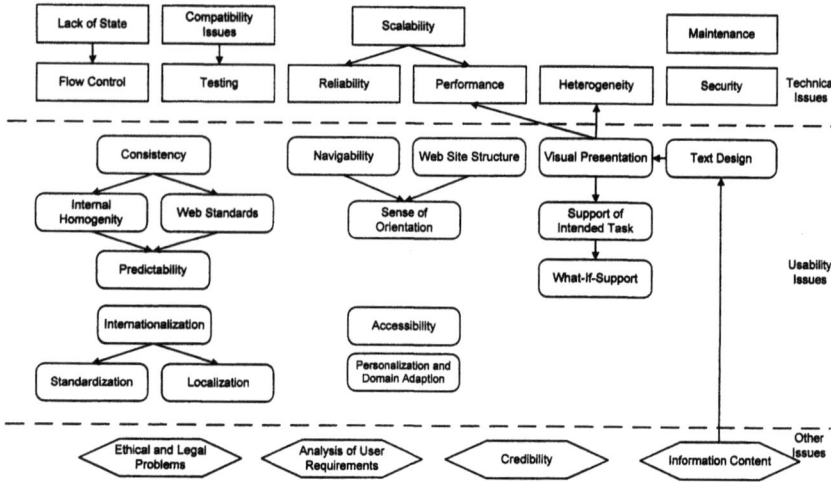

Figure 22 - An Overview of Different Web Application Issues

4.2.1 Web Design Languages

Web design languages are an established tool for the creation of hypermedia systems. While some researchers criticize the insufficient capabilities of the modeling languages with regard to the representation of dynamic aspects in Web applications ([160], [184]), recent publications have addressed this shortcoming by introducing interactive aspects beyond navigation, such as modeling constructs for fill-in forms (cf. [24], [184]). Due to these additions, Web design languages are also of interest in the context of dynamic Web applications as opposed to merely static Web sites. This section discusses the potential of Web design languages with regard to the problems identified above and describes some existing examples.

Web design languages can help facilitate solving some of the aforementioned issues by providing suitable design primitives. While the aspired level of abstraction requires a transparency with regard to most *technical problems*, such as compatibility issues, it might be possible to include model elements to support such things as the design of scalable software with deployment diagrams. Also, it might be argued that a powerful modeling language allows for the description of solutions, which are then easier to implement.

On the other hand, the design languages are far more useful with regard to *usability problems*. Many researchers are convinced that usability has to be considered from the beginning to avoid costly changes or support later on (cf. [28], [50]). For example, by modeling standard layouts available for pages throughout the site (in their first incarnation called tabletops, cf. Trigg [207]) and other reusable model components, the *consistency* of a Web site can be promoted. Similarly, ***personalization*** can be modeled by introducing parameters and rules based on their values. Links and page elements can be tied to constraints, which relate to some sort of user data (cf. [60], [74]).

The true strength of the Web design languages, however, lies in the support for ***navigation***, the importance of which has already been stressed in section 4.1.2. It should be intuitively obvious that a graph-like model can be very helpful in designing and understanding a Web site. However, such a solution only scales to a certain degree and more complex sites will produce a tight lattice of links, which will be hard to discern (cf. [78]). This problem has been addressed in the early days of hypertext research through the use of ***abstract navigational contexts***. While it is hard to identify the original source, the ***browser*** and the index-like ***filebox*** concepts of Notecards [105] as well as the ***guided tour*** as proposed by Trigg [207] are among the earliest examples. The idea is to define access structures to collections of pages, which imply certain links but do not show them explicitly in the model. Good examples are ***indices*** (i.e., pages listing all pages they reference in a linear manner) and guided tours (in this context considered a linear list of linked pages arranged to address a certain topic of interest). By using indices hierarchically, a tree-like structure can be imposed on a Web site. Figure 23 illustrates the relationship between explicit links, shown on the right, and abstract navigational contexts on the left side. When the indices are included in all subpages, as it is often done to show the tree-like structure, the explicit link model quickly mushrooms.

Abstract navigational contexts can also help to avoid the problem of links that only make sense in a certain context (cf. Paolini [173], Trigg [207]). For example, if a page is part of two contexts, any links to the context root or other elements of one context will be confusing if they appear in a page, which was reached as part of the other context. In the explicit link model on the right side

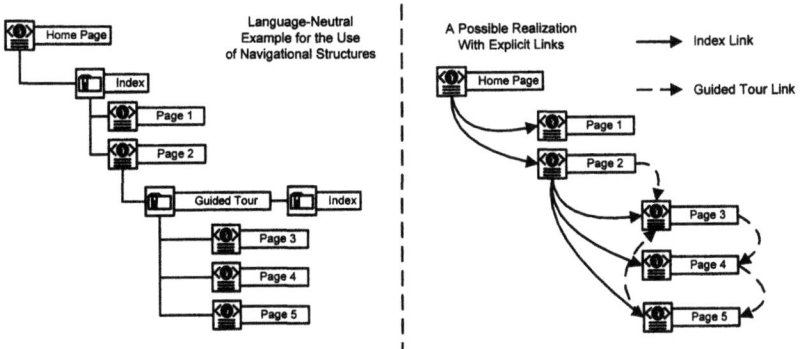

Figure 23 - Navigational Structures Versus Explicit Links

of Figure 24, for example, page 3, which is part of two contexts, has a link to each context root. However, if the page is accessed from the index of the homepage, the link to page 2 will be confusing. Navigational contexts help avoid such problems, because the correct link is included implicitly. Contexts can have other uses, for example, when modeling *dynamic behavior*, context information can be used as an implicit parameter for an operation performed by the user (cf. to the concept of constrained navigation in [24])

While Web design languages are capable of addressing some of the important issues of Web application design, they are not without their *problems*. For example, Catarci and Little feel that in many cases, people will be unwilling to learn a new language [40] and it seems as if Web design languages are often ignored by practitioners. This is clearly a social or organizational problem, which is beyond the scope of this discussion, however.

As an impressive number of Web design languages exist, it is not possible to do this group of notations justice in this context. For illustration purposes, one of the classical languages, the Object-Oriented Hypermedia Design Method, is briefly described, followed by one of the more recent languages called the Web Modeling Language. The section concludes with some examples of alternative approaches. For additional information on Web design languages see Koch [135] or Gellersen and Gaedke [83]. It should be mentioned that some of the languages described here are actually part of a methodology. However, these aspects are not relevant in this context.

4.2.1.1 The Object-Oriented Hypermedia Design Method

One of the most popular examples of a Web design language is the *Object-Oriented Hypermedia Design Method (OOHDM)* (see Schwabe and Rossi [185] for details). While it is an older approach, it is still often quoted as an inspiration or as related work, because it nicely illustrates how a model can ab-

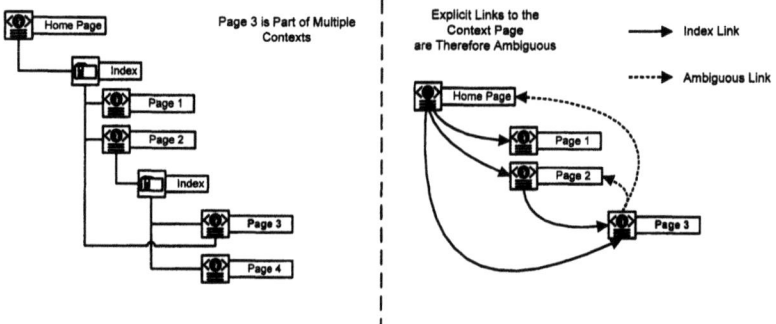

Figure 24 - Pages With Multiple Contexts

stract from the implementation details without requiring additional creative input for an implementation.

The basis for a hypertext system in OOHDM is the *conceptual model*, i.e., a UML class diagram describing the data and program logic on which the application will be based. The associations between the different classes suggest possible but not actual navigational connections.

The *navigational model* plays a central role in OOHDM and can be seen as one of many possible views on the conceptual model. The design primitives are nodes, links, and access structures. A node is a view on or an observer of one or more conceptual classes and has several attributes and link anchors. Links can originate from anchors and are otherwise self-explanatory navigation primitives. Access structures provide a more sophisticated form of navigation, allowing access to sets of links called navigational contexts. The access structures help in avoiding a tight web of individual links in the model.

A navigational context is a set of nodes and nested contexts. The nodes contained within a context may be defined via an enumeration of its members or via certain properties. For example, a context may be defined to contain all objects of a class, all targets of an n-ary link, or a dynamic set such as the history of pages accessed so far. More complex models are the "class based group", a context that contains (probably disjunctive) subsets of objects of a class, separated according to some criterion, and "link based groups", which follow the same principle for links. The content of a context is considered ordered and is accessible via an access structure, i.e., a collection of implicit links that can take several forms. Typical examples are indices, guided tours, and index guided tours as described above.

By defining a separate *interface model*, the navigational design is kept clean of interface-related concerns. Interface objects mask the navigational constructs, at least from the end users point of view. These objects are based on the concept of Abstract Data Views (ADV) (Cowan [53]). Each ADV can be customized via parameters and can handle certain events (such as a user clicking on a link). It defines the behavior and organization (i.e., layout) of the interface. An ADV may be composed of other ADVs based on the composite pattern (see [76]). The ADV displays the data provided by a navigational node and can follow the links provided by it. The events handled by an ADV can have two main effects. First, they can lead to a transition to another node, the typical behavior expected for clicking a link. However, more complex behavior may also be modeled with OOHDM, e.g., changes to the display of the current node.

A recent extension to OOHDM, proposed by Schmid and Rossi, enables the modeling of *processes* in a Web application. The approach is based on entities, which store information and business processes with activities. A business process is a special context, which can be considered a statechart diagram and can be left at any point, leading either to a suspension or a restart of the process [184].

4.2.1.2 The Web Modeling Language

Ceri et al. propose a "notation for specifying complex Web sites at a conceptual level" [42] called the *Web Modeling Language (WebML)*, which builds upon the Hypertext Design Model, the Relationship Management Methodology (see 4.2.1.3 for both), OOHDM, and other previous languages. WebML consists of four orthogonal perspectives.

The first is the *structural model*, which describes the data foundation of the site, e.g., as a UML class diagram. Since it basically corresponds to the conceptual model of OOHMD, it need not be addressed further.

The most important aspect is the *hypertext model*, which encompasses two submodels. The *composition model* defines views on the data called data units, which consist of subsets of the attributes found in classes of the structural model. Other units, such as the index unit or the scroller unit, define access structures on specific data units. The units can be grouped in pages. The *navigational model* links the units to provide a logically connected entirety. These links do not only represent the application's hyperlinks but can also occur between related elements, which are within a single page. Contextual links allow one unit to give a context for the other, e.g., the correct index of students can be identified due to a contextual link to a certain class. Non-contextual links ignore the context of the originating unit. There are also shortcuts for certain Web patterns, such as a multi-step index, which is an index pointing to several indices.

The *presentation model* is based on style sheets, which can be defined for the pages found in the navigational model. Of greater interest, however, is the *personalization model*, which is based on a user and group principle. The group information can serve as a basis for business rules and other mechanisms to alter the presentation of the application to the user. Also, due to the separation of structural and navigational model, different views on a site can easily be established. WebML can be used as a basis for model-driven development of Web applications, as the models can be represented in an XML-based format [42].

4.2.1.3 Other Web Design Languages

Besides the two examples described above, many other Web design languages exist. Due to a large conceptual overlap, these languages are not discussed in detail, for example, the *Relationship Management Methodology (RMM)* [122] is similar to OOHDM regarding its structure and model elements. For a more detailed discussion of these similarities see Gitzel et al. [89].

One of the earlier examples of a Web modeling language is the *Hypertext Design Model (HDM)*. Focusing heavily on a hierarchical definition of the data forming the hypertext application's foundation, HDM does not offer the different layers typical for other languages (see sections 4.2.1.1 and 4.2.1.2). Rather it makes many assumptions about the navigational structure of the application by providing implicit links, which allow one to navigate the tree of data and switch between the different perspectives of tree leaves called units. An application can consist of several "data trees" called entities, which can be connected by so-called application links and are, in turn, organized by a tree-like structure called an outline, which allows an initial access to the application [78].

An interesting group of Web languages is that of the *object-oriented languages*. Besides the prominent example of OOHDM described above, there are other examples such as *WebComposition* [84]. Fröhlich et al. propose a *metamodel for hypermedia design*, which is fairly similar to the other Web design languages of that time and can use a class diagram as a basis for its conceptual model [74]. In contrast to the other languages, the definition of a formal metamodel offers the advantages described in section 3.5.4.1. While an object-oriented approach might initially seem counterintuitive due to the special paradigm of the Web, it becomes more interesting in the light of object-based frameworks (see section 4.2.2).

Some languages focus on a particular aspect of usability. For example, the *Web Site Design Method (WSDM)* is, in the words of its authors, a "'user centered' rather than 'data driven'" approach [60], which focuses on personalization using different perspectives on the data, each with a focus on the needs of a particular user. The metamodel proposed by Fröhlich (see above or [74]) also allows for personalization by using a model of user data to design constraints.

The dynamic behavior of Web applications as opposed to Web sites is a recent issue, which is addressed by some extensions to existing languages (cf. [184]) or new language variants. *W2000*, for example, proposes to add new kinds of navigation, i.e., free and constrained, that identify the data to be used by the operations attached to a link [24].

4.2.2 Web Application Frameworks

The Web design languages discussed so far are quite useful for the handling of certain usability issues, especially with regard to navigation, but are unsuitable to address most of the technical problems described in section 4.1.1. This section examines the potential of Web application frameworks in this regard and describes several existing examples, analyzing to what extent they live up to this potential.

Generally speaking, a framework improves the quality of the resulting software by raising the level of abstraction of the solution domain ([103], pp. 60-66). In other words, when solving the problems involved in the creation of new software based on the framework, the need to address complex details is reduced.

Judging by the most popular open-source products, the increase in abstraction provided by Web application frameworks mainly addresses *technical issues*. For example, by building upon middleware to transparently realize an N-tier architecture, improved security, scalability, and maintainability can be ensured (cf. Offut [160]). In addition, advantages described by practitioners such as Wang encompass automatic validation and transfer of client-side data into objects, the support for cross-browser rendering and internationalization, and the provision of a controller component as the key advantages of Web application frameworks [213]. While the internationalization support mentioned by Wang seems to address a usability issue, it is typically limited to a mere technical infrastructure for providing several versions of a Web site, for example with resource bundles.

Going beyond the actual existing implementations, a mental analysis shows the great potential offered by frameworks with regard to the technical problems identified in section 4.1.1. The *introduction of state* into the normally stateless HTTP protocol was a major challenge for Web application implementation but can be solved with cookies and the (possibly persistent) server-side storage of user and state information. This approach can be improved by adding a time-out scheme for sessions as well as a clear recovery path (see Kolawa et al. [136], chapter 3). Web application frameworks can encapsulate the technical details and provide complex *flow control* on a higher level of abstraction. Similarly, the level of abstraction for *security* can be raised by providing features at a higher level of granularity. Increased abstraction leads to code, which is easier to understand, in turn making *maintenance* and to some degree *testing* easier as well.

Web application frameworks can also provide several output modes, possibly transforming the content to provide a format suitable for the various client platforms. This way, the *compatibility* issues can be automatically handled to a large degree.

Solutions to *scalability*, *reliability*, and *performance* can also be provided on a general basis. One way is to automatically adapt the output to different bandwidths, to provide automatic server-side caching, and to keep down the number of requests to the server. However, the latter is difficult, as it is not possible to update parts of HTML pages without resending the entire page, unless JavaScript or a similar technology is used, which introduces other problems ([136], chapter 3).

Similarly, support for *usability* might be imagined but has not yet been a major goal of Web application framework designers. So far, there is only support for some aspects. For example, the *consistency* of Web sites can be ensured by providing uniform templates or by using *composites of subpages* to allow the reuse of elements (compare to the concept of tabletops as defined by Trigg [207]). Similarly, *internationalization* is often supported by auxiliaries such as resource bundles. Other features are not necessarily realized yet, despite the suitability of frameworks for these tasks. For example, the *navigability* of a Web site can be improved by providing a sensible, abstracted navigation scheme, possibly based on the context concept introduced by the Web design languages (cf. [89] or chapter 5) or by providing different views on the same piece of information (cf. Garzotto et al. [80]). The *"What-if" support* demanded by Nielsen [154], *per-*

sonalization, and *accessibility* might be implemented as standard modules, encouraging developers to incorporate these aspects.

It is important to note that even if there is support for these features, this does not mean that the usability of a Web site will necessarily improve. Unlike technical problems, which are quite easily measurable, usability issues are less tangible. Even if provided with the right tools, developers will still be able to produce unusable software, especially when the design, which serves as a starting point, is poor. Additionally, due to the large investment of time into the development of such a framework, it should be designed to be useable for a wide variety of problems; therefore the solutions offered by it must not be too narrow. This view is reflected in the existing examples for Web application frameworks.

Despite the fact that Web application frameworks help address quite a few of the quality criteria identified before, it should be noted that the use of frameworks incurs a few *general problems*. Greenfield et al. feel that it is a non-trivial task to map a specific intended solution to a given framework, which is in effect an unfinished application ([103], pg. 162). Speaking from personal experience, the best explanation for this mismatch is that the developer does not know the exact control flow of the application. Unlike class libraries, which are used as building blocks for a new application, frameworks take the opposite approach, making it difficult to determine the order in which methods are called and whether they are called more than once or not. This, in turn, makes it difficult to decide in which of the methods a variable should be initialized and what state to expect. While a careful documentation can help avoid such problems, it is unrealistic to expect such a support given the nature of open-source framework development. Indeed, Gamma et al. seem to favor a "learning by example" approach for their Eclipse framework, as can be seen in their book (cf. [27]).

The great popularity of the Web as a medium of communication has spawned many different frameworks and APIs, which are intended to support the implementation of Web applications. There are many different types of approaches, and again only a small subset can be presented in this context. For further information see Wang [213] or the overview presented by the Barracuda project [25].

Many Web application frameworks focus heavily on interactivity, to some extent neglecting the hypermedia paradigm. The well-known framework *Apache Struts* (cf. [12]), for example, focuses strongly on Web forms and the processes behind them, offering no navigational support for the non-interactive pages of the Web application. Struts's core concept is the Model 2 architecture, which is a variant of the MVC pattern, and provides a controller that can use various technologies for its model and view. The technological requirements for the model are quite lax, allowing for a wide variety of concepts, including Java Database Connectivity (JDBC) [201] and EJBs. While originally the choice for view technologies was limited to the problematic JavaServer Pages (JSP) [181], leading to the proposal of Struts variants such as *Struts CX* [124] or the *Model 2X* [144], the recent addition of XSLT [48] and Java ServerFaces (see below) capability has helped to increase the decoupling of data and presentation, the lack of which was criticized by Gitzel et al. [89]. Also, the new Tiles concept for reusable page elements helps to provide more consistency and maintainability to a Web page. Yet, even though Struts's focus is on interactivity, Kamm and Klein criticize the concept for storing state in Struts as insufficient for true user dialog. They propose an extension to solve this problem [130].

The Apache Foundation is very active in the field of Web application frameworks, offering several different ones, each with a slightly different focus. *Turbine* [14], for example, provides many services to support the creation of a Web application. These include a simple security service and services for the presentation of data using JSPs or Velocity templates (cf. [15]). It also includes a limited navigational support, which allows using simpler abstract links instead of concrete URLs. *Apache Cocoon* is a publishing / Web application framework, which uses XML and XSLT to prepare data for output. As is it based on a pipeline principle, several transformations can be performed along with aggregations of different XML sources, all of which can be defined in the so-called sitemap [11].

Other frameworks are intended to provide a *simulation of a windows-based graphical user interface*. The most well-known example is probably SUN's JavaServer Faces (JSF) [202]. Other examples include the framework proposed by Puder [176], Echo [148], Jakarta Tapestry [13], and Swinglets [127]. While it is to some extent a question of personal taste, trying to emulate the event-based paradigm of a windows-based GUI with the stateless Web technology can be considered problematic. Despite the arguments in favor, such as improved portability and a richer user interface, it is doubtful as to whether or not the potential compatibility problems are worth the benefits. Also, custom GUI components, which make use of low level events (such as mouse movement), will either be not supported or result in massive traffic, a problem that Puder admits in his paper [176]. In addition, Nielsen sees pull-down menus in Web applications as a usability problem, because they violate the established paradigms (cf. [152], pg. 195). It is reasonable to assume that the same argument can be applied to other non-Web GUI features as well.

Besides the general frameworks of the Apache Foundation and the GUI-based approaches, there are many other solutions on the market. Of some interest are the Expresso Framework, which is based on a finite state machine (called controller object) [128], the OONavigator, which is based on OOHDM but which is unfortunately not available to the public (cf. [185]), and the academic project called JESSICA [26] by Bartha and Schranz, which focuses on content management.

4.3 MDD Approaches to Web Engineering

In section 3.5 it was suggested that MDD works best for domain-specific approaches. Given the fact that there are already popular solutions in the field of Web engineering in the form of Web design languages and Web application frameworks, it is important to show how the weaknesses of these existing solutions can be remedied with MDD without losing the advantages provided by them.

This section begins with a short analysis how frameworks and Web design languages can be incorporated into an MDD approach. After that the potential for negating the drawbacks of the conventional techniques is inspected, leading to a discussion under which circumstances it makes sense to use MDD for Web applications. The section ends with a brief survey of existing Web-MDD approaches, which can be examined in the light of the previous analysis.

4.3.1 Frameworks, Web Design Languages and MDD

Since any domain-specific language, and therefore particularly a *Web design language*, can be considered having a metamodel (see section 3.5), the benefits of using such a design language are also available in the context of MDD. Many of the Web design languages such as HDM were incorporated into CASE tools back when CASE was the state of the art for automated code generation. In particular, HDM as a basis for code generation is a good example how a degree of freedom is sacrificed to obtain simplicity. The hierarchical data structures of HDM with their implicit links allow to quickly set up things like technical documents but are less suitable when it comes to what Garzotto and Paolini call "'creative' applications" [78]. Besides these older code generation tools, there is at least one current MDD approach, which uses Web design languages as a basis; Fraternali and Paolini use a dialect of HDM in their model-driven Autoweb system [72].

Similarly, frameworks are a natural match for MDD (cf. Völter [210]) as they can help keep the code generation templates simple, moving away from the brute-force code generation approaches of CASE to the more elegant "framework completion" suggested by Greenfield et al. ([103], pg. 143). The integration of a framework into an MDD approach does not only add the benefits of frameworks to MDD, it also reduces the typical problems of frameworks, as will be explained in the next section.

4.3.2 The Contribution of MDD to Web Engineering

The idea of using code generation for Web applications is not new. Theng, for example, feels that "[i]f some *design ideas* could be automated so designers need not worry about their implementation, chances are that better applications could be produced, because designers would be freed to concentrate on their critical issues that cannot be automated" ([205], emphasis added). To make the point further, it is not only "glue code", which should be generated, but code based on rational decisions made by the template designers. Further elaborating this line of thought, it seems possible that model-driven approaches are useful in the context of the Web domain.

It has already been mentioned that both Web application frameworks and Web design languages can be incorporated into a model-driven approach to Web engineering. While the integrated approach combines the advantages of the two conventional approaches, the question remains what kind of additional contribution is made by MDD. This contribution can take the form of an added or amplifies benefit or the potential to offset a disadvantage of one of the conventional approaches.

One disadvantage, which might be reduced by MDD, is the lack of detailed instructions for using the *framework*. Roberts and Johnson suggest that the "compositions that represent applications of the framework", i.e., the application code fragments written for the framework, are "convoluted and difficult to understand and generate". They instead suggest using code generation based on a model in "standard notations present in the problem domain" to remedy this fault [178]. Since MDD can be based on domain-specific models, it therefore facilitates the use of the framework.

There are also several benefits, which are not provided by the conventional approaches. In fact, many of the usability problems can be addressed implicitly using MDD. For example, the navigation scheme of a Web application can be automatically provided based on general guidelines of a modeler. Of course, a solution at this level of abstraction can only be applied to a small subset of existing problems. Therefore, it should be easy to quickly come up with alternatives or extensions for the code generation templates. A hierarchical approach to MDD as mentioned in chapter 5 might be helpful in this context due to its unique properties.

The constant need for *maintenance* has been identified as one of the key technical problems of Web applications. While frameworks were identified as helpful for these tasks, MDD offers an even further improvement. As has been discussed in section 3.1, easier maintenance due to the focus on the model as a central artifact of the software development process is one of the major strengths of MDD. Clearly, in the Web environment, this potential can be realized to its fullest.

The *heterogeneity* of the client side platforms is a major challenge for the development of universally applicable Web sites. While general platform independence has been deemed challenging if not impossible in section 3.3.2.1, it is still possible to provide various code generation templates for a small and focused area such as the user interface.

The pronounced *need for testing* resulting from the heterogeneity is supported by the fact that the code generation templates can be tested separately and can benefit from the feedback of all projects using them. Additionally, test cases or simulation runs can be generated automatically.

A question of particular interest in the context of this dissertation is whether Web applications are suitable for a *hierarchical segmentation of the problem domain*, in order to profit from a hierarchical, domain-specific approach. Several researchers have proposed taxonomies of Web applications (cf. [43], [81]). Ceri et al. identify the categories of commerce, content, service (e.g., Web mailing), community, and context (e.g., directories and search engines), believing that these categories are orthogonal and a Web site may combine several of these business models [43]. Ginige and Murugesan identify other types of Web applications, i.e., informational (e.g. online newspapers), interactive (e.g. registration forms), transactional (online shopping), workflow (online planning), collaborative work environments, online communities and marketplaces, and Web portals [81]. These categories are a good starting point for a hierarchical analysis of the Web application domain, as proposed in chapter 5.

4.3.3 Existing Approaches

It seems that in the last few years, the Web was (re-)discovered as a domain, which easily lends itself to code generation. For this reason, only a subset of the existing examples can be presented in this context. One category of approaches has been put forward by researchers with an MDD background, who would like to illustrate the applicability of their respective approaches to the Web domain. Others come from the field of hypertext design and use the newly aroused interest in Web application generation to introduce their code generation approaches to a different audience.

The *Autoweb System* proposed by Fraternali and Paolini belongs to the latter group. It is a model-driven approach for the automatic generation of data intensive Web sites. Based on a variant of the Web design language HDM (called HDM-lite), database entries defining the navigational and presentational metadata are generated along specialized tables for the data described by the conceptual model. This information is used by a runtime environment to dynamically generate Web pages. The appearance of the Web site is defined via style sheets, which are based on presentation elements. These elements can be either built-in ones, configured via parameters, or be black boxes (i.e. code fragments provided by the designer). Legacy systems can easily be integrated using data replication tools [72].

While the approach of Fraternali and Paolini seems to be limited to CMS, it is interesting because its modeling aspects are based on one of the established Web design languages. Overall, AutoWeb's strength seems to lie in its strong Web background. However, it can only be called model-driven in the sense that it generates code from models. Many of the requirements defined in section 3.5.1 are not present. For example, there is no mechanism for modular extensions or the interchange of models with other tools.

VisualWADE, proposed by Gómez, is another model-driven tool for Web application development. It is based on a Web design method called OO-H. The tool offers three different design dimensions, structure, navigation, and presentation, each of which consists of a UML diagram, possibly with stereotypes and statements in the OCL-derived action language provided by VisualWADE. Pages are abstractly stored as XML files [102]. Again, the tool does not live up to the criteria identified for MDD in this dissertation.

Heckel and Lohmann propose a model-driven approach for Web applications based on what they call *graphical reaction rules*. They criticize the lack of dynamic modeling in most MDD approaches and propose the use of statecharts and collaboration diagrams to describe the dynamic aspects in a fashion similar to that used by Executable UML (cf. [140]). The changes incurred by the state transitions are described by model transformations. One of main problems addressed by the approach is the consistency between the PIM and the platform specific code. By generating a platform independent statechart handler class, which encapsulates the business logic, mappings to other technologies are simple and require changes in only a few classes [112]. While the approach has a certain appeal, the use of model transformations as opposed to code in an action language seems to imply too much overhead. Also, the approach does not explicitly address Web-specific problems and could be used for any kind of software domain with little adaptation.

Another tool using an executable PSM is *Netsilon* by Muller et al. Netsilon is designed to avoid changes to the working habits of the graphic designers and HTML integrators, as well as to provide a raised level of abstraction and increased productivity. Therefore, care is taken to allow the inclusion of static HTML fragments. The models around which this approach centers belong to three different views (called aspects in the paper), i.e., the business aspect, which uses an action language to describe the logic, a hypertext aspect for composition and navigation, and a presentation aspect [143]. Considering the background of some of the authors, Netsilon can be considered an example for Web MDD as a specialization of general MDD. Therefore, the model-driven aspects such as the metamodel and the transformations are stressed, and less attention is given to the Web aspects. For example, the options for navigation seem more primitive than those provided by OOHDM.

El Kaim et al. use the Netsilon tool for an *agile model-driven approach*. In their opinion "Web Engineering should cross-beneficiate from the new OMG MDA initiative and the Agile Modeling concepts and should be supported by suitable tools" ([65], pg. 299). Agile Modeling (AM) is defined by Ambler as "a collection of values, principles, and practices for modeling software that can be applied on a software development project in an effective and lightweight manner" [9]. Because of their informal nature, Ambler considers agile models to be more effective than other models [9]. The core idea of the approach by El Kaim et al. is that model transformations are used to allow the use of agile models as input, thus incorporating the advantage of lightweight models into the model-centricity of MDD approaches. They identify three different aspects in modeling, i.e., a business aspect describing the business model in UML and Xion (an action language), a presentation aspect, and a navigational aspect. The PSM level is source code, the claim being that the tool generates a 100% of the code [65].

Hera is a model-driven approach to Web information systems (WIS). The paper by Houben et al. emphasizes the information system nature of many modern Web applications, either because of their connection to legacy systems or their data-intensive nature. Hera introduces several views, which focus on different aspects of a WIS's architecture. The semantic layer consists of a conceptual model as well as an integration process that incorporates data from different sources into the model. The application layer describes the application in terms of navigation and user adaptation. The presentation layer specifies the details needed to produce a presentation suitable for a specific platform. The models undergo several transformation steps, leading to a platform dependent model (similar to the MDA's PSM), which is executable within a special Web-based interpreter. Functionality, i.e., business logic, is incorporated via callbacks [117]. The Hera approach is of interest in this context, because it makes heavy use of ontologies and the Resource Description Framework (RDF) [211]. Also, it focuses on data retrieval and manipulation as well as the integration of different data sources into a unified WIS.

Constantine and Lockwood contribute an exotic example in the form of an ***agile, usage-centered, model-driven approach for Web applications***. It is based on a model of the various user roles, abstract, simplified, and technology-free use cases, and abstract prototypes called content models, combined with secondary models of the domain, the business rules, and the working environment. An abstract prototype describes the user interface's contents without modeling the appearance and behavior as well as organizing the content into interaction contexts. The focus is on usability and interface design. Of similar importance are the navigational design and the visual and interaction scheme. The latter describes recurring visual elements, common layouts, and templates to apply to the interaction contexts [50]. Their approach is unusual in the field of model-driven development because it does not use any code generation. Still, it is interesting to see what kinds of models are considered appropriate.

Other examples include WebSA, proposed by Beigbeder and Castro, which uses a UML profile for modeling and which involves an additional PIM-to-PIM transformation [30] or the PIM for Web-based systems proposed by Smith and Shrimpton as a basis for an analysis of model transformations [197]. It is important to note that none of the examples given here supports a hierarchical approach as described in chapter 5 and that many are either weak with regard to MDD or Web aspects.

4.4 Conclusions

In this chapter, the problems unique to the domain of Web applications have been analyzed to assess the potential of MDD in this context. It has been shown that conventional approaches, such as Web design languages and Web application frameworks, already contribute to the solution of some aspects. MDD can integrate these classical solutions and also contributes additional advantages. The primary contribution is easier maintenance, which is a critical issue in Web applications. Also, the advantages offered by Web design languages are amplified in a model-driven context.

Thus, the domain of Web applications is suitable as a basis for an example of a hierarchical MDD approach. While the example will serve mainly as an illustration for the proposed extension mechanism, it should be noted that it nevertheless contributes to the field of model-driven Web development. In particular, it addresses some aspects missed by existing approaches such as a focus on the typical problems of a dynamic Web application without neglecting the progresses in the field of MDD compared to traditional CASE tools.

5 The OMEGA Approach

As chapter 3 has shown, a high quality extension mechanism for UML is a key success factor for MDD-based software engineering (see 3.5.1), and it has been argued that concepts like UML Profiles are not sufficient. After a careful analysis, it was concluded that hierarchical structures are a promising foundation for a language extension mechanism that supports reuse and therefore reduces the cost of creating new domain-specific code generation modules.

As stated in section 1.4, the main scientific contribution of this dissertation is the implementation and evaluation of such a *hierarchical extension mechanism*. The mechanism, which will be described in the first part of this chapter, is implemented using the technological concepts introduced in chapter 2. In particular, it employs a linguistic metamodel based on the design space defined in section 2.4 and implemented in MOF (see 2.2.2 and 2.3.3). The linguistic metamodel allows the definition of domain-specific ontological metamodel hierarchies, which are stored in XMI format (see 2.2.4) and are manipulated using the JMI-implementation MDR (see 2.2.3).

To evaluate the extension mechanism properly, it has to be used for a *real-life domain*, which is suitable for conventional MDD as described in chapter 3, in order to avoid accidental background factors to interfere with the evaluation. In chapter 4, the domain of Web engineering was identified as well-suited for model-driven development. The Web application domain will be used as the highest layer in an example hierarchy described in the second section. The CMS domain will be used as an example instance.

Section 5.3 gives a brief description of the *prototypical implementation*. The core part of the prototype consists of a domain-independent GUI and the extension mechanism infrastructure. For the purpose of illustration, a Web domain-specific code generator is provided, which will be extended for the CMS domain using the extension mechanism and the metamodel layers defined in section 5.2.

Employing the prototype, two *example application fragments* are designed in section 5.4. While the fragments cover the same aspect of a digital library, each of them is based on different requirements, in order to show the flexibility of the domain-specific metamodels. The examples will be used for a *critical evaluation* in the final chapter.

5.1 A Metamodel-Based Extension Mechanism for UML

In this section a metamodel-based extension mechanism for UML is described. This mechanism is domain-independent in nature but can be used to define domain-specific metamodel hierarchies, which can be applied to UML class and statechart diagrams. Figure 25 shows a schematic overview of the elements comprising the extension mechanism (shown in the box on the left) and potentially associated elements. The extension mechanism consists of three elements,

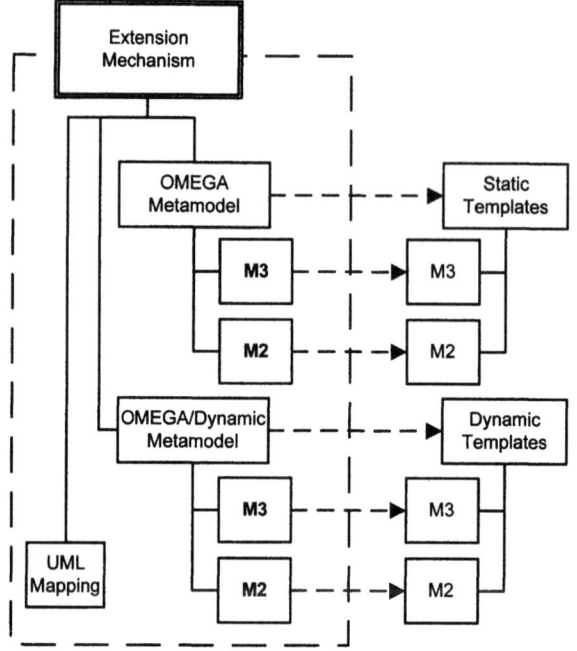

Figure 25 - The Elements of the Extension Mechanism

the static metamodel, called "OMEGA Metamodel" in the Figure, the dynamic metamodel ("OMEGA/Dynamic Metamodel") and the UML Mapping. The metamodel layers defined by the extension mechanism can be associated with code generation templates.

Each of the *metamodels* serves as a linguistic basis for an ontological metamodel hierarchy (see section 2.4.1). While an arbitrary number of layers is possible, the example discussed here uses only two ontological layers, called M3 and M2 in the Figure. These metamodel layers describe elements of the domain at different levels of abstraction and can be associated with code generation templates, which are grouped to correspond directly to the model layers defined by the linguistic metamodels. The first metamodel, called the ***Ontological Metamodel Extension for Generative Architectures (OMEGA)***, is a backward-compatible extension of the MOF metamodel. It is intended for the definition of class diagram metamodel hierarchies. OMEGA will be described in section 5.1.1. The second hierarchy, called ***OMEGA/Dynamic***, is a linguistic metamodel for statechart diagram metamodel hierarchies and will be explained in section 5.1.2.

The ***mapping to UML*** allows the use of the extension mechanism with conventional UML tools as a UML Profile with many of the associated problems described in section 3.5.3.2. An alternative is to use a tool, which appears as a normal UML tool to the user but is aware of the semantics associated with the model elements.

The extension mechanism is designed to address some of the *key requirements* for domain-specific MDD as examined in section 3.5.1. It promotes the use of a single tool for all domains, allows the interchange with other tools, and encourages the reuse of existing language elements and mappings. It also addresses one of the major problems identified by critics of the model-driven approach, which is the high initial cost due to the creation of templates (see section 3.3.2.3). The extension mechanism is intended to allow the reuse of templates found at a higher level of abstraction. A detailed examination is not possible before the details of the mechanism have been explained and is thus deferred to section 6.1.3.

As has been mentioned, the next two sections describe OMEGA and OMEGA/Dynamic. For readability, the two metamodel hierarchies are described in a non-formal manner and the technical details, which have been already described elsewhere, are omitted (see [92] or appendix A). To illustrate the difficulties associated with the design of an ontological hierarchy, OMEGA is explained in detail. The OMEGA/Dynamic statechart hierarchy is described less extensively, to avoid redundancy. After the description of the two linguistic metamodels, the mapping to UML Profiles is explained in section 5.1.3.

5.1.1 The Metamodel for OMEGA Hierarchies

This section gives a complete but informal description of OMEGA. Technical details are avoided in order to better convey the ideas behind the design.

Figure 26 shows the general structure of the OMEGA linguistic metamodel. OMEGA takes a minimalist approach, extending the MOF hierarchy to allow ontological metamodeling instead of coming up with completely new concepts. The classes in the Figure shown in white are MOF classes, which have been changed, or are superclasses for the classes newly introduced by OMEGA, which are shown in gray. All other MOF classes have been omitted for brevity but are part of the metamodel.

One of the *main goals* of OMEGA is to keep intrusion minimal and stay as close to the original MOF metamodel as possible. Generally, elements and constraints are only added as opposed to changed or moved to different places in the metamodel. However, for this reason, some of the new model elements seem less elegant than they could have been. For example, the inheritance hierarchy was not streamlined, as this would imply further changes to the MOF model. Also, for the moment, the possible metamodeling of *Operations*, which is similar to that of *Attributes*, is ignored, as it is not needed for the extension mechanism.

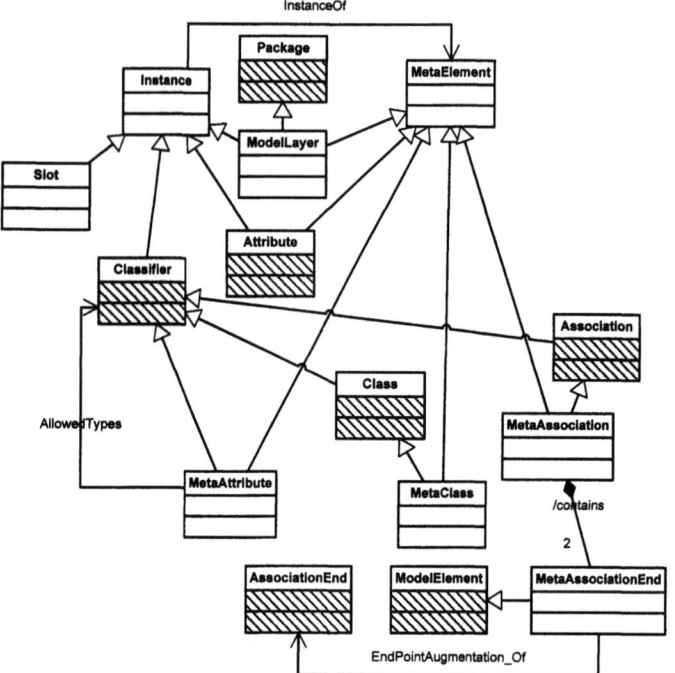

Figure 26 - OMEGA Metamodel Overview

Due to the nature of linguistic/physical metamodeling, the *terminology* is confusing. For example, the meaning of the term *"Class"* depends on the context. A clearer terminology would be helpful to separate ontological from linguistic aspects of this specification. However, this problem is not within the scope of the metamodel extension and is therefore not addressed. In ambiguous cases, the element of discussion is identified clearly. It should be noted that, for most of these explanations, it is important to understand the difference between physical and logical instantiation as described in section 2.4.1. In the case of OMEGA and OMEGA/Dynamic, the only linguistic metamodel is the physical metamodel. Therefore, the terms linguistic and physical as well as ontological and logical can be used interchangeably in this chapter.

In the element descriptions, some *notational shortcuts* are used. For example, the name of a model element X is often used as abbreviation for "a linguistic instance of X". Similarly, "X is an *InstanceOf* Y" simplifies the correct statement "X is the navigable endpoint in a linguistic instance of *InstanceOf* where Y is the non-navigable endpoint". Thus, "an *Association* must always be an *InstanceOf* a *MetaAssociation*" really means "a linguistic instance of *Association* must always be the navigable endpoint in a linguistic instance of *InstanceOf*

where a linguistic instance of *MetaAssociation* is the non-navigable endpoint."
Clearly, the short form is by far preferable to the correct long version.

Class names generally start with a capital letter and are printed in *italics* or in ***bold italics*** to indicate a section where they are explained in detail. However, the same word, when not used as a class name will be written normally, e.g., "*Type* is an attribute of *Attribute*" means that *Type* is the name of an attribute found in the *Attribute* class.

In the following subsections, the changes to the MOF standard are briefly explained. Each section starts with a brief ***conceptual description*** that sacrifices accuracy in favor of simplicity, before describing the ***actual implementation***. The exact definition of the constraints and model elements can be found on the Web (see [92]), a summary of the constraints in appendix A.

5.1.1.1 MetaElements and Instances

The core addition to the original MOF model discussed in section 2.3.3 is the introduction of a logical instantiation relationship as shown in Figure 27. The main purpose of the instantiation relationship in OMEGA is to allow a metamodel designer to create a set of *MetaElements*, which impose certain rules on their *Instances*, mainly limiting the features an *Instance* is allowed to have. In the case of *Classes*, these features are *Attributes* and *References*, in the case of *Associations*, the attributes of their *AssociationEnds*. Since some classes are both *Instances* and *MetaElements*, some *MetaElements* have both direct and indirect *Instances*. Instantiation in OMEGA is defined as transitive, allowing *MetaElements* to influence both their direct and indirect *Instances*.

As the concept of instantiation affects most elements found in OMEGA in some way, two special baseclasses, *MetaElement* and *Instance* are introduced, allowing the other elements to inherit the instantiation concept defined here.

The mechanism informally described above is implemented in the following way. An *Instance* is connected to a *MetaElement* via the *InstanceOf* relationship. This arrangement roughly corresponds to the architecture depicted in Figure 9, introducing *InstanceOf* as a new association, which represents an instantiation

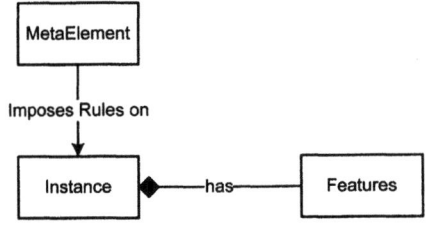

Figure 27 - OMEGA Instantiation Concept

relationship between two model elements. The *Instance* and *MetaElement* classes are both abstract and describe only the generic structure needed for logical instantiation of various kinds. Some classes, e.g., *MetaAttribute*, inherit from both *Instance* and *MetaElement*, which means they can fill both roles in logical inheritance. For this reason, the abstract *MetaElement* class has an attribute *CanSpawnMeta*, which determines whether a particular *MetaElement* may have another *MetaElement* as logical instance or not. The *CanSpawnMeta* attribute will be further elaborated on in section 5.1.1.3.

The *Instance* class contains several constraints to avoid some illogical situations. For example, *Instances* may not instantiate themselves or any of their *Instances* and abstract *MetaElements* may not be instantiated at all. The latter constraint is needed because, while the concept of abstract model elements exists in MOF, it is used in a purely physical fashion and a constraint is required to achieve the same effect logically.

The *InstanceOf* association connects a *MetaElement* to its *Instances*. An interesting aspect of *InstanceOf* is the unidirectional navigability from the *Instance* to the *MetaElement*. This arrangement is necessary to allow "frozen" (i.e., immutable) types, because navigability requires a changeable *Reference* within the *MetaElement*. A disadvantage of the unidirectionality is that a *MetaElement* cannot access its *Instances*. Therefore, constraints realizing the limitations a *MetaElement* places on its *Instances* cannot be put into the *MetaElement*. Eventually, many constraints were moved to *ModelLayer* to be used in some sort of "bird's eye view".

A relaxed strictness is used for *InstanceOf*. Certain aspects of strictness are implied by the multiplicities of *InstanceOf*, i.e., there is only one *MetaClass* for each *Instance*. *InstanceOf* also ensures that the right *MetaElements* are assigned to the proper *Instances*, e.g., only a *MetaClass* can be the *MetaElement* of a *Class*. In the following sections, the various kinds of instantiation found in OMEGA as well as the model elements involved will be discussed.

5.1.1.2 Model Layers

The purpose of *ModelLayers* is to create distinct groups of elements within the metamodel hierarchy. Each *ModelLayer* can contain various model elements, which can be instances of elements in a higher layer or metaelements for elements in a lower layer. In effect, a *ModelLayer* provides a different level of aggregation to the metamodel hierarchy. As can be seen in Figure 28, relaxed strictness is used for *InstanceOf*, meaning that instantiation can skip intermediate layers. Another design choice shown in the Figure is the axiomatic top level.

More formally speaking, a *ModelLayer* is a specialized form of *Package*, which is both a *MetaElement* and an *Instance*. *ModelLayers* group the elements of a metamodel hierarchy into distinct units, which reside at the same level of abstraction. However, *ModelLayers* do not only group elements but also enforce many of the rules implied by the design choices made for the metamodel hierar-

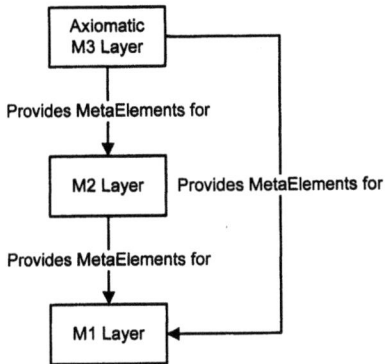

Figure 28 - OMEGA Model Layer Concept

chy. For example, elements are only allowed to instantiate elements from a *ModelLayer*, which is a transitive *MetaElement* of their own *ModelLayer*. Also, only top level elements are not required to have a *MetaElement*. This constraint reflects the design choice to have an axiomatic top level as opposed to a reflexive one. A reflexive top level would be far more complex to realize via constraints and would require more modeling effort on behalf of the OMEGA user with no immediate benefit. It is questionable if the use of recursive top levels makes sense in a logical hierarchy at all except for simulation purposes (e.g., Riehle et al. [177]). Another constraint ensures that *ModelLayers* only form a single hierarchy, i.e., that there is only one top level layer, which is the transitive *MetaElement* for all other *ModelLayers* in the instantiation tree.

While it is possible to perform MOF's *Package*-operations (*Import* etc.) on *ModelLayers*, this should be done with caution, especially if the imported *ModelLayer* is used elsewhere in the instantiation hierarchy. In most cases, one constraint or the other will be violated due to the strict requirements for the instantiation hierarchy. These operations have not been ruled out, but they will most likely be useful only to include elements into the top-most layer. The potential of these operations has to be analyzed further.

The core motivation for the introduction of *ModelLayers* is to allow for parts of the model hierarchy to be loaded in a frozen state, providing domain-specific *MetaElements* for the lower layers. A further motivation is that layers as explicit model elements are preferable to indicating levels by a counter in the model elements as proposed by Atkinson and Kühne [18], mainly because the *ModelLayers* allow a more natural aggregation of model elements.

Figure 29 provides an example for frozen layers (shown in white). An OMEGA user planning to model an online cookbook is bound to load two model layers into the model; "Web Applications" and "Content Management Systems". Both

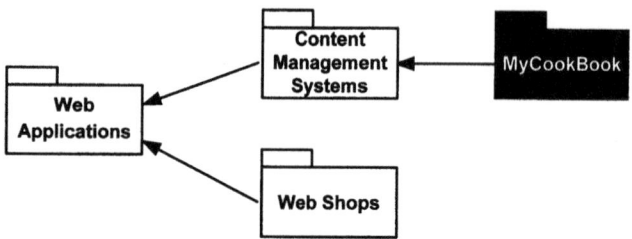

Figure 29 - Examples of Frozen Layers

ModelLayers are frozen, i.e., their contents cannot be changed. Indeed, they should not be changed to ensure coherence with other instances of the same *ModelLayer*. Since the "imported" layers are frozen, they cannot contain references to their instances (as these references could not be changed), and therefore the elements in "MyCookBook" have to refer their metaelements in their metalayers as described in section 5.1.1.1.

5.1.1.3 MetaClasses and MetaAttributes

The form of instantiation typically associated with metamodeling is that between a *MetaClass* and a *Class* shown in Figure 30, which is directly derived from Figure 27. In OMEGA, the relationship of *Classes* and *MetaClasses* is mainly based on two instantiation pairs, i.e., *MetaClass-Class* and *MetaAttribute-Attribute*. As has been mentioned before, the *MetaElements* impose certain rules on their *Instances*. In the case of *Classes*, a *MetaClass* defines the legal *Attributes* of its *Classes* and how many *Attributes* of each kind are required and allowed. A *MetaAttribute* defines which properties an *Attribute* of its type is allowed to have, e.g., a *MetaAttribute* can specify that its instances must all have a *Visibility* of *public*. Besides these core concepts, there are additional aspects, such as the *Attribute-Slot* instantiation, which will also be explained in this section but are not relevant to the fundamental understanding of *MetaClass-Class* instantiation.

In the implementation, ***MetaClass*** is a physical class, which inherits from *Class*.

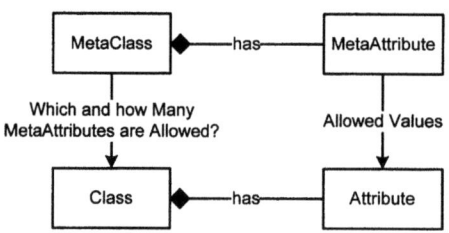

Figure 30 - OMEGA MetaClass-Class Instantiation Concept

The circular nature of the relationships between *Class* and *MetaClass* might be confusing at the first glance; a *Class* is typically *InstanceOf* a *MetaClass*, but *MetaClass* inherits from *Class*. The problem is resolved quite easily by looking at the inheritance as part of the physical metamodel. In the physical metamodel the (logical) semantics of *InstanceOf* are irrelevant and the inheritance only models the fact that a *MetaClass* is also a *Class* and therefore can have an *InstanceOf* relationship to another *MetaClass*. Without this dual nature of a *MetaClass*, a metamodel hierarchy with more than two levels would not be possible. Thus, in OMEGA the typical metamodel hierarchy will involve chains of several *MetaClasses* instantiating each other with a *Class* as the lowest instance. The *CanSpawnMeta* attribute gives the developers of metamodels some control over the length of these chains, because the *Instance* of some *MetaClass* M can only be a *MetaClass* if M's *CanSpawnMeta* is *true*. In the example in Figure 29, it is prudent to have *CanSpawnMeta* set to *false* for all *MetaClasses* in "Content Management Systems" and "Web Shops" to indicate that the next *ModelLayer* is supposed to be the final one in the hierarchy.

The class **Class** has been changed slightly from the MOF's original *Class* to allow it to be an *InstanceOf MetaClass* by making it an indirect subclass of the new *Instance* class. There are also several constraints, which ensure the *Class's Attributes* adhere to the specifications imposed by the *MetaAttributes*.

It was hinted that the instantiation hierarchy for *Attributes* consists of *MetaAttributes*, *Attributes*, and *Slots*. In this hierarchy, a *MetaAttribute* or *Attribute* can be the instance of another *MetaAtribute* and a *Slot* the instance of an *Attribute*. This means that two new classes, *MetaAttribute* and *Slot*, have to be provided in addition to MOF's *Attribute*.

The instantiation semantics of OMEGA limits the choice of *Attributes* for a *Class* through the *MetaClass*, which contains *MetaAttributes*, whose instances are the *Attributes* of the *Class*. The relationship between **Attributes** and **MetaAttributes** in OMEGA is shown in Figure 31. Each *Association* between the *MetaClass* (*Article* in the example) and a *MetaAttribute* influences the set of allowed *Attributes* in the *Class* (*MovieReview*). A *MetaAttribute* contains a number of sets of allowed values for the different properties of an *Attribute* such as its type, multiplicity, or visibility. For example, the *Attribute Date*, which is an instance of *Timestamp*, is limited to the visibilities *public* and *private*. It complies with this constraint as its visibility is *public*. The number of *Attributes* in a *Class* that are instances of the same *MetaAttribute* is governed by the multiplicities of the association between the *MetaClass* and the *MetaAttribute* (which should not be confused with the multiplicity of each *Attribute*). For example, *Synopsis* and *Review* are both instances of *Text*. Both have a multiplicity of 1..*, which means that they roughly correspond to arrays or Java Collections. A *MetaAttribute*, which is an instance of another *MetaAttribute*, must have sets of allowed values, which are subsets of those offered by its *MetaElement*.

The *MetaAttribute*'s set of values for an *Attribute*'s *Type* differs slightly from the other sets insofar as the type in MOF is not determined by an attribute but rather by a reference. As strictness forbids associations other than *InstanceOf* to cross *ModelLayer* boundaries, it is impossible for an *Attribute* to reference one of the elements in the list as type, because all these elements are in a higher model layer, i.e., the one where the *MetaAttribute* is defined. Therefore, the rule in this case is that the type of the *Attribute* must be an *InstanceOf* any of the elements in the set of allowed types as specified by the *MetaAttributes*. The avid reader might immediately identify that this is a problem in the case of *PrimitiveTypes*, which are currently treated as a special case.

The inclusion of ***Slots*** came relatively late in the development of OMEGA. It addresses a problem, which arises when *Attributes* exist on a *ModelLayer* other than the lowest one. An example is shown in Figure 32, where *Artist* has an Attribute called *Tools* and *Painter* is an instance of *Artist*. Intuitively, one might expect the class *Painter* to have an attribute slot called *Tools* in a similar fashion to the attribute slot *Name*. However, in order to include such an attribute slot, the physical metaclass *Class* would be required to have a corresponding attribute, which it of course does not have, being the standard MOF *Class*. Thus, the

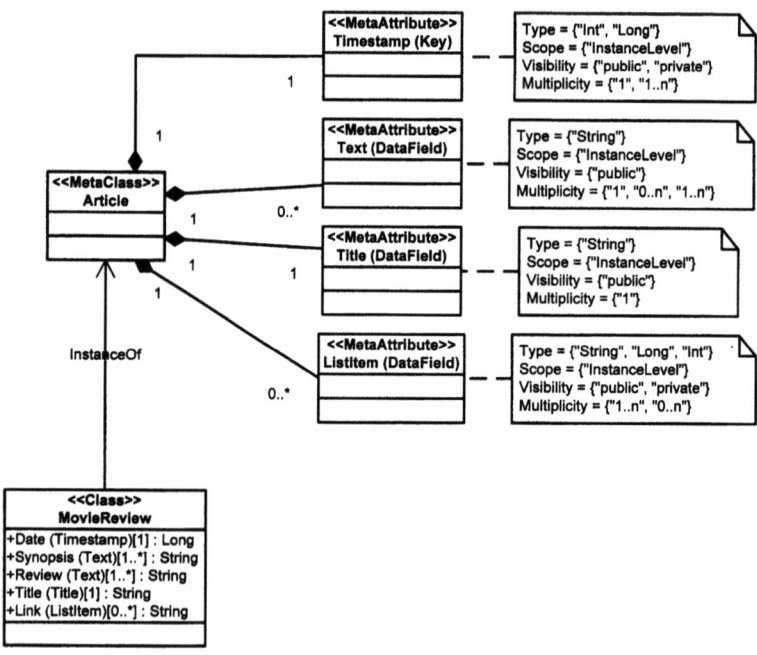

Figure 31 - MetaAttributes

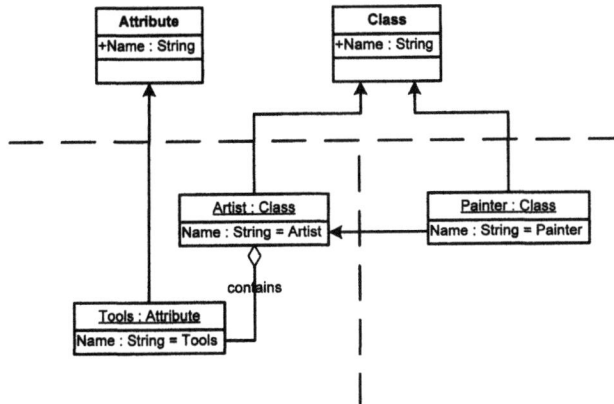

Figure 32 - Motivation for the Inclusion of Slots

new *Slot* class (which is very similar to MOF's *Constant*) is introduced in order to allow the logical instantiation of *Attributes*.

The concept of *MetaAttributes* is a unique contribution of the OMEGA approach that expands the strengths of metamodeling by providing more structure and meaning to the instances. Nevertheless, it seamlessly integrates into the MOF metamodel. The only difference is that, unlike *Attributes*, *MetaAttributes* are not contained in the *Namespace* of a *MetaClass*. Rather, they are connected to it by an association, usually as an aggregation. This way, multiplicities can be used to better control the number of instances of a *MetaAttribute* in one *Class*.

5.1.1.4 MetaAssociations

The last aspect of instantiation semantics not analyzed so far is the concept of *MetaAssociations*. In MOF the metaclass of *Association* is *Class*, however, for logical (as opposed to physical) modeling purposes such an arrangement is often not satisfactory, as it implies a purely linguistic view and makes hierarchies difficult. Thus, OMEGA introduces the concept of *MetaAssociations*, which replace *Classes* as metaelements for *Associations*. Figure 33 shows the main intention behind the new model element. Like a *MetaClass*, a *MetaAssociation* influences the nature of its *Instances*. First of all, a *MetaAssociation* limits the number of *Associations* allowed to connect to a specific type of element. More importantly, by virtue of its *MetaAssociationEnds*, the *MetaAssociation* limits the properties of its instances. For example, the *MetaAssociation* can limit the types of multiplicities and the navigability allowed for the *Associations* instantiating it.

In the implementation, the classes relevant for the instantiation of associations are *Association* and *MetaAssociation* as well as their contained elements *AssociationEnd* and *MetaAssociationEnd*. The relationship between these elements is

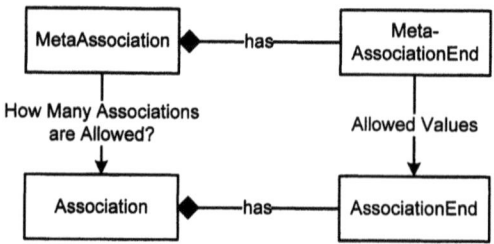

Figure 33 - MetaAssociation-Association Instantiation Concept

depicted in Figure 34. The left-hand side of the Figure shows an example of an instantiation, the right-hand side shows how the *(Meta)Associations* are represented internally (cf. Figure 6).

The instantiation of ***MetaAssociations*** is probably the most complicated aspect of OMEGA, but at the same time, it is also the most powerful metamodeling expansion proposed. The general idea is that *MetaAssociations* provide a list of allowed values for their instances the same way *MetaAttributes* do. In the example shown in Figure 34, the *MetaAssociation* called *HasCreated* restricts its instances such as *HasPainted* in two ways; via its multiplicities and via *MetaAssociationEnds*. The multiplicities of *HasCreated* behave as expected, limiting the number of instances of *HasCreated* allowed to connect to one endpoint. The *Painter* class in the example so far participates in one relationship of type *HasCreated* (i.e. *HasPainted*) but would be allowed to participate in another one (due to the 1..2 multiplicity), maybe to *Fresco*. However, a third association of type *HasCreated* with *Painter* as one of its endpoints would not be allowed.

A *MetaAssociation* does not only limit the number of allowed *Associations* of its type, it also restricts the allowed values for its properties such as multiplicity and navigability. In the example, the properties of *HasPainted* are limited by the *MetaAssociationEnds* of *HasCreated*, which are not visible in the traditional view on the left side of the Figure but are illustrated on the right. Each *Associa-*

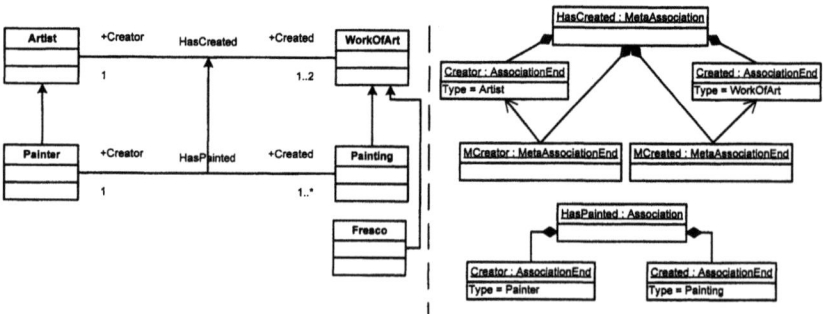

Figure 34 - MetaAssociation and Association

tionEnd in a *MetaAssociation* is referenced by one *MetaAssociationEnd*. Similar to a *MetaAttribute*, the *MetaAssociationEnd* contains a set of allowed values, in this case for multiplicity, navigability, and changeability of the end. In the example presented above, if *MCreated* had the set of {"0..*", "1"} as allowed multiplicity values, *HasPainted* would not be a valid instance of *HasCreated*, because 1..*, the multiplicity at the *Painting* end of *HasPainted*, is not an element in the set.

However, there are two important differences to *MetaAttributes*. First, there is no allowed type to be specified; the endpoint type is determined by the *AssociationEnd*. Second, while the value sets of *MetaAttributes* apply transitively, those of *MetaAssociationEnds* only affect the next level. This difference is due to the fact that *MetaAttributes* are not *Attributes* while *MetaAssociations* are also *Associations* and are therefore subject to the limitations implied by their *MetaElement*.

5.1.1.5 Implementation Notes

For convenience, the implementation of the OMEGA metamodel was based on an XMI file containing the MOF 1.4 metamodel, the changes being realized by adding new or changing existing model elements textually. The altered XMI-file containing the OMEGA metamodel definition was then used to generate interfaces representing the OMEGA metamodel using the JMI implementation MDR.

The purpose of the generated Java interfaces is to allow the creation of ontological metamodels. The JMI generated interfaces allow the creation and manipulation of instances for all the linguistic metamodel elements described in this section. A Java program, whether it is an editor or a hard-coded generator, can access the JMI repository via the interfaces and build ontological models, which can be serialized as XMI files or kept in the repository depending on the purpose of the application. The implementation and usage of OMEGA is summarized in Figure 35.

5.1.1.6 Properties of the OMEGA Metamodel

In the previous sections, the structure of the OMEGA metamodel has been described and the purpose of its elements explained. However, as has been established in section 2.4, a metamodel hierarchy has to be carefully designed to avoid a number of problems such as replication of concepts. Additionally, a

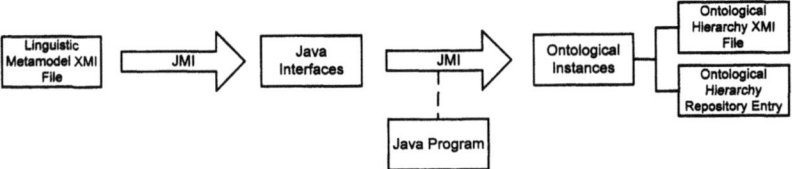

Figure 35 - OMEGA Implementation and Usage

metamodel can cause other difficulties, and it should be mentioned that OMEGA quite literally inherits some problems from MOF. Thus, to establish the properties of OMEGA, the linguistic metamodel is compared to the design space for metamodel hierarchies before discussing its problems and open questions.

In the light of the *design space* defined for metamodel hierarchies, the static OMEGA metamodel can be classified as a nonlinear hierarchy with an arbitrary number of ontological layers, an implicit real-world layer, and an axiomatic top level. It uses a relaxed strictness and a transitive *InstanceOf* relationship, which was considered one aspect of deep instantiation. The instantiation semantics are uniform and the linguistic model is fairly detailed.

One advantage of these design decisions is that the *complexity* of the resulting model is kept relatively low. The relaxed strictness might increase the perceived complexity, but solely for those, who are unfamiliar with the concept. The *consistency and precision* is improved by the use of nonlinearity and deep instantiation. As Table 1 shows, there are few choices, which have a great positive effect on *robustness to change* and *expressional strength*, and consequently the choices merely minimize potential problems in this respect. The most important of all criteria, however, is the *extensibility*, since the hierarchy is intended to serve as an extension mechanism. Thus all choices were made in favor of extensibility, unless they would lead to unacceptable results with regard to the other criteria. For example, not using any strictness would have improved extensibility further but at the price of an unacceptable reduction of precision and expressional strength.

However, while the OMEGA metamodel scores high in the criteria defined for good metamodel hierarchies, it has several *limitations*, which are either open work or were accepted in order to keep the changes to MOF minimal. Since it is important to be aware of these limitations and to understand why they exist, each of them will be addressed briefly.

One case where the original definition of MOF prevents an elegant solution is *abstract classes*. For some reasons, the designers of the MOF metamodel chose to make the attribute *IsAbstract* a feature of *GeneralizableElement*. While there is a connection between the two concepts, as abstract classes only make sense if some other class inherits from them, this choice is unfortunate. The reason is that the compliance to abstraction is a constraint, which is best enforced in the model element *Instance*. The most straightforward approach would have been to include the attribute *IsAbstract* in *MetaElement* and deny *Instances* the right to connect to *MetaElements* where the attribute value is *true*. While a similar constraint has been implemented, it is less elegant as it has to perform a type check to see whether the *MetaElement* is also a *GeneralizableElement*.

Another limitation of OMEGA is the *lack of navigability* from *MetaElements* to their instances via the *InstanceOf* association. The reason for this limitation is that the ontological metamodel layers are typically immutable as described above. Since navigability requires a reference in the *Class* instance and such a reference cannot be changed in a frozen model element, there is no such navigability. A drawback of this arrangement is that the linguistic types of metaclasses cannot define any constraints, which affect the classes' ontological instances. In the case of the prototype's hierarchy, this was not a problem, but it remains to be seen how well the system fares in the general case, possibly mandating an "unfreezing" of the metalayers.

The lack of support for metaoperations (i.e., ***behavioral features***) of any kind might strike some as problematic. However, as has been mentioned before, there are some arguments in favor of leaving out metaoperations because they are not needed. Still, for the sake of completeness, it might be useful to include metaoperations in a future version of OMEGA.

Finally, the ***encoding of values in Slots*** as character strings as opposed to the adequate primitive type is unsatisfactory. The encoding is also incomplete, because custom defined and complex types cannot be handled easily as character strings. However, the choice for value representation mirrors exactly the one used for *Constants* in the MOF standard and was adopted for consistency.

There are several ***open questions***, which will have to be addressed in future work. While OMEGA aims at being a complete metamodel for ontological metamodeling, several questions are left for future revisions of this metamodel extension.

One important question is whether ***inheritance*** should be restricted with regard to metaclasses, i.e., is it acceptable if a class inherits from another class, which does not have the same metaclass? Concepts such as powertypes [158] can be brought forth as arguments to allow cross-type inheritance. On the other hand, with the instantiation semantics chosen for OMEGA, it is questionable whether cross-class inheritance is possible at all, because the attributes a class may have depend on its metaclass. Thus, if a class inherits an attribute from a class of a different type, it is possible that a constraint violation occurs. Also, cross-type inheritance might in some respects be considered a violation of strictness as it enabled a class (indirectly) to have more than one metaclass. If one is to accept this violation, the question remains how to consolidate the constraints imposed on the multiple metaclasses. Most likely, the valid attributes would be the union of all attributes. Still, there are some problems in the details similar to those found with multiple inheritance.

Another question, which concerns instantiation semantics as much as strictness, is whether metaelements should be allowed to ***dominate multiple layers*** instead of only the next one. For example, it might be useful if a *MetaAssociation* between an entity and a (single) key has the power to ensure that all layers will always have the proper multiplicity. Rudimentary aspects of such a multi-layer dominance can be found in the instantiation semantics of *MetaAttributes*, as each consecutive *MetaAttribute* can only allow a subset of the values allowed by the *MetaAttribute* it instantiates. On the one hand, more control by the *MetaLayers* makes it easier to generate code, but, on the other hand, there is the danger of the metamodel becoming too complex or inflexible.

Since OMEGA's primary application is code generation, it is important to consider the modeling of *legacy systems*. Clearly, it should be possible to include some existing software or classes into the models created with OMEGA. However, the question as of how to implement this extension is not so easily answered. Is it preferable to have a special model element, which acts as a tag to mark classes, which already exist? Or should such decisions be made at a template level, possibly as input parameters? Each of the two approaches has its own merits and there are probably many more one could come up with.

The last open question is that of the modeling of *primitive types*. It has already been mentioned that the typing of attributes is not so straightforward with regard to primitive types, as they are neither *MetaElement* nor *Instance*. A possible solution might be to have an "invariant" *ModelLayer* containing self-instantiating elements such as primitive types or to disallow primitive types altogether, only employing domain-specific types as is encouraged in the Executable UML approach by Mellor and Balcer.

Despite these shortcomings and open questions, the OMEGA metamodel is fully functional and can be used as a basis for a hierarchical description of a domain-specific application as will be illustrated in section 5.2. The elements of the static model are complemented by the dynamic metamodel hierarchy OMEGA/Dynamic, which will be described next.

5.1.2 The Metamodel for OMEGA/Dynamic Hierarchies

It has already been mentioned that a hierarchy for statecharts is needed to complement the static hierarchy just described. The ***OMEGA/Dynamic linguistic metamodel*** described in this section fills this role. It is interesting to note that there is no example of a dynamic ontological hierarchy in the literature, although other extension mechanisms such as inheritance have been proposed for statecharts (e.g., [182]). Initial experiments quickly led to the conclusion that the traditional notion of instantiation makes little sense for dynamic metamodels. Nevertheless, the dynamic part of a software artifact can profit even more from a hierarchical extension mechanism than the static one as will be shown in the example (see section 5.2). The linguistic metamodel is particularly interesting because it stretches the boundaries of the concept of a metamodel hierarchy established in this dissertation. Nevertheless, it is still within the design space defined above (see section 5.1.2.5).

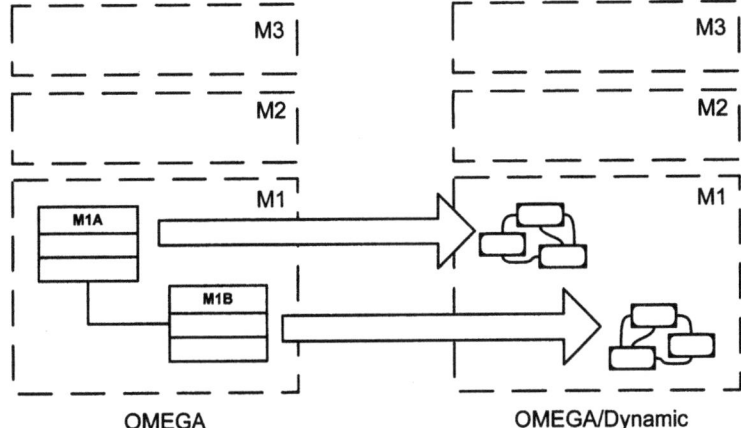

Figure 36 - OMEGA/Dynamic and OMEGA

Functionally, OMEGA/Dynamic can be seen as subservient to the OMEGA hierarchy (as shown in Figure 36). The purpose of the OMEGA/Dynamic hierarchy is to provide the infrastructure for defining the behavior associated with the OMEGA M1 level elements. Using its metaelements, the OMEGA/Dynamic hierarchy allows the definition of statechart diagrams at the M1 level. The connection between the classes of OMEGA M1 and the statecharts of OMEGA/Dynamic M1 is established via a mapping that is not part of the model definition.

The description of OMEGA/Dynamic follows the same general pattern as that of OMEGA. After the initial descriptive overview, the vital model elements are described. Afterwards, the quality of the linguistic metamodel is evaluated and design choices and open questions are addressed.

The *elements of the OMEGA/Dynamic metamodel* are shown in Figure 37 using the MOF notation. Since it is not an extension of the MOF metamodel, there are no existing classes to be considered. Thus, all elements of the OMEGA/Dynamic metamodel are shown in the Figure. As can be seen, some of the elements found in the OMEGA metamodel are also present here, i.e., the *Instance* and *MetaElement* pair and the *ModelLayer*. These elements represent the basic concepts of ontological metamodeling, which are needed in a similar way in both hierarchies. The most important elements in the metamodel are the *MetaStateCharts* and *StateCharts* as well as the different kinds of *MetaStates* and *States*. There are also some elements, which the reader might miss at this point, in particular *MetaTransitions* and *Signals*.

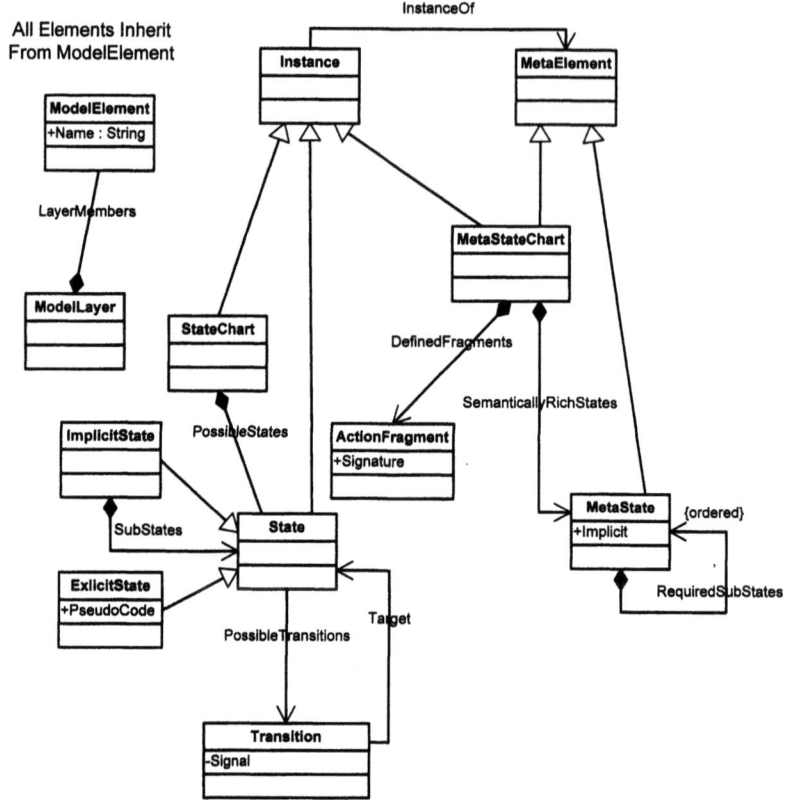

Figure 37 - The OMEGA/Dynamic Linguistic Metamodel

5.1.2.1 Instance and MetaElement

Since *Instance* and *MetaElement* exist in similar form in the OMEGA metamodel, they are not fully detailed here. Rather, it is briefly shown where the OMEGA/Dynamic version differs from the OMEGA variant. The most striking difference is that strictness is relaxed even further than in the case of OMEGA by removing the requirement for *Instances* to have a *MetaElement*. In other words, it is possible for an *Instance* class such as *State* not to have any *MetaElement*, even when not on the axiomatic top layer.

5.1.2.2 States and Transitions

States and ***Transitions*** are the main instance-level elements of an OMEGA/Dynamic hierarchy. Figure 38 shows two different kinds of *States* and a *Transition* as they are used by OMEGA/Dynamic. As can be seen, the ele-

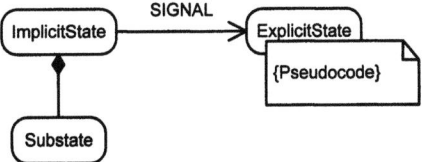

Figure 38 - OMEGA/Dynamic Instance-Level Elements

ments are similar to UML statechart diagram elements and can be easily mapped to such. Therefore, it is not necessary to explain the basic concepts underlying these elements and only the important differences are addressed. The first is that there are two different kinds of *States*. *ExplicitStates* contain a segment of pseudocode, which is interpreted as entry code. This means that every time the *State* is entered, the pseudocode is executed. *ImplicitStates*, on the other hand, do not have any pseudocode, and their behavior is determined by their *MetaState* (see next section).

Some *ImplicitStates* have substates, which can be either implicit or explicit. A *State* with substates can be considered a pattern. An example is shown in Figure 39. Depicted on the left side is an *ImplicitState* called *Condition* with two substates *True* and *False*. This triangular arrangement is a short form for an isolated part of the *StateChart*, which is entered via the *Transition* with the signal A and exited via the *Transition* called by signal B. The exact pattern replacement depends on the *MetaState* explained in the next section.

The last difference to UML statechart diagrams is the lightweight nature of *Transitions*. The only information that can be associated with a *Transition* is the signal, which leads to its execution. The most important implication of this limitation is that a *Transition* cannot have any associated pseudocode, which means that the whole behavior of a statechart is defined via the *States*.

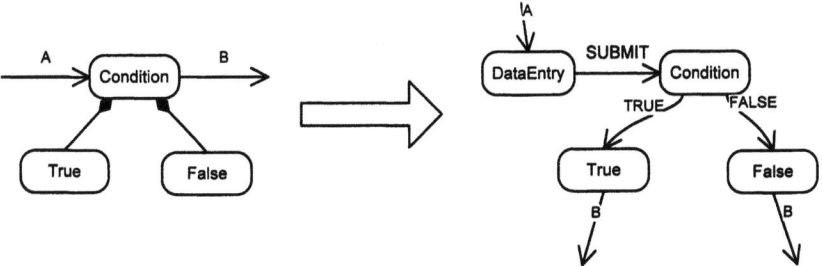

Figure 39 - An Example for the Interpretation of Substates

5.1.2.3 MetaStates and States

Of the elements described in the previous section, only *States* have a metaelement. Similar to the *MetaClass-Class* pair of OMEGA, the *MetaState* to *State* instantiation lies at the core of its linguistic metamodel. Figure 40 shows a conceptual view on the relationship between the two elements for which three different cases exist. As can be seen in the Figure, the *MetaState* does not provide a set of rules restricting its instantiating *States*. Instead, it provides semantical information. In the case of an implicit *MetaState*, i.e., a *MetaState* with the attribute value for *Implicit* set to *true*, the instance is an *ImplicitState*, whose semantics is fully defined by its *MetaState*. In the case of an explicit *MetaState*, the semantics of the instantiating *ExplicitState* is only partially defined. This distinction is important because only *ExplicitStates* are allowed to contain pseudocode.

When instantiating an implicit *MetaState*, the behavior associated with the *Instances* does not depend on pseudocode. However, this does not mean that the behavior is fixed, only that it will be determined automatically. An important factor that must not be forgotten is the static model to which a statechart belongs. Also, as has been mentioned before, some *ImplicitStates* have substates and therefore represent patterns, meaning that their exact behavior also depends on their substates. Which pattern is to be used depends on the implicit *MetaState* and the *MetaStates* of the substates.

The third case in Figure 40 is notable, because the *State* does not have a *MetaState* at all. This is due to the extreme relaxation of strictness, which does not require elements to have metaelements in an OMEGA/Dynamic hierarchy. Given the role of the *MetaStates*, i.e., adding semantic information, and the wide range of possible interpretations, the *MetaState*-less *State* represents a crucial generic element.

5.1.2.4 MetaStateCharts and StateCharts

A *StateChart* is an element that contains a complete state machine and can be associated with a single class in the static model. As shown in Figure 41, the *MetaElements* available to the elements in a *StateChart* depend on its *MetaStateChart*. Since a *MetaStateChart* is commonly associated with a *MetaClass* in the static model, it can be used to provide a "toolbox", which contains ele-

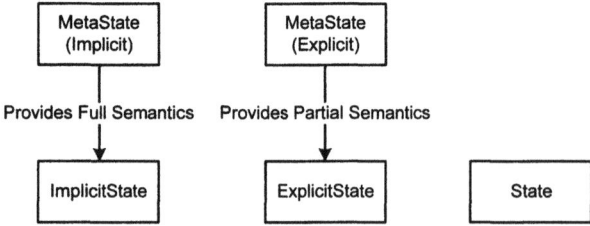

Figure 40 - OMEGA/Dynamic State Concept

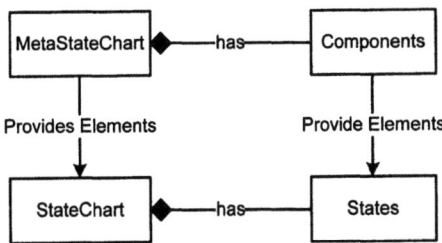

Figure 41 - OMEGA/Dynamic StateChart Concept

ments that are suitable to model the behavior typically expected by the corresponding static model element.

Besides *MetaStates*, a *MetaStateChart* can also contain *ActionFragments*. The *ActionFragments* represent a kind of "helper methods", which can be used in the pseudocode of *ExplicitStates*. In this prototypical version of OMEGA/Dynamic, the signature of a fragment is defined as text only. It is interesting to note that the *ActionFragments* have no *MetaElement* and do not form a hierarchy. Rather each *MetaStateChart* adds additional *ActionFragments*, which provide the end user with a set of elements covering all levels of abstraction.

5.1.2.5 Properties of the OMEGA/Dynamic Metamodel

In parallel to the discussion of the OMEGA metamodel, the description of OMEGA/Dynamic ends with a short analysis of its properties, again first using the metamodel hierarchy design space and then addressing other issues and open work.

At the first glance, the OMEGA/Dynamic hierarchy appears to be rather different from other metamodel hierarchies and does not seem to correspond to the *design space* defined in section 2.4. The reason is that it exhibits a very special form of relaxed strictness. Besides the relaxation suggested for class diagram hierarchies (see section 2.4.4), the requirement that a class needs to have a metaclass unless it is at the topmost level is also removed. It is interesting to see how such a minor change affects the appearance of the hierarchy.

Using the variables defined for the design space, the OMEGA/Dynamic hierarchy can be described as a nonlinear hierarchy with deep instantiation, relaxed strictness, axiomatic top level, implicit real world level, and uniform instantiation semantics. Its number of layers is arbitrary and the linguistic metamodel has a wide scope. Thus, from the standpoint of the design space, it is the same kind of metamodel hierarchy as the static one and the reasoning given in section 5.1.1.6 also applies to it.

However, there are again aspects, which are not covered by the design space. The most interesting issue is the *lack of MetaTransitions*. At the first glance, it seems curious that there are elements, which do not have metaelements, especially in the case of *Transitions*, which are an essential aspect of statechart diagrams. A naïve approach would suggest handling statecharts in a parallel way to the static diagram type. For each model element, a metamodel element is introduced, which can be used as a part of a metamodel hierarchy. However, there is little use in defining *MetaTransitions*, which basically define permissions for certain state transitions.

Due to the flexibility required for a dynamic model, the number of *MetaTransitions* would necessarily be high. There are few *Transitions*, which can be identified as invalid at higher levels of abstraction. While there are a few cases where a *Transition* never makes any sense, using *MetaTransitions* is a rather complex way of avoiding them. Also, if the domain model designer feels that a particular state sequence is an ideal solution for all domain instances, using *MetaTransitions* to enforce this path is a bad idea, because the end user will have to create a large submodel where his design input is not required. A more convenient alternative is the use of *ImplicitStates* with substates. Also, unlike *Associations* in the static case, *Transitions* contain practically no information and therefore there is no sense in limiting the allowed values for *Transitions* or in distinguishing between different types of *Transitions*.

There are also several **open questions** related to OMEGA/Dynamic. For example, the constraints of the model have not been defined formally. The main reason is that the dynamic metamodel has undergone several drastic changes, as it embodies a more radical departure from existing hierarchies than OMEGA. There are also many other aspects, which would profit from future work, for example, the facilities to formally specify the nature of *Signals, ActionFragment* signatures, and *ImplicitStates* with substates. However, since there are no examples of dynamic metamodel hierarchies, more experience with its concepts is required before well-founded extensions can be proposed.

5.1.3 Mapping to UML Profiles

In chapter 3, the lack of standards has been identified as one of the reasons for the problems often associated with CASE tools and visual programming languages. Therefore, the extension mechanism proposed here must be compatible with existing solutions. An end user is not interested in the details of the extension mechanism and most likely unwilling to learn a completely new modeling language. Therefore, it would be helpful to provide a mapping to stereotypes, the extension mechanism used by UML.

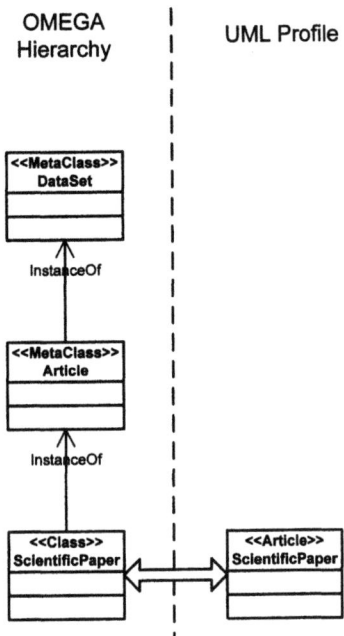

Figure 42 - OMEGA to UML Profile Mapping

The core concept of the mapping to UML Profiles is shown in Figure 42. On the left, the class *ScientificPaper* is enhanced with domain-specific information by using the OMEGA metamodel hierarchy. On the right, the whole hierarchy is replaced with a single UML stereotype, which has the name of the immediate ontological type of *ScientificPaper*. Similarly, stereotypes can be used on attributes and associations. Any attribute *Slots* of the ontological type can be represented as attributes of the stereotype, colloquially known as tagged values.

Even though it might initially seem so, no information is lost, because a UML diagram using the stereotype can always be matched to the appropriate elements in the OMEGA or OMEGA/Dynamic hierarchy. The metamodeling details are completely transparent to end users and possibly even their modeling tools. However, if the name of the stereotype is unambiguous, it is possible to use a hierarchy definition as the one shown in the next section to expand the model to the level of detail needed for code generation.

5.1.4 Using the Extension Mechanism for Code Generation

In order to understand how the extension mechanism for UML described in this section can benefit code generation, let us briefly recapitulate its core concept. The mechanism is based on two metamodel hierarchies. OMEGA is used to add domain-specific, hierarchically arranged information to class diagrams, while OMEGA/Dynamic does the same for statecharts. Similarly to Executable UML, the statechart diagrams are associated with those classes of the model that display complex behavior.

A code generation tool can use the additional information provided by the metaelements to pick the right kinds of code templates, add or remove classes from the design model, and generate documentation among other things. In order to be able to better describe how these improvements become possible, an example hierarchy is presented in the next section and is used in the context of a prototype described in section 5.3.

5.2 A Metamodel Hierarchy for MDD

In this section, an ontological metamodel hierarchy is described, which uses the linguistic metamodels of the extension mechanism introduced in section 5.1. The metamodel hierarchy will not only help to understand the practical applicability of the extension mechanism but will also serve as a basis for the evaluation of the prototype detailed in section 5.3.

Figure 43 shows the example hierarchy used for the remainder of this chapter. At the M3 level is a metamodel for *Web applications*. This technology-oriented but platform independent metamodel is used as a basis for the creation of metamodels specific to a particular business domain. There are many possibilities for M2 metamodels, and the ones shown are only examples. As a proof of concept, the *domain of Content Management* has been prototypically implemented. The models, representing individual software projects in the M2 domain, can be found at the lowest level of the hierarchy. M1 is the only level that an end-user of a domain-specific extension needs to manipulate.

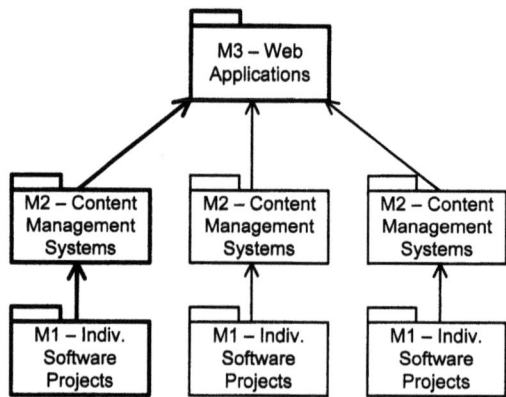

Figure 43 - An Example Metamodel Hierarchy for OMEGA

There are two reasons why the Content Management domain was chosen. On the one hand, it can be considered a good example domain, because it "illustrates an application that is fairly complex in terms of the number and types of users and the complexity of the process that is automated" (cf. Albin [6], chapter 11). On the other hand, it is less extensive than other E-Commerce-related domains, which would be hard to cover in a brief fashion. Content Management is considered E-Commerce-related because it encompasses the sale of virtual (i.e., non-physical) goods, allowing subscribers or passing customers to download text documents, such as scientific papers or newspaper articles, music files, or multimedia content.

The example hierarchy consists of four ontological metamodels, i.e., a static and dynamic metamodel for both the M3 and the M2 layer. These layers are described in the next subsections starting with the static metamodels.

5.2.1 The Static Metamodels

The *static ontological metamodels* are based on the linguistic metamodel provided by OMEGA as described in section 5.1.1. For the sake of clarity, each level is shown separately and therefore *InstanceOf* relationships are not visible. To show both the ontological and the linguistic type-instance relationships, the notation depicted in Figure 44 is used for the following discussion. The stereotype notation in guillemets indicates the linguistic metaclass and the ontological metaclass is shown in brackets. In cases where a metaclass of either type does not exist, is obvious, or is irrelevant, it is omitted.

5.2.1.1 The M3 Layer: Web Application Structure

The M3 layer, as shown in Figure 45, provides elements, which represent a *general static data structure for Web applications*. The elements of the metamodel will not be explained in detail and some information is omitted in the Figure. Instead, a brief overview is given and several interesting aspects are discussed.

The static structure of a Web application as described by the metamodel can be divided into two aspects. On the one hand, there are elements, which represent the static navigation and the presentation of data. On the other hand, there are elements, which represent the data model of the application.

View and its subclasses represent the *static navigation and data presentation*. *StaticViews* represent *Views* with no dynamic behavior, displaying static content

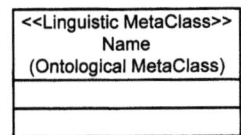

Figure 44 - Type-Instance Relationship Notation

such as that of an XML file. A *DynamicView*'s content is generated from a database entry and can most likely be manipulated by users as defined in the corresponding dynamic model. The content of a *DynamicView* depends on its state and on the *DataSet* referenced via the *Data* link.

The **data model of the application** is represented by *DataSet* instances. A *DataSet* describes a persistent entry in a generic database, not necessarily a relational one. Its attributes are modeled using *DataFields*. Like all *MetaAttributes*, a *DataField* defines a set of allowed types, multiplicities, and scopes for its instances. For example, *DataField* limits the type of its transitive instances to *String*, *Long*, *Integer*, *Double*, or any instance of *DataSet*. A *Key* is similar to a *DataField* but is slightly more restricted and carries special semantics because each key value has to be unique.

The M3 metamodel has been designed to emulate the **Web design languages** discussed in chapter 4 and thus most of its elements have equivalents in one or more of these languages. As has been mentioned in section 4.3.1, this way the strength of Web design languages can be incorporated into an MDD approach. Furthermore, each of the model elements can be mapped to one or more classes of the complementing *framework* (see section 5.3.5). By creating a direct correspondence between model elements and framework classes, the mapping from model elements to code fragments is vastly simplified.

A good example for these relationships is the *View* element. A *View* is a Web page or fragment of a Web page. It corresponds roughly to both the ADVs and navigational nodes used by OOHDM (see 4.2.1.1), because it can be part of a navigational hierarchy (via the *Child* association) and can contain other fragments (via the *Sub* association). Additionally, *View* and its subclasses corre-

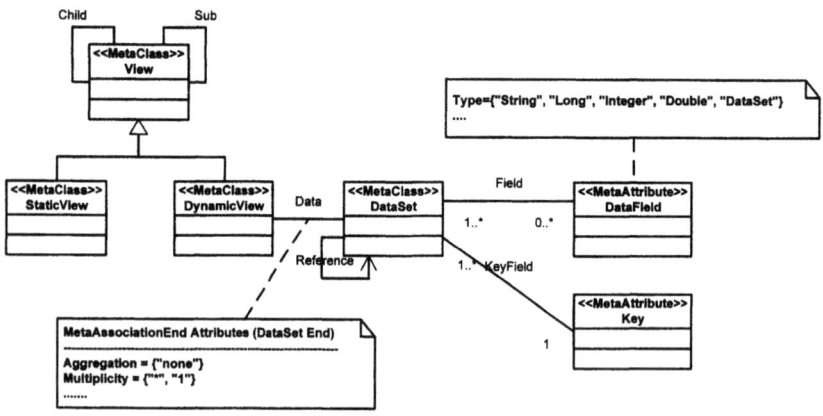

Figure 45 - The Static M3 Layer

spond exactly to the concept of views in the Context-Based Navigation (COBANA) Web application framework (see 5.3.5).

It is an interesting feature of the M3 model that it does not represent a strict class-to-class representation of a Web application but rather uses a *higher level of abstraction* by employing patterns. In particular, the *DynamicView-DataSet* group in the model represents a pattern simplifying the actual relationship between a single *View* and a group of *DataSet* instances. For the purposes of pseudocode, the model "interpretation" shown in Figure 46 is assumed, which introduces a helper class. Thus, the pseudocode in a state belonging to an instance of *DynamicView* uses a reference on a management object, which allows access to individual instances as well as the whole extent of the *DataSet*.

The *MetaAssociations*, which are part of the M3 metamodel, are relatively unrestrictive, to allow a wide variety of M2 metamodels. However, it should be noted that the ability to impose restrictions can be a powerful supporting factor for code generation. For example, the fact that *KeyField* limits the multiplicity allowed for its instances to exactly 1 on the *Key* side implies that the primary keys of all data elements in the application will be limited to a single attribute. This restriction can vastly simplify code generation because a rare special case with impact on many aspects of the generated code is ruled out.

Overall, the M3 static metamodel is relatively simple due to its high level of abstraction. As can be seen in the next section, it forms a good basis for metamodels addressing specific sub-domains of Web applications in general.

5.2.1.2 The M2 Layer: Content Management System Structure

The CMS static model is an *instance of the M3 Web model* described in the previous section, enriching the generic Web domain with more specific elements. It is important to remember that the metamodel exists mainly to illustrate the extension mechanism and that it has not been tested extensively. In other words, it is a proof of concept and, like all domain-specific metamodels, would most likely require changes after a thorough practical evaluation. Nevertheless, despite its limited scope, it aptly illustrates the strengths of the hierarchical approach. Figure 47 shows the most important aspects of the M2 layer.

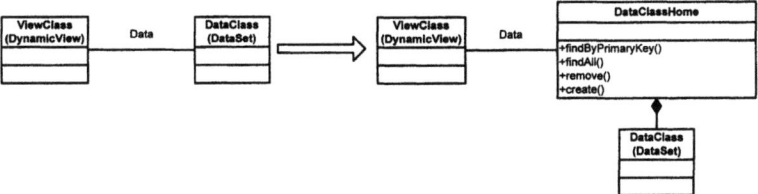

Figure 46 - Replacement Pattern for DynamicView and DataSet

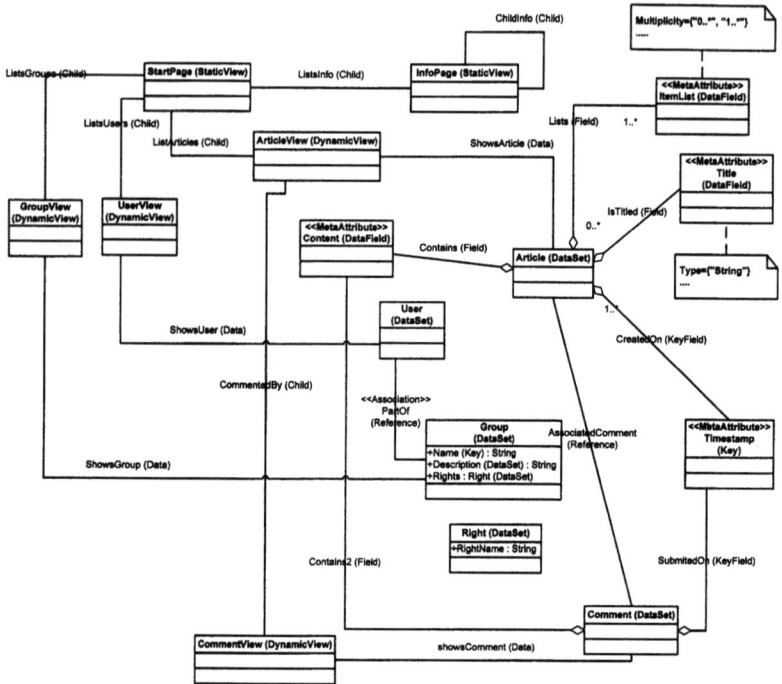

Figure 47 - The Static M2 Layer

The CMS metamodel has several subsystems with special semantics, the most important of which are the system for displaying and editing the content managed by the application, the static information aspects, and the user management. Since it is not used in the examples, the latter is not discussed further.

The *static information aspects* of the metamodel are represented by those elements, which are instances of *StaticView*, i.e., *StartPage* and *InfoPage*. A *StartPage* is a *StaticView*, which is designed to be an entry point for the user of a site. It can lead to the articles of the CMS, pages with static information, and pages, which allow the management of user data. An *InfoPage* is a simple static page with all different kinds of information such as contact information or disclaimers.

The *content management classes*, as the name implies, form the core of the CMS metamodel. *ArticleView* represents a dynamic access point to a specific kind of *Article*. As such, most of its semantics is defined in the dynamic model's description. An *ArticleView* is little more than a container for a state machine.

The *Article* associated with the *ArticleView* is a *DataSet*, which describes the CMS-managed content. All of its *MetaAttributes* carry domain-specific meaning, for example, a *Title* is a short text giving an overview of an *Article* and *Con-*

tent represents some piece of core information. There is also a special purpose *MetaAttribute* called *ItemList* used for the creation of lists of items, e.g., steps in a user manual, ingredients of a recipe, or bibliographical references.

The CMS metamodel is a good example how a generic metamodel, in this case the M3 Web application metamodel, can be enriched using instantiation. Due to the fact that the elements of the CMS metamodel have more specific semantics, they are more suitable for any kind of automated task that requires a program to make assumptions about its data such as code generation or providing semantic data about a Web application.

The ***support of semantic Web applications*** is a direction, which can only be skirted here because it is beyond the scope of this work. Briefly, a model of a Web application based on a metamodel as specific as the CMS metamodel can serve as a good basis for the creation of RDF documents to support semantic Web browsers. Even the simple distinction between a *StartPage*, an *ArticleView*, and an *InfoPage* can allow intelligent browsers to assemble a site summary. More sophisticated versions of the M2 metamodel might distinguish between page fragments displaying legal information, advertisements, and other categories of static information.

The benefit for ***code generation***, on the other hand, is a major focus of the discussion later in the next chapter. Looking at the example of the *Article* class, it is possible to point out several beneficial aspects of the added semantics, in particular due to the concept of *MetaAttributes* unique to OMEGA. The existence of M2 *MetaAttributes* implies that each attribute found in the persistent objects of a designed application will have an interpretation the code generator can use to automatically produce business logic. For example, an *Article* might be represented by its *Title* in a list. Also, the primary key of an object can be generated automatically since it is a *Timestamp*. Input fields for *Content* attributes will be given larger text areas than other *String*-based attributes such as *Title*. There are even more benefits for the dynamic metamodels that will be discussed in section 5.2.2.2.

5.2.2 The Dynamic Metamodels

The dynamic metamodel hierarchy defines the behavior associated with the elements of the static models described in the previous two sections. The ontological metamodels are all instances of the linguistic OMEGA/Dynamic metamodel. The M3 layer metamodel is described first, followed by the Content Management elements of M2.

5.2.2.1 The M3 Layer: Web Application Behavior

There is only one *MetaClass* at the M3 layer with an inherent dynamic behavior and therefore only a single *MetaStateChart* has to be defined. Figure 48 shows the metamodel for *DynamicViewBehavior*, which serves as a metaelement for the *StateCharts* used by instances of *DynamicView*.

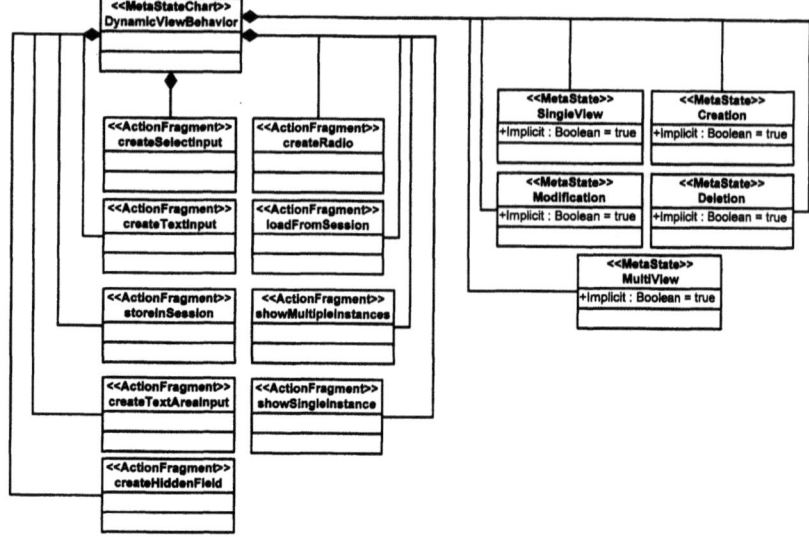

Figure 48 - The Dynamic M3 Layer

For the Web context, special *semantics* is associated with the linguistic metamodel elements provided by OMEGA/Dynamic. The generic parameters and return types of OMEGA/Dynamic are replaced by tables with key-value pairs. Since not all *States* need the same parameters, the exact nature of both the parameters and return types have to be described for all implicit *MetaStates*. Only *States*, whose expected input and provided output match, can succeed each other meaningfully. While the implicit *MetaStates* provided by the M3 metamodel generally fulfill this criterion where needed, care has to be taken by a modeler when creating instances, which define their own pseudocode. The return value of these explicit *MetaStates* is created automatically based on the *ActionFragments* called and must provide all values required by the successor.

The *semantics of Signals* is divided into two special cases, *user input* and *internal signals*. *View* and its instances are the only elements that directly receive signals from the user. The code generator is responsible for providing links, sending the proper signal to allow all the defined transitions. The rest of the *Signals* are considered internal, a case, which does not occur in the examples and is therefore not explained in detail.

The *DynamicViewBehavior MetaStateChart* provides many *ActionFragments* to facilitate the writing of pseudocode, for example, allowing the creation of Web page form elements. The *createTextInput ActionFragment* creates a text field on the output Web page of the *State*, passing the text field's content to the next *State* in the key-value table parameter. However, there is no *ActionFragment* for the creation of submit buttons. The buttons available in the Web page for a particular *State* are created automatically based on the signals of all outgoing *Transitions*. Depending on which of the buttons in a Web page is chosen, the *Signal* associated with it is sent to the Web application's controller, initiating a transition to another *State*.

The *loadFromSession* and *storeInSession* fragments represent an alternative way to pass information to other states. Unlike an entry in the key-value table, information stored in the session is accessible to *States* beyond the immediate successor.

ShowSingleInstance is an *ActionFragment* that takes a *Key* as a parameter and lets the *DynamicView* display the named instance as soon as the entry code is finished. *ShowMultipleInstances* shows a list instead of a single instance.

In addition to the fragments, there are also complete implicit *MetaStates*, which define a certain behavior. There is a slight overlap between the functionalities of the two concepts. However, this is only for convenience. If no custom pseudocode is required at all, an implicit *MetaState* is generally preferable to an *ActionFragment*.

The **Creation** *MetaState* creates a new instance of the *DataSet* belonging to its *DynamicView*. When this *State* is entered, a form with fields for all *Attributes* of the *DataSet* appears in the browser and its results are used to create a new instance with the given values. *Creation* does not expect any parameters and does not send any to the next state.

Creation is a good example of how a *MetaState* can save time during development. If the same behavior had to be realized using only explicit *States*, it would be required to create two *States* with a relatively large amount of pseudocode. The first *State* would be responsible for the creation of the input form and the second for the instantiation of the new persistent object.

Modification is a *State* that allows the manipulation of existing objects. It expects a key value as a parameter in the value table and will display the element with that key in a form. The element's values can be changed and will replace the original ones. A *Modification State* passes on the key value it received in the table sent to the next state.

Deletion expects the same parameter as *Modification* and will delete the *DataSet* instance with the corresponding *Key*. The next state depends on the links defined in the statechart but is not passed a parameter table entry.

SingleView and **MultiView** correspond to the *ActionFragments* described above but are full *States*. *SingleView* expects the same parameter as *Deletion* and *Modification*. *MultiView* does not expect any parameter entries. Both add an "instance" entry with the *Key* of the currently active object to the table that will be passed to the next state.

5.2.2.2 The M2 Layer: Content Management System Behavior

The CMS layer adds some additional functionality to the basic Web behavior defined in the M3 layer. Figure 49 shows the three *MetaStateCharts* introduced by the M2 layer. Of particular interest, as a proof-of-concept, is the *ArticleBehavior*, the first non-Web element to display dynamic behavior. The elements of the metamodel necessary for the further discussion are explained below.

Several *ActionFragments* are defined for the M2 layer. The *ActionFragments* **getApproved** and **setApproved** can be used to set and read the implicit *Boolean* variable *Approved*, which is automatically added to all *Articles*. Both fragments are intended to be called by other classes to allow distinguishing between these two different "modes" of *Article*. Of course, the approval mechanism can also be modeled using states, setting the *Approved* value internally, if more complex review processes have to be modeled. The approval flag is used by some of the *MetaStates* defined for M2.

In addition to the *ActionFragments*, there are also several *MetaStates*. **ShowApprovedArticles** is a *MetaState*, which only shows those Articles where *Approved* is *true*, otherwise it behaves like an M3 *MultiView*. **ShowUnapprovedArticles** is

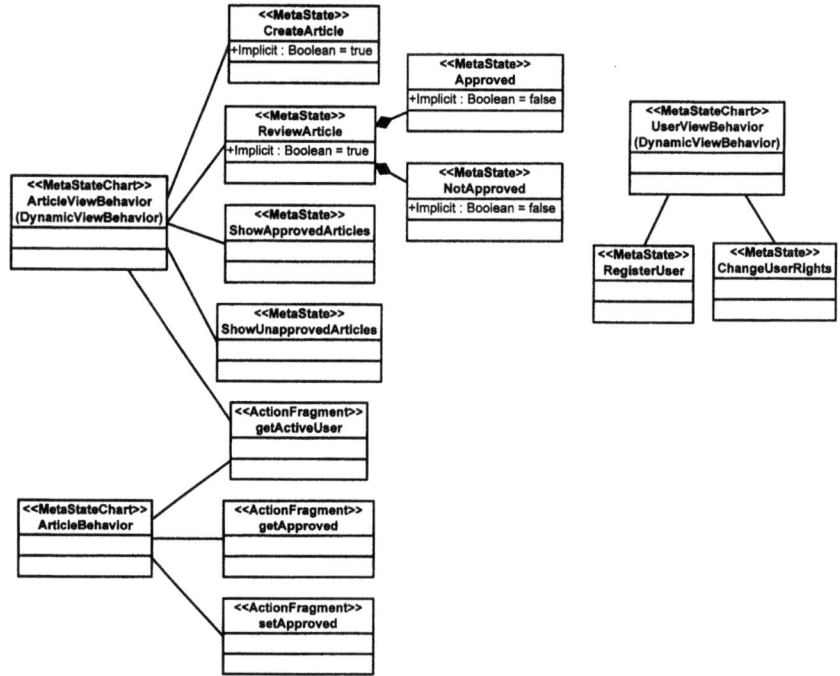

Figure 49 - The Dynamic M2 Layer

another *MetaState* that only shows those *Articles*, which are not approved. Both *MetaStates* do not expect any parameters but upon exit will pass a string consisting of the *Timestamp* and the *Title* of the selected *Article* to their follow-up *State* in the key-value table.

ReviewArticle is a *State* that represents a Web page very similar to that used by *Modification* but offers two exits, one for approval and one for rejection. There are two different *requiredSubstates*, one that will be reached when the *Article* is approved and one that is reached when it is not. The *Timestamp* of the *Article* is passed as a parameter to the next *State*. *ReviewArticle* can be interpreted as a pattern flexibly applicable to many similar situations as can be seen in the examples shown in section 5.4.

5.3 Prototypical Implementations

While the example in the previous section shows that the extension mechanism described in this chapter can be used to model domain-specific hierarchies, the question is whether these hierarchies can be used to facilitate the generation of application code. In order to be able to evaluate to what extent the intended improvements of the OMEGA extension mechanism are realized, it is necessary to provide a prototypical tool implementation.

The ***prototype***, which will be described in this section, consists of three plugins for the Eclipse tool integration platform [63], some stand-alone support tools, code generation templates, and a Web application framework. However, due to the purpose of the prototype as a test bed for the evaluation in section 6.1, not all of these elements are given the same amount of attention. Instead the following approach is taken.

First, the ***general plugin architecture*** is briefly described to explain the overall structure of the prototype. For this purpose the defined plugin interfaces are explained and it is described which plugins implement which interfaces.

The first plugin to be discussed is a generic ***modeling tool***. Not being tied to the OMEGA metamodels in particular, it provides an interface, which allows the registration of generic metamodels.

Described next, is a ***metamodel data structure*** implementing this interface. The plugin can load models, which use an ontological metamodel based on the OMEGA and OMEGA/Dynamic linguistic metamodels.

Extending both the modeling tool and the data structure plugin is a ***code generation module***. Since the goal of this dissertation is to improve the input provided to code generators and not the code generators themselves, the module is of a purely proof-of-concept nature and should not be considered complete or stable beyond the test cases. Nevertheless, it is described in some detail to be able to evaluate the ability of the extension mechanism to support code generation.

Finally, to show the advantages of a close relationship between models and coding infrastructure, a ***Web application framework*** had to be implemented. The COBANA framework has been tested and extended in the context of several non-model-driven student projects. Since COBANA is merely used as an example framework, it is only examined in so far as is relevant for the evaluation of the prototype.

5.3.1 General Plugin Architecture

Figure 50 shows the conceptual structure of the plugins developed for the prototype. OMEGAPlugin is the main plugin, which provides three extension points that allow other plugins to use its infrastructure. As shown in the Figure, it is also possible that a single plugin implements more than one point. Not shown is the fact that an extension point can be implemented multiple times. The DefaultExtension implements both *IMetaModel* and *IOMEGAeditPartFactory* twice, once for OMEGA and once for OMEGA/Dynamic.

OMEGAPlugin is a generic editor for drawing models. The concrete syntax or look of these models is variable and depends on an external object factory, which implements the ***IOMEGAeditPartFactory*** interface. By providing a different factory, the look of the graphical elements can be changed. In the prototype, the *IOMEGAeditPartFactory* interface is implemented twice, providing graphical elements for both the static and the dynamic models.

The abstract syntax of the model is determined by the plugins implementing the ***IMetaModel***, which define the types of nodes and edges allowed in the model. This interface is also implemented twice, once for each model type.

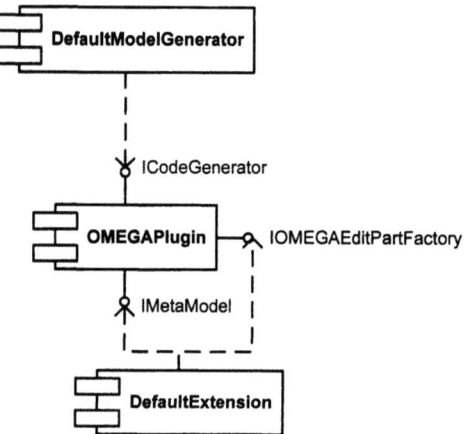

Figure 50 - Prototype Plugin Structure

The final interface is *ICodeGenerator*. The interface is used to pass the model information on to the code generator. While the interface itself is independent of the *IMetaModel* interface and there is technically no coupling between *IMetaModel* and *ICodeGenerator*, the two aspects are generally co-dependent and should be developed accordingly.

The three plugins shown in the Figure form the core application of the prototype and are therefore non-trivial. Since there is no room for a detailed discussion of their 355 classes and interfaces (see the online documentation [94] for details), only overviews can be given for each of the plugins in the next three sections. The OMEGAPlugin is described first, followed by the data structure and the code generation plugin.

5.3.2 The OMEGA Modeling Tool

The OMEGA modeling tool, realized by the OMEGAPlugin, is a highly configurable graphical user interface for the creation of models. As has been mentioned before, the look of its model elements depends mostly on the plugins implementing the *IOMEGAEditorPartFactory* extension interface. Figure 51 is a screenshot of the configuration used for the prototype. For the discussion at the end of this chapter, a detailed description of the user interface is not required. For anybody, who has ever used a UML-based or similar modeling tool, the use

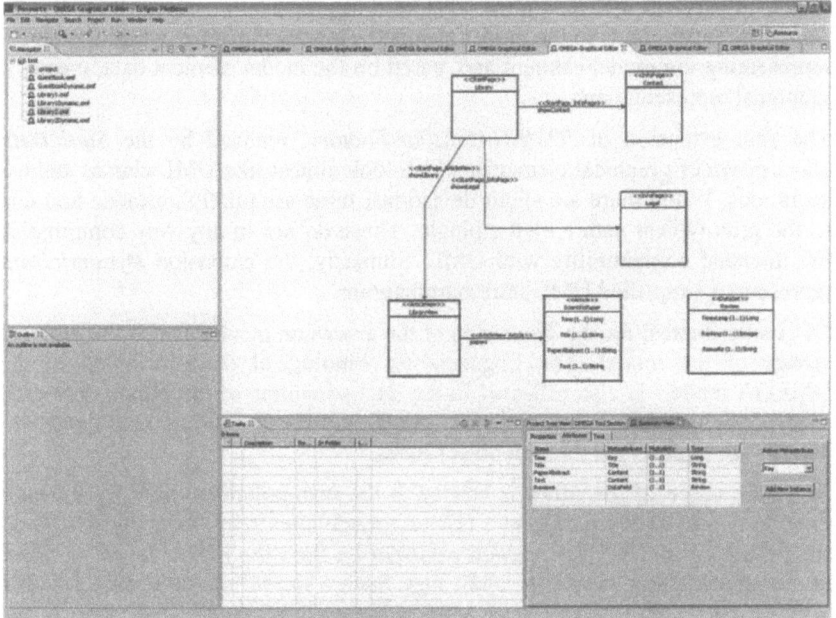

Figure 51 - Screenshot of the Plugin

of the plugin should be intuitive. Since the plugin is intended for an end user of a metamodel hierarchy, it does not support a graphical editing of the metamodels. The creation, saving, and loading of custom metamodels is realized through rudimentary helper tools, existing outside of the plugin.

As discussed in the previous section, the OMEGAPlugin provides three extension points, which require the implementation of specific interfaces. Since the interfaces and their actual implementations are best explained together, they are not discussed in the context of the main plugin and are instead delegated to the sections presenting their corresponding implementations.

5.3.3 The OMEGA Data Structure Plugin

The plugin containing the data structure needed for OMEGA is called DefaultExtension. It implements both the *IOMEGAEditPartFactory* and the *IMetaModel* interface twice, providing the concrete and abstract syntax for both the static and the dynamic metamodel. Since its functionality comprises two aspects, both are discussed separately.

The *concrete syntax* of the metamodel depends on so-called *EditParts*, a concept defined for the Draw2D Eclipse plugin. An *EditPart* contains the rules for creating a graphical representation of a model element. The principle of these wrappers is simple. Every time the editor is asked to display a model element, a lookup is performed to determine what kind of graphical element (and therefore *EditPart*) corresponds to the model element. The new *EditPart* wraps the object representing the model element and, based on the model element data, creates a graphical representation.

The first extension of *IOMEGAEditPartFactory*, realized by the **StaticData** class, provides graphical elements, which look almost like UML classes and associations. While there are slight deviations, these are purely cosmetic and due to the prototypical nature of the plugin. These do not in any way compromise the intended compatibility with UML. Similarly, the extension **DynamicData** represents a simplified UML statechart diagram.

Of greater interest for the discussion of the extension mechanism is the *abstract syntax* of the model. The linguistic vs. ontological dualism found in the OMEGA models is also reflected in the data structures of the plugin. For each kind of metamodel, a data structure exists, and the individual ontological instances are represented through object states.

Since the scope of the editor is limited to the manipulations made by the end-user, its model does not support a full metamodel hierarchy, focusing instead on the lowest layer. Only the relevant information from the higher layers is added as metainformation, similar to UML tags. Such a simplification is only possible because the metalevels are "read-only" at the end user level. Thus, most of the information described in the metamodel hierarchy can be ignored in this special case, being relevant only when new metamodels are designed, which is a task beyond the scope of the plugin.

The most important classes and interfaces of the data structure for the simplified metamodels, called Simplified OMEGA (S-OMEGA), are shown in Figure 52. The classes above the dashed line represent metaelements and the classes below are the actual instances, which will be shown in the GUI's diagrams.

A detailed explanation of these classes is not necessary in this context. Therefore, the description is limited to a few key elements. Basically, a model consists of edges (*IEdge*) and nodes (*INode*), whose properties are limited by the classes implementing *IMetaEdge* and *IMetaNode*. A metamodel can contain several elements of each category, all of which together are the types defined for the metamodel.

In the default implementation, there are two types of metamodels registered with the OMEGAPlugin, one for OMEGA-type metamodels and one for OMEGA/Dynamic metamodels. Based on an ontological instance of either of these linguistic metamodels, a new empty model can be created with a helper tool and then edited in the plugin. Thus, it is possible to work with different do-

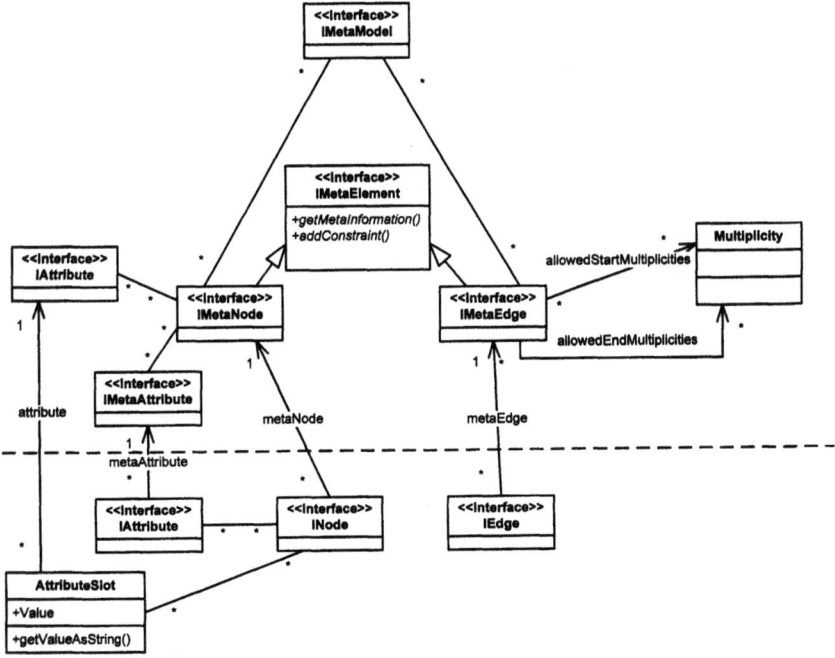

Figure 52 - S-OMEGA

main hierarchies. The exact details of the implementation are not relevant in this context, and therefore only very brief descriptions are given to convey the basic principles of the mappings of the full metamodels to S-OMEGA. Note that due to its prototypical nature, the DefaultExtension does not check any model constraints yet, i.e., it is up to the user to create valid models.

5.3.3.1 The Mapping From OMEGA to S-OMEGA

The mapping between OMEGA and S-OMEGA is almost trivial. The OMEGA element *MetaClass* is mapped to the S-OMEGA concept of *MetaNode*. Due to the relaxed strictness, all *MetaClasses*, regardless of their *ModelLayer*, are included in the metamodel. The *MetaNode* contains a *MetaAttribute* for each *MetaAttribute* of the corresponding *MetaClass* as well as its transitive metaelements, again due to the relaxed strictness. Each *MetaNode* contains the names of the *MetaClasses* of its corresponding *MetaClass* as metainformation, which gives a code generator the necessary pointers to exploit the domain-specific information encoded in the metalayers. Figure 53 shows an example of the OMEGA to S-OMEGA mapping for *Classes*.

The OMEGA *MetaAssociation* is translated into a *MetaEdge*. The *IMetaEdge* interface allows manipulation of data, which forms a subset of that found in a *MetaAssociation*. However, the values not covered are MOF-specific and do not add to the expressional strength of the model for the purpose of code generation.

Due to its prototypical nature, the current version of the plugin incorporates several simplifications. For example, inheritance is ignored. Also, *Attributes*, unlike *MetaAttributes*, are not added transitively. While these omissions do not impair most modeling activity, they are considered future work for a fully functional version of the plugin.

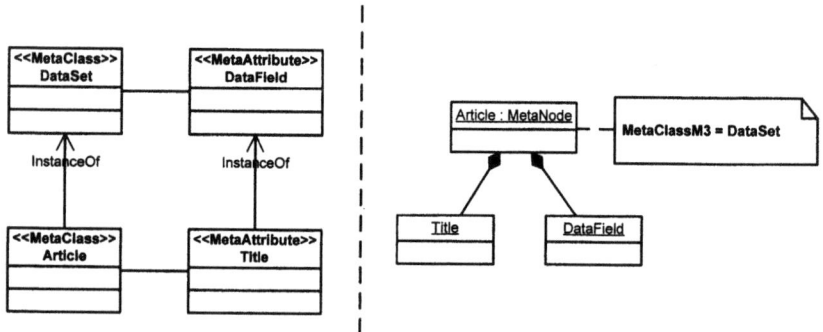

Figure 53 - OMEGA to S-OMEGA Mapping

5.3.3.2 The Mapping From OMEGA/Dynamic to S-OMEGA

The mapping from OMEGA/Dynamic to S-OMEGA follows similar principles but is a lot simpler due to the limited nature of the OMEGA/Dynamic linguistic metamodel. There are two different *INode* implementations, the *ImplicitState* and the *ExplicitState*, representing the corresponding elements in the OMEGA/Dynamic metamodel. Since the metamodel does not contain any elements related to transitions, there are only two different types of edges in the S-OMEGA metamodel; *Transition* and *ContainsSubState*. *MetaState* information is added similarly to the strategy used for *MetaClasses* as described in the previous section.

5.3.4 The Code Generation Module

As has already been mentioned, the actual details of code generation are beyond the scope of this work and therefore the code generator has only been realized as a rudimentary skeleton implementation. In particular, it does not yet support multiplicities, non-primitive types for attributes, and the use of Java classes not in *java.lang* or *java.util* in the pseudocode.

Nevertheless, the code generator is sufficient to show several interesting examples. In order to allow a profound discussion about the potential of the extension mechanism, the code generation concepts relevant for the further discussion are described. First, the overall process is explained. Then the basic concepts underlying both the static and the dynamic templates are analyzed. Finally, peculiarities of the Web domain with regard to code generation are discussed in section 5.3.4.4.

5.3.4.1 Code Generation Process

The code generation process is started by the OMEGAPlugin, which passes the model data to the code generator. The code generator performs a transformation on the data it receives to give it a form more suitable for its processing steps. The simplified data structure is summarized in Figure 54. Of particular interest are the attributes of *Element*, which identify the metatypes defined in the domain-specific hierarchy.

The **code generation process** consists of three steps, shown in Figure 55. First, the statecharts passed to the code generator are transformed, resolving the patterns implied by the *ImplicitStates* (see Figure 39). Since both the M3 and the M2 level can contain *ImplicitStates*, configuration input is required from both layers for all relevant states.

In the next step, called *feature weaving*, features are added to the classes of the static model. These features can be attributes or methods relevant for the M2 domain. Since the static templates depend solely on the M3 elements, a weaving mechanism for M3 features is not required.

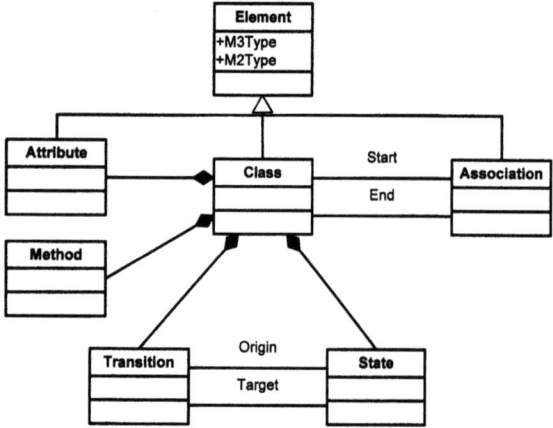

Figure 54 - Code Generator Input

After the input has been modified to resolve patterns and to add domain-specific information, the actual *code generation* can be started. This process is based on a list of tasks associated with either an M3 or M2 type. Each task uses a template and generates either a single file for all instances (e.g., a deployment descriptor) or a file for each (e.g., a Java file). Since multiple tasks may be associated with a single type, it is possible to generate multiple files for a single element, a feature useful for technologies such as EJB, which require multiple interfaces for a single element. The exact code generated depends on the templates, which are discussed in the next sections.

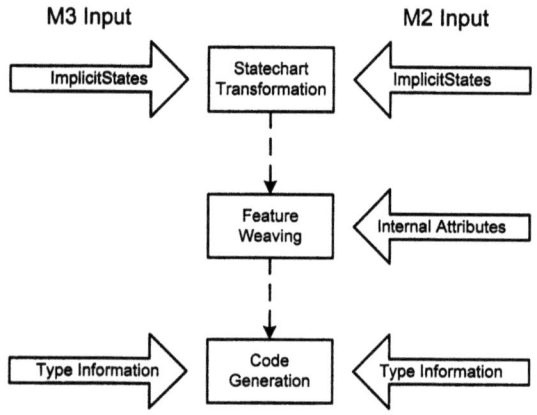

Figure 55 - Code Generation Process

5.3.4.2 Static Code Generation Templates

It should come as no surprise that the generation of the data structures needed for the application is very straightforward. Static code generation enjoys widespread use, and it is trivial to come up with a mapping from class diagrams to the static aspects of the code. However, should the need arise, some or all parts of the class diagram can be interpreted in different fashions. For example, in the hierarchy for Web applications, the class diagram combines the conceptual and navigational aspects of a Web application, using model elements from the Web design languages described in section 4.2.1.

Since the M3 layer of the metamodel hierarchies is technically oriented, it makes sense to use the M3 types for the static templates. In the example hierarchy, all static code could be generated using M3 information only.

5.3.4.3 Dynamic Generation Templates

The dynamic aspects of an application are harder to generate. The most promising approach is to use the ideas proposed by Harel and Gery [106], associating *statecharts* with individual *classes* and sending *events* to other classes' objects via references, which can lead to changes in the associated statechart instances. In the literature, there are many approaches to code generation based on statecharts (see for example [4], [47], [106], [149], or [189]), which will be discussed briefly.

Dynamic code generation is often realized by a combination of statecharts and an action language of some kind, although other approaches exist (see for example Engels et al. [66]). While typically the action language code to be executed is associated with state transitions (e.g., Harel and Gery [106]), it is also possible to put the *action language statements* into the states, executing them when the state is entered. This arrangement is favored by the Executable UML approach (as described in section 3.2.2.3) and it is also adopted for OMEGA.

Even when using the basic structure described above, there are several detail questions, which have to be answered. The two *central problems* in this context are how to represent the state of an object and how to implement the signals that trigger the transitions.

Normally, the *state of an object* is considered to be the combination of values of all its attributes. However, the resulting states are too fine-grained to map well to those in a typical statechart. While states encompassing certain ranges of values can be defined, the generated code would be complex to understand. An easier way is to represent the object state through a single *enumerative variable*, which can have a limited number of values (e.g., an *enum* in Java 1.5, cf. Chow et al. [47]). Finally, it is possible to represent the state through a *helper object*, which is based on a different class for each state, all of which implement the same interface (cf. Gamma et. al. [76] and such examples as Niaz and Tanaka [149] or Sane and Campell [182]). This approach has a few advantages with regard to the handling of signals and is therefore used for the DefaultCodeGenerator.

It is generally agreed upon that there are two basic ways to realize *signals* in an environment, which is mainly single-threaded or makes thread-related questions transparent to the developer. The first is to use an event-based approach, and the second is to use method calls (e.g., Harel and Gery [106] or Ali and Tanaka [4]). In the case of *method calls*, sending a signal means calling a method of that name in the target object. *Events*, on the other hand, rely on a central dispatcher, which is fed new events and distributes them to their target objects. The main difference between the two concepts is that in one case the execution of the object's action statements is frozen until the method call is finished, while an event will only pass control to the target as soon as its own statechart is stable, i.e., not executing any statements.

Using a helper object for the representation of states also facilitates signal handling. The reason is that each helper class can implement the methods or event listeners required for the state it represents and implement the behavior required in that particular state. Thereby, a clean separation of state code is achieved in the implementation. In the code generator plugin, both types of signals are used, depending on their role in the model.

Figure 56 shows the code generation approach chosen for OMEGA. The pseudo-UML model on the right shows a static class from the OMEGA model and its associated statechart, represented by a package. On the right, a simplified representation of the generated code is shown. As mentioned above, each state is realized by a helper class. In the example, signals are passed as events to the *changeState()* method, a realization of signals as method calls would include a method *mySignal()* in the generated class called *MyClass*.

An interesting aspect of the generated code is the *MyStateBaseClass*. A common baseclass for all states is useful, because it is the ideal location for all kinds of

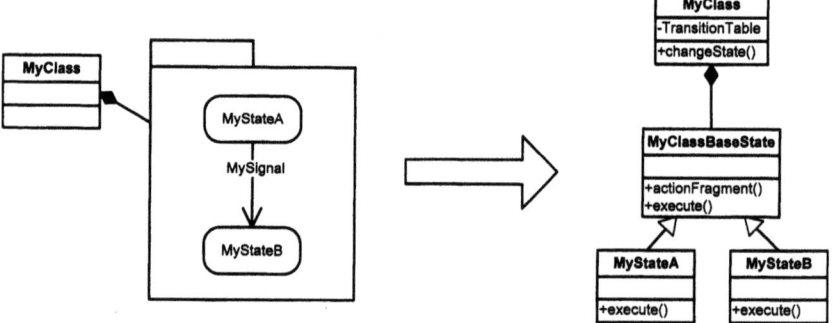

Figure 56 - Code Generation Concept

helper methods. In particular, *ActionFragments* are realized as method calls in the baseclass.

The code generated for a *State* depends on both of its *MetaStates*. Should a *State* have both an M2 and M3 type, the M2 type is used, but in most cases there is only one type. Typically a different template is provided for each *MetaState*. If the state is based on a ***non-implicit MetaState***, the pseudocode associated with the state is added. Otherwise the behavior is determined by the template.

The action language used for the *pseudocode* sections in the plugin is a subset of Java, since it makes little sense to define a new language for the purposes of a prototype. Similar arguments are brought forth by Harel and Gery, who use C++ in their O-MATE tool [106].

It should be obvious that there are some *limitations* to the chosen approach. In particular, the statecharts used as input for the code generator are somewhat simplistic. However, it can be argued that the concepts tested here will be usable with more complex statecharts as well. In particular, by using helper objects to represent the states, the code generation techniques devised by Ali and Tanaka can easily be added. Thus it becomes possible to cover more advanced features such as concurrency or substates (cf. [4]).

5.3.4.4 Code Generation for the Web Domain

While the code templates designed for the Web domain use the same basic principles as the general case described above, a few slight alterations are needed to accommodate some particularities. The ***Web M3 model*** used in the examples implies the following assumptions.

Any (transitive) instance of *View* is considered to be part of the navigational model of the application. The concepts of "childviews" and "subviews" correspond to the equivalent constructs already explained in the context of Web design languages. Thus, the whole static navigation is encoded in the static diagram.

The various *ActionFragments* of the *DynamicViewBehavior* are used to assemble a page consisting of text information, links, and edit fields. After a code block has been finished, the page is assumed to be visible to the user, who can use the various links provided. Each of the links represents a single possible signal to change the *State* of the currently active *DynamicView*. All "static" navigation is defined in the static diagram.

A *DynamicView* starts in the *State*, which is identified as the initial state due to its name, whenever the user navigates to this *DynamicView*. This implies that leaving the *DynamicView* via static navigation will reset the state.

5.3.5 A Brief Introduction to the COBANA Framework

One of the core ideas of the code generation strategy used in this context is the use of a ***suitable framework***, which allows fast and easy template implementation, to avoid the problems encountered by past approaches (see section 3.2.1). The Context-Based Navigation (COBANA) Web application framework has been designed for this purpose and is briefly described in this section. Since a general discussion is not required in this context, only the aspects, which actively support the code generation effort are shown. For further information see [86] and [89].

5.3.5.1 Basic Concept

COBANA is a framework based on the J2EE technology family. It employs a Servlet for communication with the user, utilizing XSLT templates to translate the XML data extracted either from static files or *EntityBeans* into a desired output format such as HTML. COBANA's internal structure is inspired by the Web design languages described in section 4.2.1, which allows a straightforward transformation of OMEGA models into COBANA code.

5.3.5.2 Framework Architecture

Figure 57 describes the core Java classes of COBANA in a simplified form. As in many other Web application frameworks based on the so-called "Model 2" architecture [196], the controller is a Servlet (shown as *ControllerServlet*), which delegates a client request to the relevant *View* element and returns a textual document to be sent as a reply. Due to utilization of the Composite pattern (cf. [76]), *Views* can be composed in a hierarchy similar to the navigational context concept described in section 4.2.1. When comparing Figure 57 to Figure 45,

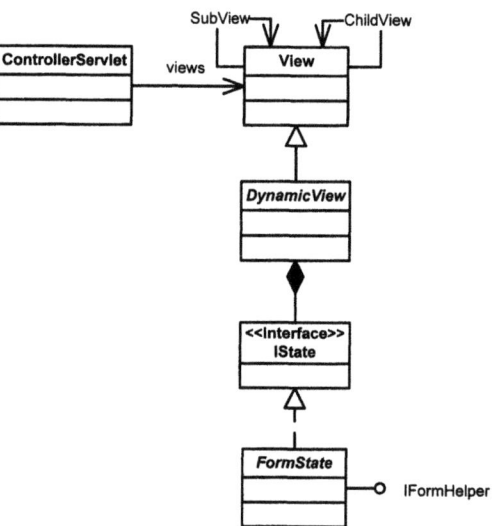

Figure 57 - Core Classes of COBANA

it is possible to see the parallel between OMEGA and COBANA in its static aspects, especially with regard to navigation. Additionally, the *DynamicView* supports the statechart code generation as shown in Figure 56.

5.3.5.3 Navigation

The left side of Figure 58 shows an example of the hierarchical organization of the views based on the associations defined in the class diagram of Figure 57. There are two hierarchies, which are interleaved but have different interpretations. Tree edges based on the *SubView* association represent elements to be included into their parent node and correspond to the concept of nested ADVs in OOHDM. *ChildView* based edges implement the OOHDM's concept of navigational contexts. Dynamic behavior is handled by statecharts within the *DynamicViews* and is therefore not part of the tree shown in the Figure.

When the *ControllerServlet* returns a document to the client, the decision which *Views* to include depends on the user input, the process state, and the *View* hierarchy. These factors identify a pruned subtree of *Views*, which is assembled into a document. The *ChildView* edges of the view hierarchy represent a nested tree of navigational contexts (cp. Figure 23). In the Web application corresponding to the example tree, the main context contains a welcome page and a products page. When viewing one of these pages, it is possible to navigate to all other pages on the same level. When the products page is active, one can also navigate to its children, the books and the DVDs page.

The right side of Figure 58 shows an example where a user has navigated to the page showing books and the tree is reduced accordingly, ignoring the *ChildViews* of all other paths. The complete page is assembled by traversing the pruned tree in a depth-first order. For each relevant node, the static or dynamically generated XML content along with the XML-based transformation results of any relevant subnodes is transformed using an XSLT style sheet. The transformation result is passed on to the parent node.

The dynamic navigation is contained entirely within the *DynamicView* class and is based on a statemachine concept, which corresponds on a one-to-one basis to

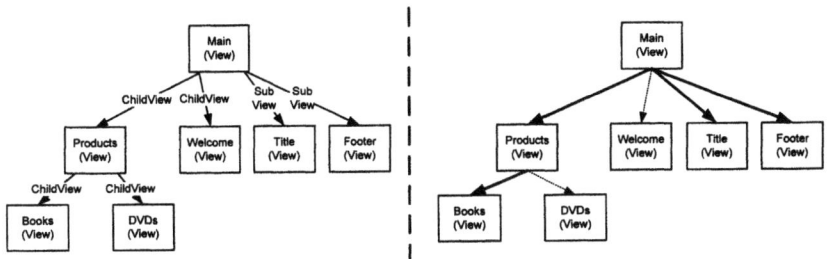

Figure 58 - COBANA Page Assembly Strategy

the code generation rules suggested for OMEGA/Dynamic. In Figure 57, *Form-State* represents a baseclass for all states that allow user input or dynamic navigation. The *IFormHelper* interface contains methods, which correspond to the *ActionFragments* defined in OMEGA/Dynamic. Since the dynamic OMEGA metamodel is explained in detail in section 5.1.2, this aspect is not discussed further.

5.3.5.4 Addressed Problems

The COBANA framework as described above is strongly oriented towards the structure of the OMEGA models. This unique focus results in several technical difficulties that require special attention. In particular, the hierarchical page assembly through multiple XLST transformations, while conceptually simple, causes some complications in the details. Primarily, the performance of the transformations was initially poor and the use of a caching mechanism, in this case the Translet technology (see [10]), was necessary. The use of Translets led to a measured performance improvement of factor 34 in the worst case and factor 170 in the average case for hierarchical transformations (cf. [86]) and thus can be used to solve the performance problem. Another difficulty was caused by special characters, such as umlauts (e.g., "ä"). While so-called entities can be used in both HTML and XML, the multiple transformations led to the entities being replaced with the special characters too early in the transformation chain. A converter class, which replaces a predefined set of special characters with entities using regular expressions, had to be developed to overcome these problems.

5.4 The Digital Library Example

In order to help the reader understand the metamodel concepts described in the previous sections and also to provide a basis for the evaluation of the extension mechanism, a small example is introduced, which uses the domain subset implemented for the prototype. As has been mentioned before, CMS, which are part of the domain of E-Commerce, are used to illustrate the capabilities of the new extension mechanism. Electronic publishing has advanced with great strides, in particular in the context of scholarly journals, which require an extensive pre-publishing process with reviews, editing etc. but have a relatively small readership. Therefore, a digital library was chosen as the particular instance used to test the prototype.

While the main advantage of the electronic publishing of scientific journals seems to be a reduction of cost, for example by eliminating the upkeep required for libraries ([109] and [159]), others feel that the cost reduction will be minimal as most of the cost concentrates on the *first-copy cost*, i.e., the cost before reproduction and distribution ([129], chapter 9).

Rather, according to Kahin and Varian, the advantages can be seen in the potential to introduce **new added value** for the customer and to allow **new product** *strategies* for the publisher. Among the advantages for the customer are the ability to follow hyperlinks between different articles, the ability to add community comments, and finally to automatically determine which papers could be interesting for a particular reader. The publishers, on the other hand, profit mainly from their ability to provide new kinds of products by creating different *bundles* of articles. This is a significant advantage over a print medium, where all readers are offered the same journal. Those not interested in the majority of the articles offered might be unwilling to pay for a package that does not suit their needs and are therefore lost as customers. Another advantage is the increased ability to employ *price discrimination*, for example by charging different amounts of money for an abstract as opposed to a full paper. Generally, a price discrimination strategy allows the publisher to extract more value than a uniform pricing strategy ([129], chapter 9-2). Harnad sees electronic publishing as a way to bypass the overhead of traditional publishers, particularly stressing the potential for improved forms of peer reviews based on public commentary [109].

While this short section cannot do justice to the complex field of digital libraries, it should be enough to illustrate that the example highlights aspects of a real-life problem. Due to space constraints, the discussion concentrates on a submission mechanism for papers to a digital library, including two different kinds of review processes, which are both described next.

5.4.1 Submission Mechanism Variant 1

The models in this section describe a simple submission mechanism embedded into a very rudimentary digital library site, which consists of a start page, legal and contact information, and a page for accessing the scientific papers in the database.

The papers in the database will be shown in a list and can be viewed individually. New papers can be submitted but will not be shown in the list of papers before they have been approved.

Papers can be approved by changing into the "admin mode", which only shows those papers that are yet to be reviewed. A paper can be selected and be accepted or rejected. Accepted papers will be added to the main list, rejected papers will be deleted without further notice to the author.

This example was chosen primarily because it represents a typical example from the domain that uses most of the concepts found in the linguistic metamodels. Furthermore, the example highlights several interesting aspects of the proposed extension mechanism, e.g., it shows that it is possible to use M3 and M2 metaelements in the same model without problems and illustrates the pattern concept introduced by *ImplicitStates*.

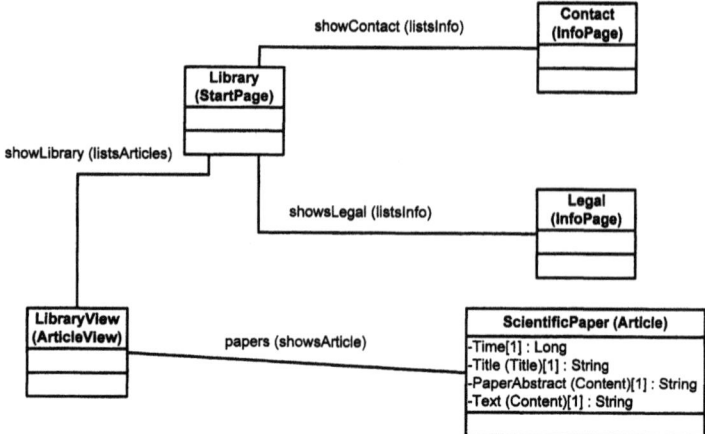

Figure 59 - Static Library Model (Variant 1)

5.4.1.1 Static Model

Figure 59 shows the static structure of the rudimentary library. The model is largely self-explanatory; it describes a simple Web application with some static pages and a single dynamic page, which allows access to the scientific papers stored in the database.

5.4.1.2 Dynamic Model

The dynamic model in Figure 60 defines the behavior of the *LibraryView* as described in the introduction. The *InitialOverview* and *RefereeMode States* both display a list of papers to the user and allow the selection of individual entries, either to view them (see *ViewPaper*) or to review them (see *Review*). Note that *SubmitPaper* uses the M3 *MetaState Creation* to illustrate how *MetaStates* from both layers can be combined.

The two substates of *Review* called *Approved* and *NotApproved* are used to define the exact behavior of the application based on whether a paper was accepted or not. The behavior is defined using the pseudocode shown below.

```
// Pseudocode for Approved
Long currKey = (Long) loadFromSession("CurrentArticleKey");
ScientificPaper curr = papers.findByPrimaryKey(currKey);
curr.setApproved(new Boolean(true));
```

The pseudocode for *NotApproved* is a very naïve way to deal with rejected papers. However, due to the modularity of the M2 *ReviewArticle* state, it is also possible to take more appropriate action, e.g., create an email, which will be sent to the author of the paper etc.

```
// Pseudocode for NotApproved
```

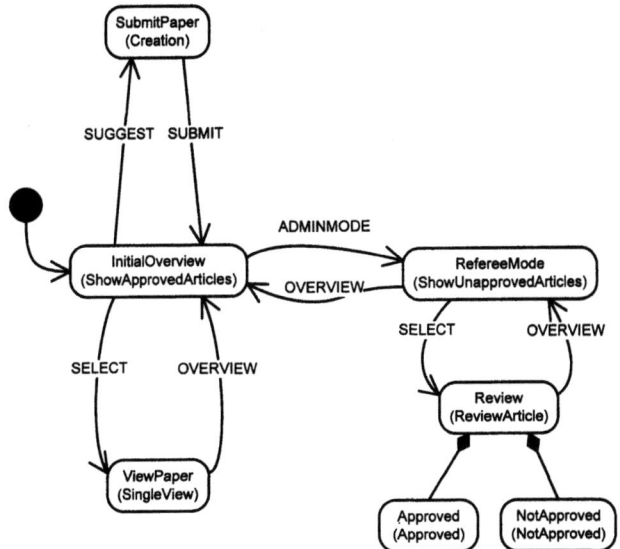

Figure 60 – Dynamic Library Model (Variant 1)

```
Long currKey = (Long) loadFromSession("CurrentArticleKey");
papers.remove(currKey);
```

5.4.2 Submission Mechanism Variant 2

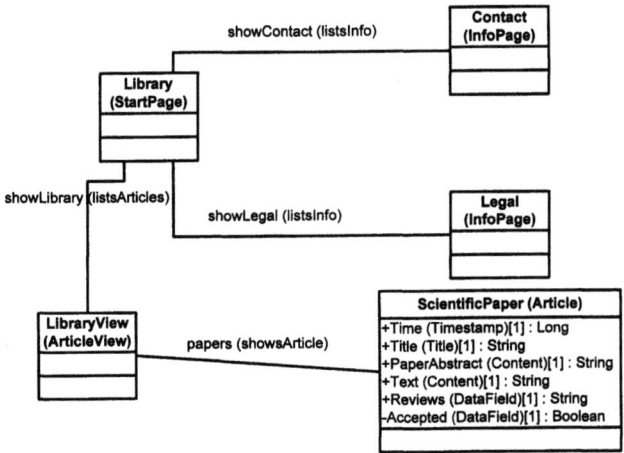

Figure 61 – Static Library Model (Variant 2)

The second example in this section also models a submission mechanism. Its main purpose is to show that the domain-specific metamodels are not too restrictive and still allow a designer to address the specific customization needs in the context of a particular project.

The model shown here addresses the fact that a digital library has a far more stringent acceptance policy and more involved review process than the typical CMS. Thus, acceptance or rejection of a paper is not decided by a single person with the click of a button. Instead two positive reviews are needed for a paper to be accepted.

5.4.2.1 Static Model

The only change in Figure 61 as opposed to the previous example in Figure 59 is the addition of two new attributes in the *ScientificPaper* class. The *Reviews* attribute is a string that contains all reviews associated with the paper. The *Accepted* attribute is a *Boolean* value that is *true*, if one of the reviewers has already submitted a positive review of the paper. It should be noted that these new attributes are kept simple, mostly due to the limitations of the prototype, but nevertheless illustrate the possibility of implementing custom solutions.

5.4.2.2 Dynamic Model

Figure 62 shows the statechart used for the customized submission mechanism. While the behavior differs significantly from the first variant, there is still only one statechart needed. As has been mentioned, the default review mechanism provided by the M2 layer is replaced with a custom implementation. In this case, the paper to be reviewed is selected in a read-mode first before reviewing it. Af-

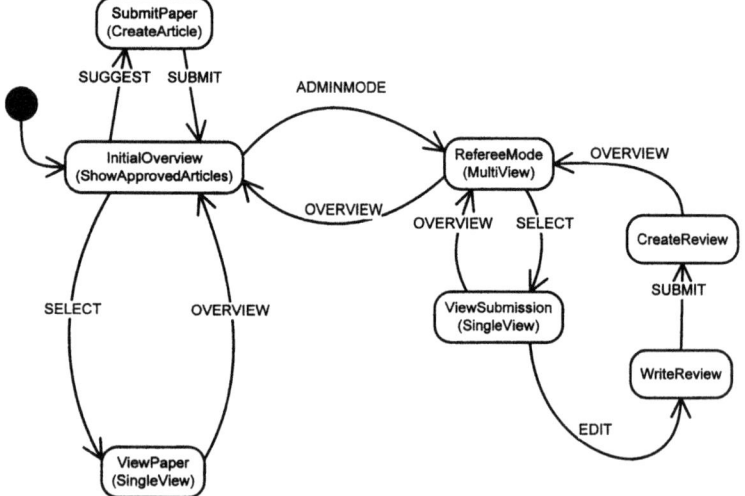

Figure 62 - Dynamic Library Model (Variant 2)

ter writing the review, an intermediate step is taken, which creates the review and accepts the paper, if both the current and one of the previous reviews were positive.

The pseudocode for *WriteReview* represents a customized Web form that allows a reviewer to accept or reject a paper and to write a short review about it.

```
// Pseudocode for WriteReview
Map data = (Map) param;
Long key = new Long((String) data.get("instance"));
String[] answers = {"yes", "no"};
createSelectInput(
    "Do you think this paper should be accepted for the online Library?",
    answers, 0);
createTextAreaInput("Please briefly state the reasons for your decision:",
    "");
createHiddenField("instance", key.toString());
```

The pseudocode for *CreateReview* is slightly more complex. It describes the behavior explained above with most of the code representing the extraction of information from the Web form.

```
// Pseudocode for CreateReview
Map data = (Map) param;
Long key = new Long((String) data.get("instance"));
ScientificPaper paper = papers.findByPrimaryKey(key);
Boolean accept = null;
String acc = (String) data.get("Do you think this paper should be accepted for the online Library?");
if (acc.equals("yes")) accept = new Boolean(true);
else accept = new Boolean(false);
String remarks = (String) data.get("Please briefly state the reasons for your decision:");
if (paper.getAcceptance().booleanValue() && accept.booleanValue())
{
    // this is the second acceptance
    paper.setApproved(new Boolean(true));
}
else
{
    paper.setAcceptance(accept);
}
String allReviews = paper.getReviews();
allReviews = allReviews.concat("\n\n"+remarks);
paper.setReviews(allReviews);
```

While the pseudocode of this example is slightly more complex than the one in the first submission mechanism, it is still quite simple compared to the code required to program the same application from scratch, even when using the same framework. The code generated for the example above is more than 25 pages long, excluding the deployment descriptors[3].

5.5 Summary

In this chapter, the extension mechanism based on the OMEGA and OMEGA/Dynamic metamodel hierarchies has been introduced. While technical details are omitted, its core features were shown, in particular, the ability to add hierarchical metainformation to all elements in a model.

To illustrate the functionality of the extension mechanism, both dynamic and static metamodels from the Web application domain were designed and extended for the CMS subdomain. For the prototype, also examined in this chapter, a Web domain code generator module was implemented and extension templates for the CMS subdomain were developed. The prototype was used to create two model fragments describing variants of a paper submission mechanism for a scientific online journal. The two fragments will be used as core examples for the evaluation process in the next chapter.

---

[3] See http://www.wifo.uni-mannheim.de/~gitzel/research/OMEGA/SecondExample.pdf

6 Conclusions and Future Work

Having presented the concepts of the hierarchical extension mechanism for UML and the prototypical code generation environment used for its evaluation, there are only a few issues left to address. First, the example fragments described in the previous chapter will be used for a critical evaluation of the extension mechanism. Using a list of criteria, it will be shown that the extension mechanism enables a reduction of the overall software development cost in a domain by pointing out particular aspects of the example implementation. It will be examined whether the prototype contains all the crucial elements of a full implementation, in order to show the general applicability of the cost reduction potentials identified.

In section 6.2, the OMEGA approach as a whole is critically assessed, addressing aspects, which have provoked differing views during discussion at conferences or seminars. After that, related and future work will be discussed before providing a brief conclusion.

6.1 Theoretical and Practical Evaluation

In order to judge the quality of the proposed extension mechanism, its prototype has to be tested to determine whether the goal defined for the extension mechanism is reached. As has been mentioned in the introduction, this goal is the *reduction of the total cost of all projects* conducted in a specific domain as opposed to the same software implemented based on a custom-developed domain tool.

Going back to Figure 1, it can be seen that the total cost consists of two factors, i.e., the fixed cost involved in the creation of and training with the tool environment and the cost per project. While the Figure is a simplification, in particular with regard to the linear cost development per project, the model is a suitable basis for an evaluation of the prototype, since the variable costs are not relevant for the comparison (see section 6.1.3).

The remainder of this section is structured as follows. First, the approach used for the evaluation of the prototype is described and care is taken to explain why its results are considered representative of the general case. Next, it is shown why the example described in sections 5.2 through 5.4 can be used as a basis for the chosen approach. In section 6.1.3, the concrete realization of the chosen evaluation technique is described. Based on these foundations, the results are presented and explained afterwards.

6.1.1 Evaluation Approach

There are several types of software engineering research validation, ranging from "blatant assertion" to formal analysis (cf. Shaw [193], in particular Table 5). However, since no statistically significant body of data provided by experiments using the prototype exists yet or can be produced in the context of this work, most of these methods are not applicable. For these reasons, the "'slice of life' example based on a real system" approach is adopted here ([193], pg. 732).

Shaw states that an example can be used to validate research, if it represents a realistic instance of the problem, which contains all relevant aspects [193]. It can be argued that this reasoning implies that the scalability of the example to real-life problems has to be considered as well even though it is not mentioned explicitly.

For the concrete reasoning about the example, several ideas proposed by Schweiggert are adopted. Schweiggert suggests the identification of a *list of criteria*, starting with the defined goal and iteratively partitioning the criteria further until they can be used to establish a collection of *precise questions*, whose answer does not depend primarily on personal opinion. The answers to the questions provide a good basis for the validation of the example [186].

In order to be able to apply the advice given by Shaw and Schweiggert, the evaluation approach will be divided into two steps. First, it is shown that the example is both scalable and representative of the general case. In the second step, a list of criteria is developed and applied to the example.

6.1.2 Scalability and General Applicability of the Example

If the example is to be considered adequate for the purposes of the evaluation, it has to be scalable and generally applicable. In this context, both the prototype and the example models have to meet these requirements because it is the combination of the two that influences the results of the evaluation.

The *prototype*, while being limited to a subset of the required functionality, only leaves out features, which have been shown to work by other researchers. For example, automatic constraint checking is trivial but time-consuming to implement. Similarly, the missing code generation features such as multi-valued attributes are part of other code generators, e.g., those based on Executable UML or the work of Harel and Gery [106]. Therefore, the prototype can be considered *scalable* and *generally applicable* based on other, real-world examples. In particular, it can be used for the creation of professional and fully functional software.

Same arguments apply to the *submission mechanism example*. The example can be considered a good representation of the general case, because it contains both dynamic and static aspects, which will be encountered in real life and uses all of the aspects newly introduced due to the extension mechanism. For these reasons, other examples will be, in principle, variations using the same elements as the paper submission example. In the light of these arguments, the example can be considered *generally applicable* for the purpose of the evaluation.

The *scalability* of the example can be assumed, if it can be interpreted as a subsystem of a more complex project. Since a subsystem consisting of a class diagram and statecharts can be linked with other subsystems using the techniques presented in the Executable UML context, larger applications can be generated from models that use the extension mechanism. The integration of legacy software can be added by using well-known interfaces to other domains as domain elements (cf. Macala et al. [138]).

To sum up the arguments given above, the example used for the evaluation is both scalable and generally applicable, because the mechanisms created in the context of other works are also applicable to the example. Hence, even though these qualities cannot be formally shown, there are strong indicators that both required conditions are met.

6.1.3 Quality Criteria for the Extension Mechanism

As has been described in section 6.1.1, a list of criteria has to be determined, which can serve as a basis for a list of critical questions that can be used to reason the degree to which the goal described by the criteria is achieved. In the case of the extension mechanism, the overall goal is to reduce the total cost of software development not per project but per domain or software product line.

In order to determine a cost reduction potential, the state of the art and the newly proposed mechanism have to be compared. In the comparison (as shown in Figure 63), a hypothetical custom tool and a tool using the OMEGA-based extension mechanism, i.e., the prototype described in this chapter, are used as specimens. The *custom tool* is an MDD development tool created without the use of an extension mechanism, possibly implemented from scratch. The *prototype*, on the other hand, is a configurable environment supporting modeling for a specific domain (in the example Web application design). The configuration for a specific sub-domain is performed by loading the relevant metamodel via the extension mechanism and deploying the corresponding templates in the code generator.

Figure 64 shows a partitioning of the total product line cost into its two top level criteria, i.e., the fixed costs and the costs per project. The *costs per project* are not further analyzed based on the assumption that they are at least equal regard-

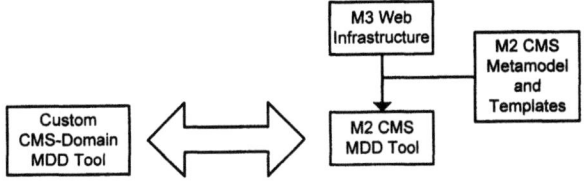

Figure 63 - Comparison Between a Custom and an Extended Tool

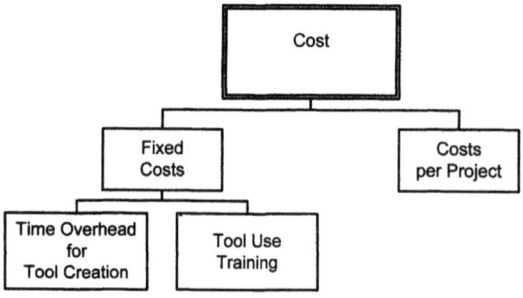

Figure 64 - Cost Factors

less of whether a custom tool or the prototype is used. The applicability of this assumption is discussed in section 6.1.3.1.

Assuming that the extension mechanism will be used primarily for software development projects where human resources are the driving cost factor (cf. [23], pg. 74), the *fixed costs* depend on two major aspects. The first is the time needed for the creation of either the custom tool or the M2 metamodel and templates for the prototype. The second is the time needed to train the development teams how to use the newly created or customized domain-specific tool.

6.1.3.1 Assessing the Variable Costs

In order to be able to ignore them, the variable costs have to be identified as invariant with regard to the environment used. In the simplest model, the costs per project are influenced by the lines of code and the productivity of the developers (cf. [23], pp. 74-75). As the final product is in both cases the same, the lines of code are identical. If it can be argued that the productivity also remains unchanged, the variable costs can be ignored.

This means that a tool using the extension mechanism such as the prototype has to be functionally similar to a tool that has been custom-designed for the same M2 domain. The question to ask in this context is, whether the two tools will appear different to the user or not and, if there are any differences, whether they will significantly affect the users ability to create models.

It is very likely that a hypothetical custom tool is not fundamentally different to use than the prototype for two reasons. With regard to the graphical user interface, the OMEGAPlugin does not greatly deviate from other modeling tools (see Figure 51). Also, as has been shown, it is possible to map the metaelements of the extension mechanism to a UML Profile (see section 5.1.3) and to use the Profile in a standard UML modeling tool. Therefore, there is no fundamental difference between the two cases and no change in variable costs.

6.1.3.2 Assessing the Fixed Costs Due to Time Overhead

The general strategy for assessing the fixed costs has already been described. The main intention of the extension mechanism is to greatly reduce the *time overhead* for the creation of a new domain-specific tool. The questions in this context, shown below, examine the degree of reuse made possible due to the extension mechanism.

- Is the creation of the M2 metamodel simplified due to the existence of the M3 model?
- Is the creation of the M2 templates simplified due to the existence of the M3 templates?
- Is the structured reuse made possible by the extension mechanism preferable to the ad hoc reuse of templates?

The first two questions were chosen, because they address the two core aspects of the creation of a new MDD tool, assuming that a suitable editor already exists. If it is possible to reuse either model elements or templates of the M3 level, the time overhead for tool creation will be reduced. Yet, if the creation of either is complicated by the requirements of the M3 infrastructure, the overhead will be increased. The last question addresses the fact that there are other forms of reuse as well, i.e., a custom tool can be based on existing templates belonging to related domains, which are manually adapted for the new purpose.

Regarding the first question, it can be argued that the creation of the M2 *metamodel* is simplified by the existence of the M3 metamodel. First of all, the existing elements provide *guidance* for the developer. Since the M3 metamodel can be interpreted as a more abstract view on its M2 metamodels, the basic structure of M2 is already mapped out and it is less likely that elements are forgotten or will be defined poorly. For example, the OMEGA M3 Web application model already contains and enforces for its instances the basic concepts found in both the Web design languages and the COBANA framework with the concepts of dynamic and static views and navigational contexts realized via *Child* associations.

Besides the guidance provided by the M3 metamodel, in many cases *model elements can be reused directly*, especially in the case of the dynamic metamodel. The M3 *ActionFragments* represent common technology-oriented activity of the M3 domain and are therefore essential elements of any domain using the M3 technology. In the example hierarchy, most of the *ActionFragments* are defined at the M3 level. Their essential contribution to the M2 domain can be seen when looking at the pseudocode of the example models, which makes heavy use of the *ActionFragments* provided.

Model element reuse is less common in the static metamodel. While all elements of the M3 layer are available as metaclasses in the model due to relaxed strictness, it is generally advisable to provide specialized M2 metaelements. For example, the *Article* metaclass, while not inherently different to the pure *DataSet*, carries a lot of semantics, which can be used in the business logic found in the dynamic M2 models. For instance, the *CreateArticle MetaState* relies on the ability to interpret the attributes of the persistent data. In particular, the *Timestamp* attribute differs from the other attributes, because it is not initialized through user input but automatically assigned the current system time. The *Creation MetaState* of M3 on the other hand is unable to interpret attributes. Thus, an M2 static metamodel cannot generally reuse many M3 model elements. However, a special situation occurs when a modeled system deviates in some aspects from the intended M2 domain. In that case, the M3 model elements are useful because of their higher level of abstraction.

Similarly, the creation of M2 *templates* is simplified by existence of the M3 metamodel and templates. First of all, a high degree of *template reuse* is possible. In the case of *static models*, there is a very high potential for reuse. In the example, no static M2 templates were needed at all, the M3 templates and the ability to weave new attributes into the model being sufficient to generate all static code. While there might be specific cases, which do require specialized M2 level templates, it can be assumed that static reuse is generally going to be high.

In the case of *dynamic models*, the saving was more restricted. While some generic M3 *MetaStates* exist, most behavior is "business logic" and therefore has to be defined at the M2 level. Also, the definition of M2-level implicit *MetaStates* is not simplified by the existence of the M3 *MetaStates*. For example, *CreateArticle* requires a template that does not profit from the existence of similar M3 *MetaStates* such as *Creation*, even though conceptually, they seem related. However, the new *MetaStates* benefit from the *ActionFragments* defined at M3 level, because they are realized as methods and can be called by the templates implementing the M2 *States*. It is hard to give a good estimate of the savings implied by this kind of reuse. However, since the *ActionFragments* in the example represent basic Web page related activity such as the creation of HTML forms, it is likely that most new *MetaStates* can reuse code created for the M3 level.

The M2 *ActionFragments*, on the other hand, profit little from the M3 templates in the example. Still, the M2 *ActionsFragments* were relatively small and more evolved domains are likely to include larger fragments, which might use M3-level template code. It is difficult to exactly assess this potential at this stage but since *ActionFragments* are conceptually similar to *MetaStates* (e.g., consider *showSingleInstance* and *SingleView*) it is likely that a comparable leverage effect will occur.

However, artifacts available for reuse as described above only lead to a simplification, if they are easily incorporated. For example, if reusable code can only be located after a long search, its potential is greatly diminished. In the case of the example hierarchy's templates, most reuse involves the use of complete templates, which are well-defined due to the M3 metamodel. In the more complex cases, the interaction between the layers is largely limited to method calls corresponding to *ActionFragments*. The only information that the M2 template programmer needs that is not described in the M3 metamodel is the name of the baseclass, which implements the M3 *ActionFragments*.

One problem involved in the creation of the M2 templates is that the designers have to know how to implement code for the M3 domain and the details of the technology used for the M3 templates. In the original concept of the code generator, it was intended to transform largely technology-independent M2 template code to accommodate the technology used at the M3 level using aspect-oriented programming techniques and weave the resulting fragments into the M3 templates. Since the plan had to be abandoned due to problems with the existing code weaving tools, the deficit as described arises and any attempts to reduce *feature delocalization* (see section 3.1.2) have to be considered future work.

The *third question* related to the time overhead is whether it is really necessary to use a formalized reuse mechanism instead of simply adapting artifacts produced in the context of other software product lines. Since this is essentially the same question as whether code reuse in general should be formalized or is possible ad hoc and strong arguments against the latter can be found in the literature (e.g., see Greenfield et al. [103]), the question will be addressed only briefly.

In the example, the structured way of reuse provided by the extension mechanism is preferable to manually adjusting generic templates, which correspond to the generic M3 Web application templates, to fit the M2 CMS domain. The primary advantage in this context is the maintenance of the templates. Since the M2 templates are largely independent of the M3 templates, interacting only through well-known "interfaces", the M3 template logic need only be maintained at a single point instead of for each project. Also, due to the fact that the code generation logic for all transitive instances of an M3 element is concentrated in a single template, inconsistencies can be avoided.

Overall, the extension mechanism seems to hold a great potential for the reduction of the overhead involved in the creation of a new domain-specific modeling tool. It allows a substantial reuse of both templates and model elements, and while at the current stage the technology of the M3 templates has to be understood by the designers working at the M2 level, it is at least theoretically possible to eliminate this problem.

6.1.3.3 Assessing the Fixed Costs due to Initial Training

After the creation of a new domain-specific tool, it is necessary to train the development team in the use of the metamodel and the semantics provided by the templates. The initial training is required for both the custom tool and the prototype, which can be compared using the following questions.

- Is a generic tool more difficult to use than a custom tool?
- Is the training time reduced by the existence of a generic M3 infrastructure?

Both questions seem to overlap slightly but cover different aspects newly introduced by the prototype. Since a generic tool has to cover more than a particular domain, it is possible that this additional requirement makes the tool more difficult to understand. The second question refers to the fact that the generic tool provides a largely uniform interface to the user regardless of domain, which might influence the training time.

The first questions can be answered briefly. As has been explained in section 6.1.3.1, the prototype's user interface is not fundamentally different from that of a custom tool. Therefore, the learning effort for both should be the same.

For similar reasons, the training time reduction due to the generic infrastructure is minimal or non-existent. Both the custom tools for different domains and the prototype configured for the same domains change by the same degree. The only potential advantage is that all sub-domains of the Web domain will be based on consistent Web principles due to the M3 metamodel, whereas different custom tools might behave inconsistently. As has already been mentioned, the static M3 metaclasses correspond to the concepts found in Web design languages and, therefore, all M2 metamodels will be consistent with these concepts.

Overall, it can be said that the training cost is not adversely affected by the introduction of the extension mechanism. On the other hand, it is questionable whether the training time can be improved significantly.

6.1.4 Explanations and Conclusions

In this section, the linguistic metamodels required for the proposed extension mechanism have been validated using an example consisting of a prototypical plugin and an example hierarchy. By analyzing three different criteria, variable cost, creation overhead cost, and training cost, it was shown that the extension mechanism offers a substantial improvement regarding the creation overhead while maintaining the status quo in the other two cases. The findings were supported by examples taken from the prototype and the sample hierarchy.

While the benefit due to the reduced overhead cost is substantial, I feel that this is still a very conservative assumption, adopted because of the lack of empirical data. It is my opinion that there are other areas where the extension mechanism incurs large savings. For example, if it were possible to write technology-independent M2 templates and pseudocode, both the creation of the M2 templates and the training time would be reduced.

Also, according to case studies conducted in the past, the quality of the domain-specific tool improves over the time, i.e., with each iteration (cf. Macala et al. [138]). Since all domains reuse M3 templates, the quality of all M2 domains will be improved, reducing the need for maintenance and therefore costs at later stages of the software's lifecycle.

6.2 General Assessment of the OMEGA Approach

While the evaluation in the previous section has shown that the proposed extension mechanism facilitates the creation of new domain-specific MDD modules, there are other aspects, which should at least be briefly addressed. Since in the previous chapters, the different concepts and technologies used for the scientific contributions of this dissertation have already been discussed and the diverse opinions on each subject have been presented, they are not revisited here. Instead, this section concentrates on those arguments brought forth especially against the OMEGA approach.

6.2.1 Complexity of the Approach

At this point, it should be clear that metamodeling is far from trivial. At a superficial glance, the concern might arise that the OMEGA approach could be too complex to offer an alternative to manual software development. This feeling is similar to that professed by many critics of MDD approaches, as the following quotation illustrates:

"Any technology that deals in meta-meta-models is going to be hard to sell, no matter how many analyst's reports have been written." [110]

I feel this statement is misguiding, because it is not important how complex a system is "under the hood". To stay within the analogy, the AFS (Active Front Steering) technology makes driving a car easier and safer, without the user being required to understand the technical details, which are far from simple (cf. [69]). What counts in the end is how complex and reliable the system is to the user. The hierarchical approach described here does not result in complex modeling tasks. As can be seen in the prototype, the part visible to the user is identical to the stereotype concept of UML. While there are some extra rules, other UML Profiles, such as EDOC, imply similar constraints and thus are as complex as the approach described here (see section 3.5.3.2 for details). Also, section 6.1 suggests that the improved organization and more extensive reuse of code-generation infrastructure made possible by a hierarchical approach will improve reliability in the long run rather then make matters more complex.

6.2.2 The General Layout of the Model Hierarchy

The layout of the model hierarchy presented in section 5.2, when seen as the equivalent of the OMG's refinement process from CIMs to PSMs, features a notable deviation by placing the technology layer at the top. It might be argued that this arrangement is problematic because of the life expectancy of technology as opposed to that of business logic. In other words, if the technology of the uppermost layer becomes obsolete, so will all of its instances. Therefore, the layer arrangement will reduce the potential of reuse.

However, the comparison to the MDA model transformation stages is problematic. In particular, the PSMs of the OMG are not instances of the PIMs. Rather, a model transformation is needed to get from the PIM to the PSM. Also, the PIM is the main point of input from the designer, whereas the M3 layer is not edited by an end user. Thus, a PIM and a M3 metamodel are unrelated concepts.

The argument that the M3 layer relies on a specific technology is only partially true and not as critical as it might seem. The technological concepts found on the M3 layer of the OMEGA and OMEGA/Dynamic hierarchies are very abstract. They are not tied to a certain technology but rather to a paradigm such as that of the Web, putting them somewhere between MDA's PIMs and PSMs with regard to level of abstraction (cf. the detailed example given in [134]). On this level of abstraction, there is still a choice whether to generate code for Servlet-based applications or PHP scripts, as well as a choice whether to use HTML, WAP, or some future format yet to be defined. Should the basic paradigm become obsolete, it is still possible to switch to another metamodel by using transformation rules, which shift instances from the current metamodel to the new one. Granted, this task is not trivial but with the advent of transformation languages, it will be feasible with reasonable effort. Indeed, the OMG's MDA reference document explicitly mentions PIM to PIM and PSM to PSM transformations (see [142], pg. 13).

However, it is also debatable whether the life expectancy of a technology, especially a technological paradigm, really is a critical factor. Not everybody agrees on the concept that technology is in constant flux (see section 3.3.2.1). The target groups for OMEGA are Small and Medium-sized Enterprises (SME), which act as "software factories", producing and maintaining many variations of their basic product. In such a setting, a technology layer at the bottom would be a terrible mistake. It has been argued that a change at a higher model layer requires changes at all lower layers. Thus, with the domain layer above the technology layer, each problem domain would need its own technology templates, even if all projects were intended for the same technological target platform. This situation is the exact opposite of the intentions associated with the hierarchical extension mechanism.

6.2.3 Conceptual Issues

One aspect of the OMEGA ontological metamodel that has caused other researchers in the same field to pronounce their disagreement is the definition of instantiation as transitive. In particular, the concern was raised that this would make instantiation indistinguishable from inheritance. Similarly, any of the other deviations from the established metamodeling rules could lead to comparable discussions.

It is true that some of the definitions and concepts have been changed and that a metamodeling purist can locate aspects where the definitions used in this dissertation run counter to some previously established ones. However, the linguistic metamodels described are an extension of existing concepts and the deviations are not methodological mistakes but intentional modifications, identified as such.

The concern of a lack of distinction between inheritance and transitive instantiation to me seems to be unwarranted, especially in the light of the delimitation provided in section 3.5. Maybe the problem is that to its opponents, transitive instantiation is closer to inheritance than to their (non-transitive) concept of instantiation. However, as the proverb goes: "What's in a name?" As the evaluation of the prototype has shown, the extension mechanism does provide an improvement over the existing extension mechanisms because it allows the reuse of more abstract domains. This improvement is independent of the names used to describe the concepts. Therefore, any discussion in this context is purely academic.

6.3 Open Questions and Future Work

As shown in the previous section, the open details found in the extension mechanism have already been discussed elsewhere (e.g., in section 5.1.1.6) and the discussion of future work at this point will be limited to the conceptual level. While a lot of work has been put into both the theoretical foundation and the actual prototype, there were still areas too specific to individual aspects of the problem or too labor-intensive to be fully addressed.

The *example hierarchy* provided for the evaluation of the extension mechanism is one of the aspects that could profit from future work. Domain specific languages of any kind are difficult to come up with and have to be improved iteratively (cf. Völter [210] and Macala et al. [138]). Since the Web application hierarchy used was only for illustrative purposes and has not seen a lot of use, it should be clear that it might need further refinement and expansions.

This problem is a result of the fact that the whole approach could not be tested extensively in the context of this work, in particular in the context of an *empirical evaluation* based on real-life Web projects. It would be interesting to see which of the inherent benefits of the approach would be perceived as most useful by practitioners and what further development paths would be discovered.

However, before such an evaluation could be conducted, many of the tool's modules would have to be improved. In particular, the *code generation mechanisms* were mostly neglected, since the goal of this dissertation was not to improve code generation algorithms but to improve the input given to them. Aspect-oriented code weavers such as InjectJ [70] developed at the Forschungszentrum Informatik (FZI) in Karlsruhe would complement the concepts found in the metamodel hierarchy nicely. At the current stage, InjectJ in particular still lacks a few key capabilities, such as metadata input, making integration into the OMEGA plugin an interesting target of future work.

Finally, not all aspects of the metamodel hierarchies have a *formal definition*. OMEGA/Dynamic has not been formally documented in the same detail as the original OMEGA metamodel. The main reason is that OMEGA/Dynamic is a metamodel, which departs from the other hierarchies typically found in the literature, and it is therefore necessary to define all constraints from scratch. For the same reason, the model was prone to changes and testing its capabilities was deemed more important than formally defining its technical details.

Overall, the ideas presented in this dissertation are limited to a very specific aspect of MDD and it is surprising how many different ideas, standards, and even fields of research had to be considered to propose an improved variant. In some ways, the work completed felt like fundamental research in so far as many infrastructural tools were developed. Hopefully, at least some of the software components created for the prototype will enable others to build upon the ideas presented here.

6.4 Related Work

Since the ideas proposed in this dissertation come from a very active field of research, which rejuvenates many ideas of its predecessors and overlaps with other fields, it is a difficult decision which publications to consider as related. Also, many of the individual chapters already present related work, e.g., chapter 4 discusses other MDD efforts in the domain of Web applications.

The primary goal of this dissertation was identified as the proposal of a new extension mechanism for UML. Therefore, it might be prudent to limit related work to UML extension mechanisms only. However, these approaches have been discussed in detail in section 3.5. More importantly, there are other projects, which have the same purpose as the extension mechanism described in this dissertation, which should also be considered in this context.

Therefore, the discussion of related work focuses on any kind of tool or software development process, which aims at providing an infrastructure to rapidly establish domain-specific code generation environments. As has been mentioned, a lot of the other work referenced throughout the chapters could be considered related work but is not repeated here for space reasons.

6.4.1 UML as a Family of Languages

The catchphrase "UML as a family of languages", which applies to the works of Duddy [62], Atkinson and Kühne [18], Völter [209], Nordstrom ([155], [156]), Frankel [73], Kent [132], Clark et al. [49] and many others, has already been discussed before. Without going into the details, it can be said that these approaches see UML as a generic extensible language suitable for a wide range of domains. Based on UML's metametamodel, it is possible to use the same infrastructure to design models for domains, which have vastly different or even contradictory semantics (cf. Cook [51]), without having to resort to lightweight extension mechanisms such as UML Profiles. A custom metamodel can be used with all the benefits a specialized modeling language offers within a known tool framework. Duddy [62] proposes a vision for MDA where models based on custom metamodels can be designed, then transformed to a PSM common to all metamodels to use for code generation.

Some of the "family of languages" approaches are very similar to the ideas proposed in this work, in particular those using a nonlinear hierarchy. However, the OMEGA-based extension mechanism expands those concepts, introducing a static and a dynamic hierarchy for metamodel elements. The related work here often stays closer to the original UML concepts even in aspects that will be transparent for the end user and therefore not require such a conservative approach.

6.4.2 Software Product Lines

The concept of *domain-specific, product-line software development* can be considered to be a precursor of some of the ideas presented here. Its core idea is that domain-specific infrastructures are created in a separate development process to be used as an infrastructure for software development within a specific domain (cf. [138]). However, this approach lacks a focus on modern standards, thus providing no base-line infrastructure for the creation of new domain tools. In fact, in the case study by Macala et al. [138], the analysis which tools will be required is considered to be a vital step. In the OMEGA-based prototype, the infrastructure is fixed and only the domain-specific information has to be developed.

6.4.3 MetaCASE Tools

The idea of providing an infrastructure for a code generation environment is also not new; an early example is the metaCASE concept. In his review of metaCASE tools, Isazadeh identifies the labor-intensity involved in the creation of CASE tools as a major problem, warranting the use of tools, which allow the automatic generation of CASE tools as a solution. While metaCASE tools seem to offer many advantages over traditional CASE tools, they lack good metamodel languages for the creation of modeling languages to be used in the CASE tools [123].

There are two major differences between the metaCASE concept and the OMEGA prototype. First, the metaCASE tools do not produce domain-specific tools but rather tools that are centered on a specific software development methodology or process. In contrast, OMEGA's prototype is not tied to a specific software process. Instead, its extension mechanism focuses on the hierarchical creation of domain-specific languages. Second, the core problem of metaCASE tools, the poor quality of the metamodeling language, is avoided by using a variant to the well-established MOF standard as metamodel.

6.4.4 Software Factories

Among all the related work, *Software Factories* come closest to the OMEGA approach described in this dissertation. Greenfield et al. describe this vision of the future of software development in their book of the same title [103].

Briefly speaking, Software Factories are a specialized form of software product lines. Greenfield et al. aim at defining an infrastructure of concepts that allows the fast and professional development of a software factory schema, a general analysis of a problem domain (e.g., financial services or health care). The schema consists of several viewpoints and their relationships to each other. Each viewpoint is associated with certain artifacts such as models or code and the relationships show the required synchronization in the case of changes. Based on the schema, a set of tools, domain-specific modeling languages, frameworks, patterns, and processes can be developed, which can then be integrated into a generic IDE to allow the development of a very specific type of product. A product is finished as soon as all the artifacts defined in the schema are implemented or generated.

The goal of the software factory concept is to maximize the amount of reuse by creating a synthesis of existing concepts such as development by assembly, model-driven development, or process frameworks. Its progenitors hope that this approach will lead to component standards, which in turn lead to the emergence of software supply chains and ultimately a mass customization of software.

While the approach shares many similarities with OMEGA, especially the concept of using suitable domain-specific frameworks as a basis for code generation, its scope is far wider and its solutions differ in important details. For example, Software Factories' MDD concepts are elaborationist, requiring a (possibly manual) synchronization of different artifacts such as models and code. This situation cannot occur in OMEGA, due to its translationist nature. Also, most of the effort put into OMEGA focuses on the improvement of UML's extension mechanism, rather than sharing the wider scope of the software factory approach.

6.5 *Conclusion*

As stated in chapter 1, the main objective of this dissertation is to provide a *hierarchical extension mechanism for UML*, which allows for a more efficient development of code generation modules for a specific domain. The mechanism was evaluated using a *prototypical code generation environment* using a problem domain suitable for MDD, in this case, Web applications.

Secondary scientific contributions were the creation of a design space covering the options of metamodeling hierarchy creation, a critical analysis of the goals as well as the state of the art of MDD, and the analysis of the Web application domain to determine its suitability for MDD.

By analyzing several different criteria, it was shown that the extension mechanism offers a substantial improvement regarding the creation overhead of domain-specific tools while at least maintaining the status quo in the other two cases. The findings were supported by examples taken from the prototype and the sample hierarchy.

The evaluation results show that the proposed extension mechanism is an interesting avenue for the improvement of contemporary software development. Since it nicely integrates with existing MDD-related standards, it is not a purely academic exercise but has practical relevance, offering a systematic solution that might help domestic SME software developers to stay competitive against offshore competition.

Appendix A: OMEGA Constraints

This appendix formally describes the model elements and constraints in the OMEGA linguistic metamodel. The elements are grouped by type and the constraints are listed at the end.

Changed Classes

In this section, the changes made to the existing classes of the original MOF metamodel are described. For reasons of brevity, I only describe the actual changes and not the whole classes.

Classifier

Super Classes
- Instance
- GeneralizableElement

Constraints
$\Omega-1$

Class

Constraints
$\Omega-2, \Omega-3, \Omega-4, \Omega-5$

Attribute

Super Classes
- Instance
- StructuralFeature
- MetaElement

Constraints
$\Omega-6, \Omega-7$

Association

Constraints
$\Omega-8, \Omega-9, \Omega-10, \Omega-11$

Package

While Package has not been changed in any way, it is included here, because OMEGA looks for a tag named ValidationTag in the outermost Package. If such a tag does not exist, the software will check whether the model complies to the constraints defined for the ontological hierarchy and include the tag with a value of true if the model is valid and false otherwise. If the tag exists, a check will only be performed if its value is false and it will be updated accordingly.

New Classes

These classes are new additions to the MOF metamodel, which allow the modeling of metamodel hierarchies. Their position in the class hierarchy can be seen in Figure 26.

ModelLayer

A model layer contains all elements of a single ontological level. Its use is not enforced by any kind of constraints. However, it can vastly help the understanding of a hierarchy and also can be used to provide "frozen" metalayers for a model.

Super Classes
- Package
- Instance
- MetaElement

Contained Elements
MetaClass, Class, Association, MetaAssociation, MetaAttribute, Exception, Constant, Constraint, Tag, DataType

Attributes
None.

References
None.

Operations
None.

Constraints
Ω–12, Ω–13, Ω–14, Ω–15, Ω–16, Ω–17, Ω–18, Ω–19

MetaElement

This class has been introduced to allow for a single InstanceOf relationship as opposed to several different ones. Due to this fact, MetaElement does not really have any properties at all save for the fact that it can be used as a target for the InstanceOf relationship. In this respect it is not so much unlike the GeneralizableElement for inheritance.
`isAbstract = true`

Super Classes
None

Contained Elements
None

Attributes
- canSpawnMeta:boolean. If true, instances of this MetaElement can be MetaElements as well.

References
None

Operations
None

Constraints
None

MetaClass
This model element is used to describe ontological metaclasses.

Super Classes
- MetaElement
- Class. This might seem ironic, but a MetaClass is really a class that has the additional property of being a MetaElement.

Contained Elements
None.

Attributes
None.

References
None.

Operations
None.

Constraints
None.

MetaAttribute
This class constrains the possible Attributes contained by a Class. All MetaAttributes that have an Association with a MetaClass are used as a basis for the attributes of its instances (see Class for details). Figure 31 shows how MetaAttributes influence the attributes of a class.

Super Classes
- MetaElement
- Classifier MetaAttributes differ from Attributes in several ways, one of which is the fact that they are not contained by the element they belong to but have an aggregation-type Association with it. This difference results in a greater expressiveness of MetaAttributes, e.g., by setting the right multiplicity, a MetaAttribute can be the type for several similar Attributes. Thus, unlike Attributes, MetaAttributes must be able to participate in Associations, which requires Classifier as a superclass. While the concept of inheritance (which is implicitly possible for all subclasses of Classifier) is of limited usefulness for MetaAttributes, there are special cases where it could be utilized and thus the transitively inherited GeneralizableElement-Properties are not of "undefined" behavior.

Contained Elements
None.

Attributes

- AllowedVisibilities: VisibilityKind [0..n]. The visibility kinds that are allowed for Attribute instances. An empty list means free choice.
- AllowedMultiplicities: MultiplicityKind [0..n]. The multiplicity kinds that are allowed for Attribute instances. Again, an empty list means free choice.
- AllowedScopes: ScopeKind [1..2]. The scope kinds that are allowed for Attribute instances.

References

- AllowedTypes: Classifier [0..n]. The Types, which are allowed for Attributes. If this reference is not set, the type is not restricted.

Operations
None.

Constraints
Ω–20, Ω–21, Ω–32

MetaAssociation
This linguistic class is used to describe ontological MetaAssociations.

Super Classes

- MetaElement
- Association. Again, this might seem ironic, but a MetaAssociation is really an Association that has additional properties (such as being the target for the InstanceOf Association and describing some kind of "meta constraints", which limit the multiplicities and aggregation types of its ontological instances). While such metaconstraints are not necessarily required for a metamodel hierarchy, it seems reasonable to offer this option, especially in the context of the requirements of our other projects involving metamodeling.

Contained Elements

- MetaAssociationEnd

Attributes
None.

References
None.

Operations
None.

Constraints
Ω–22, Ω–23

MetaAssociationEnd

This class describes allowed values for ontological instances of a MetaAssociation. This is done via collections, which contain all the allowed values for each of the AssociationEnd attributes. The required constraints can be found in the MetaAssociation class.

Super Classes
- ModelElement

Contained Elements
None.

Attributes
- isNavigable:boolean [0..2]
- aggregation:AggregationKind [0..n]
- multiplicity:MultiplicityType [0..n]
- isChangeable:boolean [0..2]

References
- associationEnd : AssociationEnd [1] - this reference is used in conjunction with the EndpointAugmentationOf association.

Operations
None.

Constraints
Ω–24

Instance

This abstract class allows other classes to inherit a reference useable with the InstanceOf relationship. While we originally put this functionality into Classifier, we had to extract it to an extra class with the introduction of the class MetaAttribute, which is separate from the existing inheritance structure.
`isAbstract = true`

Super Classes
None

Contained Elements
None

Attributes
None

References
- isInstanceOf : MetaElement [0..1]

Operations
None

Constraints
Ω–25, Ω–26, Ω–27

Slot

A Slot is the instance of an Attribute. Obviously, most Slots will occur on the user data level, which is normally not modeled. However, in some situations, it might be prudent to have attributes at a higher level (Mn, n > 1), which will result in slots (containing an attribute value) at the next level (Mn-1). In effect, a Slot represents some sort of constant within the context of the class. Note that attribute slots at a level higher than M0 are also used in the MOF metamodel, e.g., the attribute "abstract" of MofClass.

Super Classes
- Instance
- ModelElement. Constant was not chosen as a superclass for reasons of simplicity— this way the type of a slot is solely defined by its attribute and, thus, there is no need to store a redundant type.

Contained Elements
None

Attributes
- value: String [1] The value of the Slot encoded as text. This solution corresponds to the one chosen for Constants in the MOF standard.

References
None

Operations
None

Constraints
Ω–28, Ω–29

New Associations

AllowedTypes
This Association provides the connection between MetaAttribute and the multiple Types, which are possible for its ontological instances. Unlike MetaAttribute's other sets of allowed options, the Type is not an enumeration and thus needs to be modeled via an Association.

Ends
- Restrictor [0..n]: MetaAttribute.
- AllowedType [0..n]: Classifier

Constraints
None

InstanceOf
This association denotes a type-instance relationship between a MetaElement and an Instance.

Ends

- Level [0..n]: Instance, not navigable. The reason for the non-navigability is that the meta element will most likely be frozen and thus cannot have a changeable reference corresponding to this association.
- Metalevel [0..1]: MetaElement

Constraints

Ω–30, Ω–31,

EndpointAugmentationOf

This association connects a MetaAssociationEnd and an AssociationEnd. The MetaAssociationEnd provides rules, which restrict the instance of the endpoint corresponding to the AssociationEnd.

Ends

- MetaInfo [0..1]: MetaAssociationEnd, not navigable.
- Endpoint [1]: AssociationEnd. Every MetaAssociationEnd is associated with exactly one AssociationEnd.

Constraints

None

Constraints

Ω–1. Given the set A of all Associations and MetaAssociations associated with a class C, and given a set A' of all MetaAssociations associated with its MetaClass C', the following must be true: For each $x \in A$ there must be an $x' \in A'$, which is the MetaElement of x. The other restrictions imposed on Associations are enforced in the Association class and the multiplicities are enforced by .

Ω–2. Given the set A of all Attributes contained in and all MetaAttributes associated with a class C, and given a set A' of all MetaAttributes associated with its MetaClass C', the following must be true: For each $x \in A$ there must be an $x' \in A'$, which is the MetaElement of x. Furthermore, for each $x' \in A'$ the number of elements in A, which are its instances must be higher or equal to the minimum multiplicity and lower or equal to the maximum multiplicity of the Association, which connects x' to C'. This constraint can be easily implemented by using a hashmap with the MetaElements as keys and the (Meta)Attributes as values.

Ω–3. The Slots a Class C contains depend on its MetaClass C' (as identified by isInstanceOf). For each attribute contained in C', C must contain exactly one Slot, which is an instance of the Attribute. Attributes differ from MetaAttributes in many ways; one of them is the fact that they are contained in a Class as opposed to having a "composite" Association with it.

Ω–4. Each Class that is not a MetaClass must participate in exactly one InstanceOf relationship. A MetaClass is also a Class due to inheritance.

Ω–5. Augment rule C-15: A Class may contain only Classes, DataTypes, Attributes, *Slots*, References, Operations, Exceptions, Constants, Constraints, and Tags.

Ω–6. The properties of an Attribute (e.g., type or visibility) depend on its MetaAttribute (as identified by isInstanceOf). An Attribute must have values for multiplicity, visibility, and scope, which are elements in the corresponding lists of allowed values given in the MetaAttribute reachable via the InstanceOf relationship. The type of an attribute must be an InstanceOf one of the elements referenced by AllowedTypes of its MetaAttribute.

Ω–7. Each Attribute A being a Feature of some ModelElement M must participate in exactly one InstanceOf relationship with a MetaAttribute A' being a Feature of some ModelElement M', for which is true that M has an InstanceOf relationship with M'.

Ω–8. Despite the introduction of MetaAssociation, which inherits from Association, Rule C-34 is unchanged. This might seem confusing at the first glance as the rule states that Associations may not have subclasses. However, it is important to realize that Association is an instance_of Class and not an instance_of Association!

Ω–9. Augment rule C-33: An Association may only contain AssociationEnds, Constraints, and Tags with "... plus any elements specified by any of its subclasses.". If this rule was not changed, MetaAssociations could not contain MetaAssociationEnds as they inherit C-33 from this class.

Ω–10. If an Association A is an InstanceOf a MetaAssociation A' (i.e., the reference isInstanceOf is set) the attribute values of the AssociationEnds of A must each be an element of the corresponding set of allowed values found in the MetaAssociationEnds of A'.

Ω–11. Each Association that is not a MetaAssociation must participate in exactly one InstanceOf relationship. A MetaAssociation is also an Association due to inheritance.

Ω–12. For all Instances contained within a ModelLayer M, the reference isInstanceOf is null if and only if the reference isInstanceOf of M is also null. In other words, only the topmost model layer can contain elements, which have no metaelements.

Ω–13. *Each ModelLayer must be contained in a package.*

Ω–14. A ModelLayer may only contain the following elements: MetaClass, Class, Association, MetaAssociation, MetaAttribute, Exception, Constant, Constraint, Tag and DataType

Ω–15. If a ModelLayer, whose reference isInstanceOf is null is contained in a package, no other ModelLayer with a reference isInstanceOf that equals null can be in the same package. This implies that only one topmost model layer can exist in a package.

Ω–16. For all Instances contained within a ModelLayer M, the element referenced by isInstanceOf, if any, must be contained in a ModelLayer transitively reachable via M's isInstanceOf reference. This constraint is less restrictive than it could be—in effect, it describes a relaxed form of strictness. It allows metaelement to element relationships to skip model layers altogether, i.e., an element found in O1 may directly instantiate an element from O3.

Ω–17. All linguistic Associations other than InstanceOf, which involve elements within this layer, must have the other endpoint also within this layer.

Ω–18. For each MetaAssociation A', the following must hold true: Given the set $\hat{A}$ of all instances A_n, $n \in N_0$, of A' with the AssociationEnds $a_{1,n}$ (which are instances of MetaAssociationEnd ma_1, referencing AssociationEnd a_1' of A') and $a_{2,n}$ (which are instances of the MetaAssociationEnd ma_2 of A', referencing AssociationEnd a_2' of A') and the set $\hat{E}_1$ of all instances $C_{1,n}$ of the MetaClass(?) C'_1 referenced by isOfType of a_1' and the set $\hat{E}_2$ of all instances $C_{2,n}$ of the MetaClass(?) C'_2 referenced by isOfType of a_2': For each element $C_{1,n} \in \hat{E}_1$ the number of opposite elements $C_{2,n} \in \hat{E}_2$ reachable through an association $A_n \in \hat{A}$ must not exceed the lower and upper bound of the AssociationEnd a_2' of the MetaAssociation A'. For each element $C_{2,n} \in \hat{E}_2$ the number of opposite elements $C_{1,n} \in \hat{E}_1$ reachable through an association $A_n \in \hat{A}$ must not exceed the lower and upper bound of the AssociationEnd a_1' of the MetaAssociation A'. This is the standard behaviour expected of the instances of a MetaAssociation with regard to multiplicities.

Ω–19. The following rule is directly derived from ModelElement's constraints and thus implies: If the layer is frozen, none of the elements within can be changed in any way.

Ω–20. A MetaAttribute can contain Tags and Constraints.

Ω–21. A MetaAttribute, which has an InstanceOf relationship to a MetaAttribute, must have values for type, multiplicity, visibility, and scope, which are subsets of the corresponding lists of allowed values given in the MetaAttribute. If no set is given at the metalevel, any set or no set at all may be used for the instance.

Ω–22. A MetaAssociation can and must contain exactly 2 MetaAssocationEnds in addition to the elements described in C-33.

Ω–23. The Type of all AssociationEnds within a MetaAssocation must be MetaClass or MetaAttribute. MetaElement is not a valid choice, because otherwise MetaAssociations or ModelLayers would be valid endpoints as well.

Ω–24. associationEnd must point to one of the AssociationEnds contained within the MetaAssociation containing this MetaAssociationEnd. This implies that the EndpointAugmentationOf Association may only connect elements within the same MetaAssociation's namespace.

Ω–25. No Instance that is also a MetaElement, may be an InstanceOf itself or of any of its Instances.

Ω–26. No Instance that is also a MetaElement, may be an InstanceOf a MetaElement with canSpawnMeta = false.

Ω–27. No Instance may be an InstanceOf a MetaElement, which is a GeneralizableElement and has the linguistic attribute 'isAbstract' set to 'true'. The confusing nature of this constraint results from our desire to ensure backwards compatibility.

Ω–28. "value" must contain the textual representation of an attribute value, which must be of the type specified by the Attribute reachable via isInstanceOf. It should be noted that this constraint can only be enforced for the built-in primitive types. Arbitrary and complex types cannot be handled in a standardized way.

Ω–29. The name of the Slot must be the same as the name of its MetaElement.

Ω–30. A Class can only be an instance of a MetaClass, an Attribute can only be an instance of MetaAttribute, a ModelLayer can only be an instance of a ModelLayer, an Association can only be the instance of a MetaAssociation and a Slot can only be the instance of an Attribute.

Ω–31. A MetaClass can only be an instance of a MetaClass, a MetaAttribute can only be an instance of MetaAttribute, and a MetaAssociation can only be the instance of a MetaAssociation.

Ω–32. For each type referenced by the association AllowedTypes, the referenced end, i.e. element must be of type Class or DataType.

References

[1] Accelerated Technologies (2004): Nucleus Bridgepoint. http://www.acceleratedtechnology.com/embedded/nuc_modeling.html

[2] AndroMDA Community (2004): AndroMDA Homepage. http://www.andromda.org/

[3] Aleksy, M., Korthaus, A., and Schader, M. (2005): Implementing Distributed Systems with Java and CORBA. Springer Verlag, New York

[4] Ali, J. and Tanaka, J. (2000): Converting Statecharts into Java Code. In: Proceedings of the Fourth & Fifth World Conference on Integrated Design and Process Technology (IDPT 1999-2000), Dallas, Texas, June 4-8, 2000, Society for Design and Process Science (SDPS), CD-ROM

[5] Akehurst, D.H. and Patrascoiu (2003): Tooling Metamodels with Patterns and OCL. In: Proceedings of the Metamodelling for MDA Workshop, York, November 2003, Online Proceedings: http://www.cs.york.ac.uk/metamodel4mda/onlineProceedingsFinal.pdf

[6] Albin, S. (2003): The Art of Software Architecture: Design Methods and Techniques. John Wiley & Sons, New York, online version at Books24x7

[7] Álvarez, J., Evans, A., and Sammut, P. (2001): Mapping between Levels in the Metamodel Architecture. In: Gogolla, M. and Kobryn, C. (Editors): Proceedings of the The Unified Modeling Language, Modeling Languages, Concepts, and Tools, 4th International Conference (UML 2001), Toronto, Canada, October 2001, Lecture Notes in Computer Science 2185, Springer Verlag, New York, pp. 34-46

[8] Ambler, S. W. (2002): Agile Modeling: Effective Practices for eXtreme Programming and the Unified Process. Wiley & Sons, New York, online version at Books24x7

[9] Ambler, S. W. (2005): Agile Modelling Homepage. http://www.agilemodeling.com

[10] Apache Software Foundation (2005): Apache Xalan 2.5.2, http://xml.apache.org/xalan-j/

[11] Apache Software Foundation (2005): The Apache Cocoon Project. http://cocoon.apache.org/

[12] Apache Software Foundation (2005): The Apache Struts Web Application Framework. http://struts.apache.org/

[13] Apache Jakarta Project (2005): Jakarta Tapestry. http://jakarta.apache.org/tapestry/

[14] Apache Jakarta Project (2005): Jakarta Turbine Web Application Framework. http://jakarta.apache.org/turbine/

[15] Apache Jakarta Project (2005): Velocity. http://jakarta.apache.org/velocity/

[16] Atkinson, C. and Kühne, T. (2003): Calling a Spade a Spade in the MDA Infrastructure, In: Proceedings of the Metamodelling for MDA First International Workshop, York, UK, November 2003, Online Proceedings: http://www.cs.york.ac.uk/metamodel4mda/onlineProceedingsFinal.pdf

[17] Atkinson, C. and Kühne, T. (2003): Model-Driven Development: A Metamodeling Foundation. In: IEEE Software, September/October 2003 (Vol. 20, No. 5), IEEE, pp. 36-41

[18] Atkinson, C. and Kühne, T. (2002): Rearchitecting the UML Infrastructure. In: ACM Transactions on Modeling and Computer Simulation, October 2002 (Vol. 12, No. 4), pp. 290-321

[19] Atkinson, C. and Kühne, T. (2002): The Role of Metamodeling in MDA. In: Proceedings of the International Workshop in Software Model Engineering (held in conjunction with UML '02), Dresden, Germany, October 2002. http://www.metamodel.com/wisme-2002/

[20] Atkinson, C. and Kühne, T. (2001): The Essence of Multilevel Metamodeling. In: Gogolla, M. and Kobryn, C. (Editors): Proceedings of the The Unified Modeling Language, Modeling Languages, Concepts, and Tools, 4th International Conference (UML 2001), Toronto, Canada, October 2001, Lecture Notes in Computer Science 2185, Springer Verlag, New York, pp. 19-33

[21] Atkinson, C., Kühne, T., and Henderson-Sellers, B. (2002): Stereotypical Encounters of the Third Kind. In: Jézéquel, J.-M., Hussmann, H., and Cook, S. (Editors): Proceedings of the Unified Modeling Language, 5th International Conference (UML 2002), Dresden, Germany, October 2002, Lecture Notes in Computer Science 2460, Springer Verlag, New York, pp. 100-114

[22] Atkinson, C. (1997): Meta-Modeling for Distributed Object Environments. In: Proceedings of the 1st International Enterprise Distributed Object Computing Conference (EDOC'97), Gold Coast, Australia, October 1997, IEEE Computer Society, pp. 90-101

[23] Balzert, H. (2000): Lehrbuch der Softwaretechnik. Spektrum, Akademischer Verlag, Heidelberg.

[24] Baresi, L., Garzotto, F., and Paolini, P. (2000): From Web Sites to Web Applications: New Issues for Conceptual Modeling. In: Liddle, S. W., Mayr, H. C., and Thalheim, B. (Eds.): ER 2000 Workshop, LNCS 1921, Springer Verlag, New York, pp. 89-100

[25] Barracuda (2002): Surveying the Landscape. http://barracudamvc.org/Barracuda/docs/landscape.html

[26] Barta, R. and Schranz, M. (2005): JESSICA: an object-oriented hypermedia publishing processor. http://www.ra.ethz.ch/CDstore/www7/1882/com1882.htm

[27] Beck, K. and Gamma, E. (2004): Contributing to Eclipse: Principles, Patterns, and Plug-Ins. Pearson Education, 2004

[28] Becker, S. A. and Berkemeyer, A. (2002): Rapid Application Design and Testing of Web Usability. In: IEEE Multimedia, October/December 2002 (Vol. 9 No. 4), IEEE Computer Society, pp. 38-46

[29] Becker, S. A. and Mottay, F. E. (2001): A Gobal Perspective on Web Site Usability. In: IEEE Software January/February 2001 (Vol. 18 No. 1), pp. 54-61

[30] Beigbeder, S. M. and Castro, C. C. (2004): An MDA Approach for the Development of Web Applications. In: Koch, N., Fraternali, P., and Wirsing, M. (Eds.): Proceedings of the International Conference on Web Engineering (ICWE 2004), July 2004, Munich, LNCS 3140, Springer-Verlag, New York, pp. 300-305

[31] Bézivin, J. (2003): MDA: From Hype to Hope, and Reality. Invited Talk at the UML 2003, http://www.sciences.univ-nantes.fr/info/perso/permanents/bezivin/UML.2003/UML.SF.JB.GT.ppt

[32] Bézivin, J. and Lemesle, R. (1998): Ontology-Based Layered Semantics for Precise OA&D Modeling. In: J. Bosch, S. Mitchell (Editors): ECOOP'97 Workshop Reader, June 1997, Jyväskylä, Finland, LNCS 1357, Springer Verlag, New York, pp. 151-154

[33] Bézivin, J. and Lemesle, R. (1997): Ontology-Based Layered Semantics for Precise OA&D Modeling. In: J. Bosch, S. Mitchell (Editors): ECOOP'97 Workshop Reader, June 1997, Jyväskylä, Finland, LNCS 1357, Springer Verlag, New York, pp.151-154

[34] Bichler, L.: A flexible code generator for MOF-based modeling languages. In: Proceedings of the 2nd OOPSLA Workshop on Generative Techniques in the context of Model Driven Architecture. Online Proceedings: http://www.softmetaware.com/oopsla2003/ bichler.pdf

[35] Booch, G., Brown, A., Iyengar, S., and Selic, B. (2004): An MDA Manifesto. In: MDA Journal, http://www.bptrends.com/publicationfiles/05-04%20COL%20IBM%20Manifesto%20-%20Frankel%20-3.pdf

[36] Borges, J. A., Morales, I., and Rodríguez, N. J. (1996): Guidelines for Designing Usable World Wide Web Pages. In: Companion of the Proceedings of the Conference on Human Factors in Computing Systems (CHI'96), Vancouver, Canada, April 1996, ACM, pp. 277-278

[37] Breton, E. and Bézivin, J. (2001): Model-Driven Process Engineering, In: Proceedings of the 25th Annual International Computer Software and Ap-

plications Conference (COMPSAC'01), October 2001, Chicago, USA, IEEE Computer Society, pp. 225-230

[38] Breton, E. and Bézivin, J. (2002): Weaving Definition and Execution Aspects of Process Meta-models, In: Proceedings of the 35th Annual Hawaii International Conference on System Sciences (HICSS'02) – Volume 9, January 2002, Big Island, Hawaii, USA, IEEE Computer Society, pp. 290-299

[39] Brooks, F. (1987): No Silver Bullet: Essence And Accidents of Software Engineering. Originally in: IEEE Computer Magazine, 1987, online "reprint": http://www.computer.org/computer/homepage/misc/Brooks/

[40] Catarci, T. and Little, T. D. C. (2001): Guidelines for Hypermedia Usability Inspection. In: IEEE Multimedia, January/March 2001 (Vol. 8 No. 1), IEEE Computer Society, pp. 66-69

[41] CDIF Technical Committee (1994): CDIF – CASE Data Interchange Format, Extract of Interim Standard, EIA/IS-107, Electronic Industries Association, January 1994

[42] Ceri, S., Fraternali, P., and Bongio, A. (2000): Web Modeling Language (WebML): a Modeling Language for Designing Web Sites. In: Proceedings of the 9th Internation World Wide Web Conference (WWW9), Amsterdam, Holland, May 2000, CDROM.

[43] Ceri, S., Fraternali, P., and Matera, M. (2002): Conceptual Modeling of Data-Intensive Web Applications. In: IEEE Internet Computing, July/August 2002 (Vol. 6 No. 4), IEEE Computer Society, pp. 20-30

[44] Chan, Y. and Suwanda, H. (2000): Designing Multinational Online Stores: Challenges, Implementation Techniques and Experience. In: Proceedings of the 2000 Conference of the Centre for Advanced Studies on Collaborative Research, Mississauga, Canada, IBM Press, pp. 1-14

[45] Chandrasekaran, B., Josephson, J. R., and Benjamins, V. R. (1999): What Are Ontologies, and Why Do We Need Them? In: IEEE Intelligent Systems, January/February 1999 (Vol. 14 No. 1), IEEE Computer Society, pp. 20-26

[46] Chikofsky, E. J: (1988): Software Technology People Can Really Use. IEEE Software, March 1988 (Vol. 5 No. 2), IEEE Computer Society, pp. 8-10

[47] Chow, K. O., Jia, W., Chan, V. C. P., and Cao, J. (2000): Model-Based Generation of Java Code. In: Proceedings of the International Conference on Parallel and Distributed Processing Techniques and Applications (PDPTA'00), Volume V. Las Vegas, USA, CREAS, online version: http://www.dvo.ru/bbc/pdpta/vol5/p522.pdf

[48] Clark, J. (Editor) (1999): XSL Transformations (XSLT) Version 1.0 W3C Recommendation 16 November 1999. http://www.w3.org/TR/ xslt

[49] Clark, T., Evans, A., Sammut, P., and Willans, J. (2004): Applied Metamodelling – A Foundation for Language Driven Development Version 0.1. Online version: http://albini.xactium.com/content/index.php?option=com_remository&Itemid=28

[50] Constantine, L. L. and Lockwood L. A. D. (2002): Usage-Centered Engineering for Web Applications. In: IEEE Software, March/April 2002 (Vol. 19 No. 2), IEEE Computer Society, pp. 42-50

[51] Cook, S., Mellor, S., Warmer, J., Wills, A., and Evans, A. (Moderator): Advanced Methods and Tools for a Precise UML. http://www.puml.org

[52] Cook, S. (2004): Domain-Specific Modeling and Model Driven Architecture. In: MDA Journal, http://www.bptrends.com/publicationfiles/01%2D04%20COL%20Dom%20Spec%20Modeling%20Frankel%2DCook%2Epdf

[53] Cowan, D. D. and Lucena, C. J. P. (1995): Abstract Data Views: An Interface Specification Concept to Enhance Design for Reuse. In: IEEE Transactions on Software Engineering, March 1995 (Vol. 21, No. 3), IEEE Computer Society, pp. 229-243

[54] Czarnecki, K. and Helsen, S. (2003): Classification of Model Transformation Approaches, In: 2nd OOPSLA Workshop on Generative Techniques in the context of Model Driven Architecture. Online Proceedings: http://www.softmetaware.com/oopsla2003/mda-workshop.html

[55] Deitsch, A. and Czarnecki D. (2001): Java Internationalization. O'Reilly, 2001

[56] Deng, G., Lu T., Turkaye, E., Gokhale, A., Schmidt, D., and Nechypurenko, A. (2003): Model Driven Development of Inventory Tracking System, In: 3rd OOPSLA Workshop on Domain Specific Visual Languages, Anaheim, USA, October 2003, ACM, online Proceedings: http://www.cis.uab.edu/info/OOPSLA-DSM03/Papers/ index.htm

[57] Denning, P. J. (2004): The Field of Programmers Myth, In: Communications of the ACM, July 2004 (Vol. 47, No. 7), ACM, pp. 15-20

[58] DeMichiel, L. G. (2003): Enterprise JavaBeans Specification, Version 2.1. SUN Microsystems, November 2003, http://java.sun.com/products/ejb/docs.html

[59] Deshpande, Y. and Hansen S. (2001): Web Engineering: Creating a Discipline among Disciplines. In: IEEE MultiMedia, April/June 2001 (Vol. 8 No. 2), IEEE Computer Society, pp. 82-87

[60] De Troyer, O. and Leune, C.J. (1998): WSDM: a user centered design method for Web sites. In: Proceedings of the 7th International World Wide Web Confernce (WWW7), online proceedings: http://www7.scu.edu.au/programme/fullpapers/1853/com1853.htm

[61] Dirckze, R (Spec. Lead) (2002): Java™ Metadata Interface (JMI) Specification – JSR 040, Version 1.0 Final Specification. Java Community Process, June 2002, http://jcp.org/aboutJava/communityprocess/final/jsr040/index.html

[62] Duddy, K. (2002): UML2 Must Enable a Family of Languages. In: Communications of the ACM, November 2002 (Vol. 45, No. 11), ACM, pg. 73-75

[63] Eclipse Foundation (2005): Eclipse.org Main Page. http://www.eclipse.org/

[64] Ehrig, H. (1979): Introduction to the Algebraic Theory of Graph Grammars. In: Proceedings of the International Workshop on Graph Grammars and Their Application to Computer Science and Biology, LNCS 73, Springer Verlag, New York

[65] El Kaim, W., Studer, P., and Muller, P.-A. (2003): Model Driven Architecture for Agile Web Information System Engineering. In: Konstantas, D. et al. (Eds.): Proceedings of the 9th International Conference on Object-Oriented Systems (OOIS 2003), September 2003, Geneva, Switzerland, LNCS 2817, Springer Verlag, New York, pp. 299-303

[66] Engels, G., Hücking, R., Sauer, S., and Wagner, A. (1999): UML Collaboration Diagrams and Their Transformation to Java. In: France, R. and Rumpe, B. (Editors): Proceedings of the 2nd International Conference on the Unified Modeling Language (UML'99), Fort Collins, USA, October 1999, LNCS 1723, Springer Verlag, New York, pp. 473-488

[67] Ferrucci, F., Tortora, G., and Vitiello, G. (2002): Visual Programming. In: Marciniak (Ed.): Encyclopedia of Software Engineering, Second Edition, Wiley-Interscience, 2002, pp. 1867-1892

[68] Filman, R. E. (2004): Interface Pains. In: IEEE Internet Computing, September/October 2004 (Vol. 8 No. 5), IEEE Computer Society, pp. 4-6

[69] Fleck, R. (2001): PKW Lenksysteme – Vorbereitung auf die Technik von Morgen, Proceedings of the "PKW-Lenksysteme – Vorbereitung auf die Technik von morgen" Conference, Essen, Haus der Technik e.V.

[70] Forschungszentrum Informatik Karlsruhe (2005): Inject/J Homepage. http://injectj.fzi.de/

[71] Fowler, M. (2005): UML Bliki. http://www.martinfowler.com/bliki/uml.html

[72] Fraternali, P. and Paolini, P. (2000): Model-Driven Development of Web Applications: The Autoweb System. In: ACM Transactions on Information Systems, October 2000 (Vol. 28, No. 4), ACM, pp. 323-382

[73] Frankel, D. S. (2004): The MDA Marketing Message and the MDA Reality. In: MDA Journal, http://www.bptrends.com/deliver_file.cfm?fileType=publication&fileName=03%2D04%20COL%20Marketing%20Message%20%2D%20Reality%20Frankel1%2Epdf

[74] Fröhlich, P., Henze, N., and Nejdl, W. (1997): Meta Modeling for Hypermedia Design. Online Version: http://www.kbs.uni-hannover.de/Arbeiten/Publikationen/1997/metadata/pfroehlich.html

[75] Fuentes, L., Pinto, M., and Vallecillo, A. (2003): How MDA Can Help Designing Component- and Aspect-based Applications. In: Proceedings of the Seventh International Enterprise Distributed Object Computing Conference (EDOC'03), Brisbane, Australia, September 2003, IEEE Computer Society, pp. 124ff

[76] Gamma, E., Helm, R., Johnson, R., and Vlissides, J. (1996): Design Patterns. Addison-Wesley, 1996

[77] Gardner, T., Griffin, C., Koehler, J., and Hauser, R. (2003): A review of OMG MOF 2.0 Query / Views / Transformations Submissions and Recommendations towards the final Standard. OMG July 2003. http://www.omg.org/docs/ad/03-08-02.pdf

[78] Garzotte, F. and Paolini, P. (1993): HDM – A Model-Based Approach to Hypertext Application Design. In: ACM Transactions on Information Systems, January 1993 (Vol. 11, No. 1), ACM, pp. 1-26

[79] Garzotto, F., Mainetti, L., and Paolini, P. (1995): Hypermedia Design Analysis, and Evaluation Issues. In: Communications of the ACM, August 1995 (Vol. 38, No. 8), ACM, pp. 74-86

[80] Garzotto, F., Mainetti, L., and Paolini, P. (1996): Information Reuse in Hypermedia Applications. In: Proceedings of the the seventh ACM conference on Hypertext and Multimedia, Bethesda, USA, 1996, ACM, pp. 93-104

[81] Ginige, A. and Murugesan, S. (2001): Web Engineering: An Introduction. In: IEEE Multimedia, January/March 2001 (Vol. 8 No. 1), IEEE Computer Society, pp. 14-18

[82] Geisler, R., Klar, M., and Pons, C. (1998): Dimensions and Dichotomy in Metamodeling. In: Proceedings of the 3rd BCS-FACS Northern Formal Methods Workshop, Ilkley, UK, September 1998, BCS, online version: http://ewic.bcs.org/conferences/1998/3rdfacs/papers/paper10.htm

[83] Gellersen, H.-W. and Gaedke M. (1999): Object-Oriented Web Application Development. In: IEEE Internet Computing Online, January/February 1999 (Vol. 3, No. 1), IEEE Computer Society, pp. 60-68

[84] Gellersen, H.-W., Wicke, R., and Gaedke, M. (1997): WebComposition: An Object-Oriented Support System for the Web Engineering Lifecycle. In: Selected papers from the sixth international conference on World Wide Web, Santa Clara, California, United States, Elsevier Science Publishers, Essex, UK, pp. 1429-1437, online version: http://www.teco.edu/~gaedke/publication/webengineering/webcomposition.html

[85] Gitzel, R. (2004): WAM 2004 – Workshop Report. http://www.wifo.uni-mannheim.de/WAM2004/Proceedings/06_WAM 2004Protocol.pdf

[86] Gitzel, R. and Aleksy, M. (2004): Implementation of a Model-Centric Web Application Framework with J2EE. In: Proceedings of the 3rd International Conference on Principles and Practice of Programming in Java (PPPJ'04), Dublin, Ireland, Computer Science Press Trinity College / ACM International Conference Proceeding Series, pp. 529-534

[87] Gitzel, R. and Hildenbrand, T. (2005): A Taxonomy of Metamodel Hierarchies - Working Paper 1-05. http://www.wifo.uni-mannheim.de/~gitzel/publications/taxonomy.pdf

[88] Gitzel, R. and Korthaus, A. (2004): The Role of Metamodeling in Model-Driven Development. In: Proceedings of the 8th World Multi-Conference on Systemics, Cybernetics and Informatics (SCI2004), Orlando, USA, July 2004, IIIS, pp. 68-73

[89] Gitzel, R., Korthaus, A., and Mazloumi, N. (2003): Realizing Web Designs with the Cobana Framework. In: Proceedings of the 21st IASTED International Multi-Conference on Applied Informatics (AI2003), Innsbruck, Austria, February 2003, IASTED, pp. 1065-1071

[90] Gitzel, R., Korthaus, A., and Schader, M. (2004): The Potential of Automatic Code Generation for the Web Application Domain. In: WSEAS Transactions on Information Science and Applications, December 2004 (Issue 6, Volume 1), WSEAS, pp. 1617-1625

[91] Gitzel, R. and Merz, M. (2004): How a Relaxation of the Strictness Definition Can Benefit MDD Approaches With Meta Model Hierarchies. In: Proceedings of the 8th World Multi-Conference on Systemics, Cybernetics and Informatics (SCI2004), Orlando, USA, July 2004, IIIS, pp. 62-67

[92] Gitzel, R., Ott, I., and Schader, M. (2004): Ontological Metamodel Extension for Generative Architectures (OMEGA) – Working Paper 1-04. http://www.bwl.uni-mannheim.de/Schader/_files/gitzel-omega.pdf

[93] Gitzel, R. and Schader, M. (2003): Generation of XML-based Web Applications Using Metamodels. In: Proceedings of the 7th IASTED In-

ternational Conference on Internet And Multimedia Systems And Applications (IMSA'03), Honolulu, USA, August, 2003, IASTED

[94] Gitzel, R. and Schwind, M. (2005): The OMEGAPlugin JavaDocs. http://www.wifo.uni-mannheim.de/~gitzel/research/OMEGA/JavaDoc/index.html

[95] Glass, R. (2004): Learning to Distinguish a Solution from a Problem, In: IEEE Software, May/June 2004 (Vol. 21 No. 3), IEEE Computer Society, pp. 111-112

[96] Glass, R. (2004): Matching Methodology to Problem Domain, In: Communications of the ACM, May 2004 (Vol. 47, No. 5), ACM, pp. 19-21

[97] Glass, R. (2004): On Modeling and Discomfort, in: IEEE Software, March/April 2004 (Vol. 21 No. 2), IEEE Computer Society, pp. 102-103

[98] Glass, R. (2004): Some Heresy Regarding Software Engineering, In: IEEE Software, July/August 2004 (Vol. 21 No. 4), IEEE Computer Society, pp. 104, 102-103

[99] Glass, R. (2002): Project Retrospectives, and Why They Never Happen, In: IEEE Software, September/October 2002 (Vol. 19 No. 5), IEEE Computer Society, pp. 112, 111

[100] Glass R. (2001): A Story about the Creativity Involved in Software Work, In: IEEE Software, September/October 2001 (Vol. 18 No. 5), IEEE Computer Society, pp. 96-97

[101] Glass, R. (2000): The Generalization of an Application Domain. In: IEEE Software, September/October 2000 (Vol. 17 No. 5), pp. 128, 127

[102] Gómez, J. (2004): Model-Driven Web Development with VisualWADE, In: Koch, N., Fraternali, P., Wirsing, M. (Eds.): Proceedings of the International Conference on Web Engineering (ICWE2004), Munich, July 2004, LNCS 3140, Springer-Verlag New York, pp. 611-612

[103] Greenfield, J., Short, K., Cook, S., and Kent, S. (2004): Software Factories – Assembling Applications with Patterns, Models, Frameworks, and Tools. Wiley Publishing, Indianapolis.

[104] Guttmann, M. (2004): A Response to Steve Cook. In: MDA Journal, http://www.bptrends.com/deliver_file.cfm?fileType=publication&fileName=02%2D04%20COL%20Resp%20to%20Cook%20Frankel%2DGuttman2%2Epdf

[105] Halasz, F. G., Moran, T. P., and Trigg, R. H. (1987): NoteCards in a Nutshell. In: Proceedings of the SIGCHI/GI conference on Human factors in computing systems and graphics interface, Toronto Canada, October 1986, ACM, pp. 45-52

[106] Harel, D. and Gery, E. (1996): Executable Object Modeling with Statecharts. In: Proceedings of the 18th International Conference on Software Engineering (ICSE'96), Berlin, Germany, March 1996, IEEE Computer Society, pp. 246-257

[107] Harel, D. and Rumpe, B. (2000): Modeling Languages: Syntax, Semantics, and All That Stuff – Part I: The Basic Stuff. The Weizmann Institute of Science, Rehovot, Israel, MCS00-16. http://www4.in.tum.de/~rumpe/ps/Modeling-Languages.pdf

[108] Harel, D. and Rumpe, B. (2004): Meaningful Modeling: What's the Semantics of "Semantics"? In: Computer, October 2004 (Vol. 37 No. 10), IEEE Computer Society, pp. 64-72

[109] Harnad, S. (1996): Implementing Peer Review on the Net: Scientific Quality Control in Scholarly Electronic Journals. In: Peek, R. and Newby, G. (Editors): Scholarly Publication: The Electronic Frontier. Cambridge MA: MIT Press, Cambridge, pp. 103-108

[110] Haywood, D. (2004): MDA: Nice Idea, Shame about the... http://theserverside.com/articles/content/MDA_Haywood/article.html

[111] Hearnden, D., Raymond, K., and Steel, J. (2002): Anti-Yacc: MOF-to-Text, In: Proceedings of the Sixth International Enterprise Distributed Object Computing Conference (EDOC'02), Lausanne, Switzerland, September 2002, IEEE Computer Society, pp. 200-211

[112] Heckel, R. and Lohmann, M. (2003): Model-Based Development of Web Applications Using Graphical Reaction Rules. In: Pezzè, M. (Editor): Fundamental Approaches to Software Engineering, 6th International Conference (FASE 2003), Warsaw, Poland, April 2003, LNCS 2621, Springer Verlag New York, pp. 170-183

[113] Herbsleb, J. and Mockus, A. (2003): Formulation and Preliminary Test of an Empirical Theory of Coordination in Software Engineering. In: Proceedings of the European Software Engineering Conference and ACM SIGSOFT Symposium on the Foundations of Software Engineering (ESEC/FSE'03), Helsinki, Finland, September 2003, ACM, pp. 138-147

[114] Hofstede, G. (2004): Geert Hofstede Cultural Dimensions. http://www.geert-hofstede.com/

[115] Holzschlag, M. (2004): Color My World. http://www.molly.com/articles/webdesign/2000-09-colormyworld.php

[116] Horton, W. (1995): Top Ten Blunders by Visual Designers. In: ACM SIGGRAPH Computer Graphics, November 1995 (Vol. 29 Issue 4), ACM, pp. 20-24

[117] Houben, G.-J., Barna, P., Frasincar, F., and Vdovjak, R. (2003): Hera: Development of Semantic Web Information Systems, In: Lovelle, J.M.C. et

al. (Eds.): Proceedings of the 3rd International Conference of Web Engineering (ICWE 2003), Oviedo, Spain, July 2003, LNCS 2722, Springer Verlag New York, pp. 529-538

[118] Hubert, R. (2002): Convergent Architecture – Building Model-Driven J2EE Systems with UML, John Wiley & Sons, New York

[119] IO-Software (2003): ArcStyler Getting Started. IO-Software, October 2003. http://www.io-software.com/as_support/docu/QuickStart_Guide.pdf

[120] IO-Software (2005): Arcstyler Overview Page. http://www.io-software.com/products/arcstyler_overview.jsp

[121] IO-Software (2005): ArcStyler Technical Briefing – Architecture Class ROI. http://www.io-software.com/as_support/brochures/ArcStyler_Technical_Briefing.pdf

[122] Isakowitz, T., Kamis, A., and Koufaris, M. (1998): The Extended RMM Methodology for Web Publishing. Working Paper IS-98-18, Center for Research on Information Systems, 1998. http://www.dsi.unive.it/~smm/docs/isakowitz98.pdf

[123] Isazadeh, H. (1997): CASE Environments and MetaCASE Tools. External Technical Report, Department of Computing and Information Science, Queen's University, Kingston, Canada. http://www.cs.queensu.ca/Department/TechReports/Reports/1997-403.pdf

[124] IT.CappucinoNet.com (2003): Struts CX Homepage. http://it.cappuccinonet.com/strutscx/index.php

[125] Ivory, M. Y., Sinha, R. R., and Heart, M. A. (2001): Empirically Validated Web Page Design Metrics. In: Proceedings of the CHI 2001 Conference on Human Factors in Computing Systems (SIGCHI'01), Seattle, USA, March, 2001, ACM, pp. 53-60

[126] Ivory, M. Y. and Hearst M. A. (2002): Improving Web Site Design. In: IEEE Internet Computing, March/April 2002 (Vol. 6 No. 2), IEEE Computer Society, pp. 56-63

[127] Javelinsoft (2005): Swinglets Homepage. http://www.javelinsoft.com/swinglets/

[128] Jcorporate (2005): Expresso Homepage. www.jcorporate.com/expresso.html

[129] Kahin, B. and Varian, H. R. (2000): Internet Publishing and Beyond: The Economics of Digital Information and Intellectual Property. MIT Press, Cambridge, online version at Books24x7

[130] Kamm, C. and Klein, C. (2002): Komplexe Web-Anwendungen mit "Struts". In: ObjektSpektrum 03/2002, SIGS-Datacom, Troisdorf, pp. 26-31

[131] Keep, C., McLaughlin, T., Parmar, R. (1993): The Electronic Labyrinth – Vannevar Bush. http://www.iath.virginia.edu/elab/hfl0034.html

[132] Kent, S. (2002): Model Driven Engineering. In: Butler, M., Petre, L., and Sere, K. (2002): Proceedings of the 3rd International Conference on Integrated Formal Methods (IFM 2002), Turku, Finland, May 2002, LNCS 2335, Springer Verlag New York, pp. 286-298

[133] Kent, S. (2004): On code generation from models. http://blogs.msdn.com/stuart_kent/archive/2004/06/14.aspx

[134] Kleppe, A., Warmer, J., and Bast, W. (2003): MDA Explained – The Model Driven Architecture: Practice and Promise. Pearson Education, Boston

[135] Koch, N. (1999): A Comparative Study of Methods for Hypermedia Development, Technical Report 9905, Ludwig-Maximilians-Universität München, http://citeseer.nj.nec.com/koch01comparative.html

[136] Kolawa, A., Hicken, W., and Dunlop, C. (2002): Bulletproofing Web Applications. Wiley & Sons, New York, online version at Books24x7

[137] Kühne, T. (2003): Automatisierte Softwareentwicklung mit Modellkompilern, In: thema Forschung 1/2003, VMK-Verlag, pp. 116-122

[138] Macala, R. R., Stuckey, L. D., and Gross, D. C. (1996): Managing Domain-Specific, Product-Line Development. In: IEEE Software, May 1996 (Vol. 13 No. 3), IEEE Computer Society, pp. 57-67

[139] Marcus, A. and Gould E. W. (2000): Cultural Dimensions and Global Web User-Interface Design: What? So What? Now What? In: Proceedings of the 6th conference on Human Factors & the Web. Online version: http://www.tri.sbc.com/hfweb/marcus/hfweb00_marcus.html

[140] Mellor, S., Balcer, M. (2002): Executable UML – A Foundation for Model-Driven Architecture, Addison-Wesley, Hoboken

[141] Mellor, S. (2004): Agile MDA. In: MDA Journal, http://www.bptrends.com/deliver_file.cfm?fileType=publication&fileName=06%2D04%20COL%20Agile%20MDA%20%2D%20Frankel%20%2D%20Mellor%2Epdf

[142] Miller, J. and Mukerji, J. (2003): MDA Guide Version 1.0.1, OMG Document Number: omg/2003-06-01, OMG, 12.6.2003. http://www.omg.org/cgi-bin/doc?omg/2003-06-01

[143] Muller, P.-A., Studer, P., and Bézivin, J. (2003): Platform Independent Web Application Modeling. In: Stevens, P., Whittle, J., and Booch, G. (Editors): The Unified Modeling Language, Modeling, Languages, and Applications, 6th Internation Conference (UML 2003), San Francisco, USA, October 2003, LNCS 2863, Springer Verlag New York, pp. 220-233

[144] Mercay, J. and Bouzeid, G. (2002): Boost Struts with XSLT and XML. In: JavaWorld Magazine. http://www.javaworld.com/javaworld/jw-02-2002/jw-0201-strutsxslt.html

[145] National Instruments (2004): LabVIEW Homepage. http://www.ni.com/labview/

[146] Neumann, P. G. (2004): The Big Picture, In: Communications of the ACM, September 2004 (Vol. 47, No. 9), ACM, pg. 112

[147] Neuwirth, C. M. and Regli, S. H. (2002): Usability and the Web. In: IEEE Internet Computing, March/April 2002 (Vol. 6 No. 2), IEEE Computer Society, pp. 44-45

[148] NextApp (2005): Echo Homepage. http://www.nextapp.com/products/echo/

[149] Niaz, I. A. and Tanaka, J. (2003): Code Generation From UML Statecharts. In: Proceedings of the 7th IASTED International Conference on Software Engineering and Applications (SEA 2003), Marina Del Rey, USA, November 2003, IASTED, pp. 315-321

[150] Nielsen, J. (1996): Original Top Ten Mistakes in Web Design. http://www.useit.com/alertbox/9605a.html

[151] Nielsen, J. (1999): "Top Ten Mistakes" Revisited Three Years Later. http://www.useit.com/alertbox/990502.html

[152] Nielsen, J. (2000): Designing Web Usability: The Practice of Simplicity. German edition, Markt+Technik Verlag, München

[153] Nielsen, J. (2002): Top Ten Web-Design Mistakes of 2002. http://www.useit.com/alertbox/20021223.html

[154] Nielsen, J. (2003): Top Ten Web Design Mistakes of 2003. http://www.useit.com/alertbox/20031222.html

[155] Nordstrom, G., Sztipanovits, J., Karsai, G., and Ledeczi, A. (1999): Metamodeling – Rapid Design and Evolution of Domain-Specific Modeling Environments, In: Proceedings of the 6th Symposium on Engineering of Computer-Based Systems (ECBS '99), Nashville, USA, March 1999, IEEE Computer Society, pp. 68-74

[156] Nordstrom, G. (1999): Metamodeling – Rapid Design And Evolution of Domain-Specific Modeling Environments, Dissertation, Graduate School of Vanderbilt University, Nashville

[157] Obrenovic, Z., Starcevic, D., and Selic, B. (2004): A Model-Driven Approach to Content Repurposing, In: IEEE Multimedia, January/March 2004 (Vol. 11, No. 1), IEEE Computer Society, pp. 62-71

[158] Odell, J. (1994): Power Types, in: Journal of Object Oriented Programming, May 1994 (Vol. 7 No. 2), pp. 8-12

[159] Odlyzko, A. (1995): Tragic Loss or Good Riddance? The Impending Demise of Traditional Scholarly Journals. In: Journal of Universal Computer Science, 1994 (Pilot Volume Issue 0), pp. 3-52

[160] Offutt, J. (2002): Quality Attributes of Web Applications. In: IEEE Software, March/April 2002 (Vol. 19 No. 2), IEEE Computer Society, pp. 25-32

[161] OMG (2002): Meta Object Facility (MOF) Specification, Version 1.4. OMG, April 2002. http://www.omg.org/cgi-bin/doc?formal/2002-04-03

[162] OMG (2002): Request for Proposal: MOF 2.0 Query / Views / Transformations RFP. OMG, April 2002. http://www.omg.org/docs/ad/02-04-10.pdf

[163] OMG (2002): Unified Modeling Language Specification (Action Semantics). OMG, January 2002. http://www.omg.org/docs/ptc/02-01-09.pdf

[164] OMG (2003): Common Warehouse Metamodel (CWM) Specification Version 1.1, formal/03-03-02 Volume 1. OMG, March 2003. http://www.omg.org/docs/formal/03-03-02.pdf

[165] OMG (2003): Ontology Definition Metamodel Request For Proposal. ad/2003-03-40. OMG March 2003. http://www.omg.org/docs/ad/03-03-40.pdf

[166] OMG (2003): Revised Submission to OMG RFP ad/2003-04-07: Meta Object Facility (MOF) 2.0 Core Proposal. OMG, April 2003. http://www.omg.org/cgi-bin/apps/doc?ad/03-04-07.pdf

[167] OMG (2003): Unified Modeling Language Specification Version 1.5 formal/03-03-01, OMG, March 2003. http://www.omg.org/docs/formal/03-03-01.pdf

[168] OMG (2003): UML 2.0 Infrastructure Specification, ptc/03-09-15, OMG, December 2003. http://www.omg.org/docs/ptc/03-09-15.pdf

[169] OMG (2003): XML Metadata Interchange (XMI) Specification Version 2.0 formal/03-05-02. OMG, May 2003, http://www.omg.org/docs/formal/03-05-02.pdf

[170] OMG (2004): Meta Object Facility (MOF) 2.0 Core Specification. http://www.omg.org/docs/ptc/03-10-04.pdf

[171] OMG (2004): UML Profile and Interchange Models for Enterprise Application Integration (EAI) Specification. http://www.omg.org/docs/formal/04-03-26.pdf

[172] OMG (2004): UML Profile For Enterprise Distributed Object Computing (EDOC). http://www.omg.org/technology/documents/formal/edoc.htm

[173] Paolini, P. (1999): Hypermedia, the Web and Usability Issues. In: Proceedings of the IEEE International Conference on Multimedia Computing and Systems (ICMCS 1999), Florence, Italy, June 1999, IEEE Computer Society, pp. 111-115

[174] Plato: Phaedo

[175] Precise UML Group (2004): The Precise UML Group Homepage. http://www.cs.york.ac.uk/puml/

[176] Puder, A. (2004): Extending Desktop Applications to the Web. In: Proceedings of the 3rd International Symposium on Information and Communication Technologies (ISICT'04), Las Vegas, Nevada, June, 2004, ACM International Conference Proceedings Series, pp. 8-13

[177] Riehle, D., Fraleigh, S., Bucka-Lassen, D., and Omorogbe, N. (2001): The Architecture of a UML Virtual Machine. In: Proceedings of the 2001 Conference on Object-Oriented Programming Systems, Languages, and Applications (OOPSLA'01), Tampa Bay, USA, October, ACM, 2001

[178] Roberts, D. and Johnson, R. (1996): Evolving Frameworks – A Pattern Language for Developing Object-Oriented Frameworks. http://st-www.cs.uiuc.edu/users/droberts/evolve.html

[179] Rosson, M. B. and Carroll, J. M. (2002): Usability Engineering: Scenario-Based Development of Human-Computer Interaction. Morgan Kaufmann Publishers, San Francisco, online version at Books24x7

[180] Roth, E. M., Patterson, E. S., and Mumaw, R. J. (1994): Cognitive Engineering. In: Marciniak (Editor): Encyclopedia of Software Engineering, Second Edition, Wiley-Interscience, 2002, pp. 163-179

[181] Roth, M. and Pelegrí-Llopart, E. (2003): JavaServer Pages Specification Version 2.0. http://java.sun.com/products/jsp/download/index.html

[182] Sane, A. and Campell, R. (1995): Object-Oriented State Machines: Subclassing, Composition, Delegation, and Genericity. In: Proceedings of the 10th Annual ACM Conference on Object-Oriented Programming Systems, Languages, and Applications (OOPLSA'95), Austin, USA, October 1995, pp. 17-32

[183] Schneeweiss, C. (1999): Hierarchies in Distributed Decision Making. Springer Verlag New York

[184] Schmid, H. A. and Rossi, G. (2004): Modeling and Designing Processes in E-Commerce Applications. In: IEEE Internet Computing, January/February 2004 (Vol. 8 No. 1), IEEE Computer Society, pp. 19-27

[185] Schwabe, D. and Rossi, G. (1998): An Object Oriented Approach to Web-Based Application Design. In: Theory and Practice of Object Systems 4(4), 1998, revised internet version: http://www.inf.puc-rio.br/~schwabe/papers/TAPOSRevised.pdf

[186] Schweiggert, F. (2000): Qualitätsbezogene Evaluation von Software-Produkten. In: Heinrich, L., Häntschel, I. (Editors): Evaluation und Evalu-

ationsforschung in der Wirtschaftsinformatik, Oldenburg Verlag, Munich, pp. 283-298

[187] Seidewitz, E. (2003): What Models Mean. In: IEEE Software, September/October 2003 (Vol. 20, No. 5), IEEE Computer Society, pp. 26-32

[188] Seidewitz, E. (2003): What Do Models Mean? OMG Document ad/03-03-31, OMG, March 2003. http://www.omg.org/docs/ad/03-03-31.pdf

[189] Sekerinski, E. and Zurob, R. (2001): iState: A Statechart Translator. In: Gogolla, M. and Kobryn, C. (Editors): Proceedings of the 4th International Conference on the Unified Modeling Language (UML 2001), Toronto, Canada, October 2001, LNCS 2185, Springer Verlag New York, pp. 376-390

[190] Selic, B. (2003): The Pragmatics of Model-Driven Development, In: IEEE Software, September/October 2003 (Vol. 20, No. 5), IEEE Computer Society, pp. 19-25

[191] Selic B. (2004): UML ist nicht schwieriger als Java oder C. In: JavaMagazin, 8.2004, Software & Support Verlag GmbH, Frankfurt, pp. 15-16

[192] Shannon, B. (Editor) (2003): Java 2 Platform Enterprise Edition Specification, v1.4. http://java.sun.com/j2ee/j2ee-1_4-fr-spec.pdf

[193] Shaw, M. (2003): Writing Good Software Engineering Research Papers. In: Proceedings of the 25th International Conference on Software Engineering (ICSE'03), Portland, USA, May 2003, IEEE Computer Society, pp. 726-736.

[194] Shlaer, S., Mellor, S., and Lee, M. (1994): Shlaer-Mellor Method. In: Hutt, A. (Editor): Object Analysis and Design – Description of Methods. Wiley, New York, 1994, pp. 165-176

[195] Shneiderman, B. (2002): Leonardo's Laptop: Human Needs And the New Computing Technologies. MIT Press, Cambridge

[196] Singh, I., Stearns, B., Johnson, M., and others (2005): Designing Enterprise Application with the J2EE Platform, Second Edition, http://java.sun.com/blueprints/guidelines/designing_enterprise_applications_2e/titlepage.html

[197] Smith, R. P. and Shrimpton, D. H. (2004): Towards a PIM for the Model-Driven Development of Web-Based Systems. In: Workshop on Model Driven Development (WMDD 2004), online proceedings: http://heim.ifi.uio.no/~janoa/wmdd2004/papers/

[198] Snoeck, M. and Dedene, G. (1997): Experiences with Object Oriented Model-driven development, In: Proceedings of the 8th International Workshop on Software Technology and Engineering Practice (STEP '97) (including CASE '97), London, UK, July 1997, pp. 143

[199] Spinellis, D. (2003): On the Declarative Specification of Models, In: IEEE Software, March/April 2003 (Vol. 20 No. 9), IEEE Computer Society, pp. 96, 94-95

[200] Steinmann, F. and Kühne, T. (2004): Are Models the DNA of Software Construction? A Controversial Discussion. In: 3rd Workshop on Software Model Engineering WiSME@UML. Online proceedings: http://www.metamodel.com/wisme-2004/papers.html

[201] SUN (2004): JDBC Homepage. http://java.sun.com/products/jdbc/

[202] SUN (2004): Java ServerFaces Homepage. http://java.sun.com/j2ee/javaserverfaces/index.jsp

[203] Süß, C., Freitag, B., and Brössler, P. (1999): Meta-Modeling for Web-Based Teachware Management, In: Proceedings of the 18th International Conference on the World Wide Web and Conceptual Modeling, Paris, France, November 1999, LNCS 1727, Springer Verlag New York, pp. 98-102

[204] Sutcliffe, A. and Mehandjiev, N. (2004): End-User Development. In: Commnunications of the ACM, September 2004 (Vol. 47, No. 9), ACM, pg. 31-32

[205] Theng, Y. L. (2003): Designing Hypertext and the Web with the Heart and the Mind. In: Bommel, P. van (2003): Information Modeling for Internet Applications. Idea Group Publishing, Hershey, online version at Books24x7

[206] Tortora, G. (1990): Structure and Interpretation of Visual Languages. In: Chang, S.-K. (Ed.): Visual Languages and Visual Programming, Plenum, New York 1990, pp. 3-30 (as quoted in: Ferrucci, F., Tortora, G., and Vitiello, G. (2002): Visual Programming. In: Marciniak (Ed.): Encyclopedia of Software Engineering, Second Edition, Wiley-Interscience, 2002, pp. 1867-1892)

[207] Trigg, R. H. (1988): Guided Tours and Tabletops: Tools for Communicating in a Hypertext Environment. In: ACM Transactions on Office Information Systems, October 1988 (Vol. 6, No. 4), ACM, pp. 398-414

[208] Uhl, A. and Ambler, S. W.: "Point/Counterpoint, POINT: Model Driven Architecture Is Ready for Prime Time, COUNTERPOINT: Agile Model Driven Development Is Good Enough", in: IEEE Software September/October 2003 (Vol. 20, No. 5), IEEE Computer Society, pp. 70-73

[209] Völter, M. (2000): Metamodellierung, http://www.voelter.de/services/mdsd.html

[210] Völter, M. (2004): Modellgetriebene Softwareentwicklung. In: Objekt-Spektrum 4/2004, SIGS-Datacom, Troisdorf, pp. 14-21

[211] W3C (2004): Resource Description Framework. http://www.w3.org/RDF/

[212] W3C (2005): Web Services. http://www.w3.org/2002/ws/

[213] Wang, D. (2004): Bunte Rahmen. In: Javamagazin 9.2004, Software & Support Verlag GmbH, Frankfurt, pp. 36-44

[214] Watson, Andrew (2004): Integration and the Future of Middleware. Slides presented at the WAM 2004 workshop. http://www.wifo.uni-mannheim.de/WAM2004/Proceedings/01_WatsonKeynote.pdf

[215] WfMC (2005): Workflow Standards and Associated Documents. http://www.wfmc.org/standards/docs/Stds_diagram.pdf

[216] Zachman, J. A. (1987): A Framework for Information Systems Architecture. In: IBM Systems Journal, 1987 (Vol. 26, No. 3). IBM Publication G321-5298.

ENTSCHEIDUNGSUNTERSTÜTZUNG FÜR ÖKONOMISCHE PROBLEME

Herausgegeben von Wolfgang Gaul, Armin Heinzl und Martin Schader

Band 1 Ingo Böckenholt: Mehrdimensionale Skalierung qualitativer Daten. Ein Instrument zur Unterstützung von Marketingentscheidungen. 1989.

Band 2 Jürgen Joseph: Arbeitswissenschaftliche Aspekte der betrieblichen Einführung neuer Technologien am Beispiel von Computer Aided Design (CAD). Felduntersuchung zur Ermittlung arbeitswissenschaftlicher Empfehlungen für die Einführung neuer Technologien. 1990.

Band 3 Eva Schönfelder: Entwicklung eines Verfahrens zur Bewertung von Schichtsystemen nach arbeitswissenschaftlichen Kriterien. 1992.

Band 4 Michael Bargl: Akzeptanz und Effizienz computergestützter Dispositionssysteme in der Transportwirtschaft. Empirische Studien zur Implementierungsforschung von Entscheidungsunterstützungssystemen am Beispiel computergestützter Tourenplanungssysteme. 1994.

Band 5 Reinhold Decker: Analyse und Simulation des Kaufverhaltens auf Konsumgütermärkten. Konzeption eines modell- und wissensorientierten Systems zur Auswertung von Paneldaten. 1994.

Band 6 Wolfgang Gaul / Martin Schader (Hrsg.): Wissensbasierte Marketing-Datenanalyse. Das WIMDAS-Projekt. 1994.

Band 7 Daniel Baier: Konzipierung und Realisierung einer Unterstützung des kombinierten Einsatzes von Methoden bei der Positionierungsanalyse. 1994.

Band 8 Ulrich Lutz: Preispolitik im internationalen Marketing und westeuropäische Integration. 1994.

Band 9 Kirsten Petersen: Design eines Courseware-Entwicklungssystems für den computerunterstützten universitären Unterricht. CULLIS-Teilprojekt I. 1996.

Band 10 Stefan Neumann: Einsatz von Interactive Video im computerunterstützten universitären Unterricht. CULLIS Teilprojekt II. 1996.

Band 11 Eberhard Aust: Simultane Conjointanalyse, Benefitsegmentierung, Produktlinien- und Preisgestaltung. 1996.

Band 12 Peter Heydebreck: Technologische Verflechtung. Ein Instrument zum Erreichen von Produkt- und Prozeßinnovationserfolg. 1996.

Band 13 Michael Pesch: Effiziente Verkaufsplanung im Investitionsgütermarketing. 1997.

Band 14 Frank Wartenberg: Entscheidungsunterstützung im persönlichen Verkauf. 1997.

Band 15 Thomas Lechler: Erfolgsfaktoren des Projektmanagements. 1997.

Band 16 Alexandre Saad: Anbahnung und Erfolg von europäischen kooperativen F&E-Projekten. Eine empirische Analyse anhand von ESPRIT-Projekten. 1998.

Band 17 Michael Löffler: Integrierte Preisoptimierung. 1999.

Band 18 Frank Säuberlich: KDD und Data Mining als Hilfsmittel zur Entscheidungsunterstützung. 2000.

Ab Band 19 erscheint die Reihe unter dem Titel 'Informationstechnologie und Ökonomie'.

Band 19 Rainer Kiel: Dialog-gesteuerte Regelsysteme. Definition, Eigenschaften und Anwendungen. 2001.

Band 20 Axel Korthaus: Komponentenbasierte Entwicklung computergestützter betrieblicher Informationssysteme. 2001.

Band 21 Markus Aleksy: Entwicklung einer komponentenbasierten Architektur zur Implementierung paralleler Anwendungen mittels CORBA. Mit Beispielen aus den Wirtschaftswissenschaften. 2003.

Band 22 Michael Zapf: Flexible Kundeninteraktionsprozesse im Communication Center. 2003.

Band 23 Yvonne Staack: Kundenbindung im eBusiness. Eine kausalanalytische Untersuchung der Determinanten, Dimensionen und Verhaltenskonsequenzen der Kundenbindung im Online-Shopping und Online-Brokerage. 2004.

Band 24 Lars Schmidt-Thieme: Assoziationsregel-Algorithmen für Daten mit komplexer Strutkur. Mit Anwendungen im Web Mining. 2003.

Band 25 Stefan Hocke: Flexibilitätsmanagement in der Logistik. Systemtheoretische Fundierung und Simulation logistischer Gestaltungsparameter. 2004.

Band 26 Viktor Jung: Markteintrittsgestaltung neugegründeter Unternehmen. Situationsspezifische und erfolgsbezogene Analyse. 2004.

Band 27 Lars Brehm: Postimplementierungsphase von ERP-Systemen in Unternehmen. Organisatorische Gestaltung und kritische Erfolgsfaktoren. 2004.

Band 28 Ralf Gitzel: Model-Driven Software Development Using a Metamodel-Based Extension Mechanism for UML. 2006.

www.peterlang.de

Jože Florjančič / Karl Pütz (eds.)

Informatics and Management

Selected Topics

Frankfurt am Main, Berlin, Bern, Bruxelles, New York, Oxford, Wien, 2004.
421 pp., num. fig. and tab.
ISBN 3-631-51869-2 / US-ISBN 0-8204-6535-6 · pb. € 62.50*

The book is another result of the many years of co-operation between the Faculty of Organizational Sciences of the University of Maribor and the Institute of Economics and Didactics of Economics of the University of Aachen and the European Centre of Integration Research (EZI) e.V., Aachen. It is for all those who are interested in questions of management or are affected by them, as well as students who wish to discover more about IT-specific tasks and the knowledge they require. It is for workers and management staff in IT-departments who wish to critically challenge existing solutions or look beyond their own specialised field and learn about new spheres of activity, as well as for university teachers and their colleagues, who are interested in this concrete implementation of their research and teaching, in order to obtain new impulses.

Contents: Management · Informatics · E-Commerce · Organisation · Human Resource

Frankfurt am Main · Berlin · Bern · Bruxelles · New York · Oxford · Wien
Distribution: Verlag Peter Lang AG
Moosstr. 1, CH-2542 Pieterlen
Telefax 00 41 (0) 32 / 376 17 27

*The €-price includes German tax rate
Prices are subject to change without notice
Homepage http://www.peterlang.de